UWorld | COLLEGE PREP

SAT® Reading and Writing

An Illustrated Study Guide
First Edition

Acknowledgments for the First Edition

UWorld's passion for education and dedication to student success are the driving forces behind our quality products. Ensuring that the course materials in this book are accurate and up to date would not have been possible without our team of content experts, editors, illustrators, software developers, and support staff.

About the SAT

Your performance on the SAT verifies your academic abilities and commitment to learning. A higher score will enhance your college application. Scan the QR codes below to learn more about the SAT and UWorld resources.

UWorld Resources

SAT Exam Information

Prepare for the SAT with UWorld's SAT Study Guides

Preparing for the SAT can be challenging. UWorld's self-paced SAT Study Guides, written by SAT experts, were created to help you overcome this challenge and achieve your best score. Our Study Guides are designed to help you learn all course material efficiently and effectively so you can be successful on exam day.

- **VIVID ILLUSTRATIONS AID IN LONG-TERM RETENTION OF KEY EXAM CONCEPTS**

  Our SAT Study Guide brings difficult concepts to life with hundreds of engaging, high-impact visual aids that make topics easier to understand and remember.

- **TEST YOUR BASIC KNOWLEDGE WITH CHECK FOR UNDERSTANDING QUESTIONS**

  Our SAT Study Guides include hundreds of "Check for Understanding" (CFU) questions. CFUs are designed to assess your foundational knowledge. Everything you need to answer a CFU question appears in the Study Guide. So, if you're not confident about answering a CFU question, the best strategy is to reread the Study Guide. Answers and brief explanations for each CFU question are at the end of the printed Study Guide.

Enhance Learning with Our Digital SAT Study Guides

Scan to learn more

Our SAT course provides a digital version of SAT Study Guide that transforms ordinary reading into an interactive study session, including short video lessons on important topics. Key terms in our digital SAT Study Guides are highlighted in blue and can be clicked on to display illustrations that will help you learn more about a specific concept.

Words with dotted underlines can be clicked on to display a pop-up definition that provides a deeper understanding of their context.

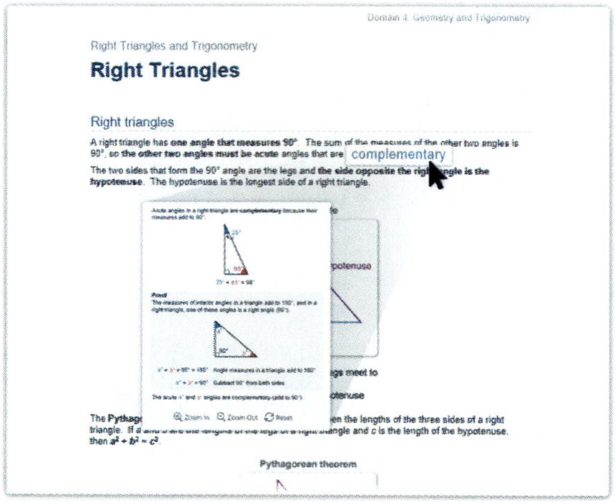

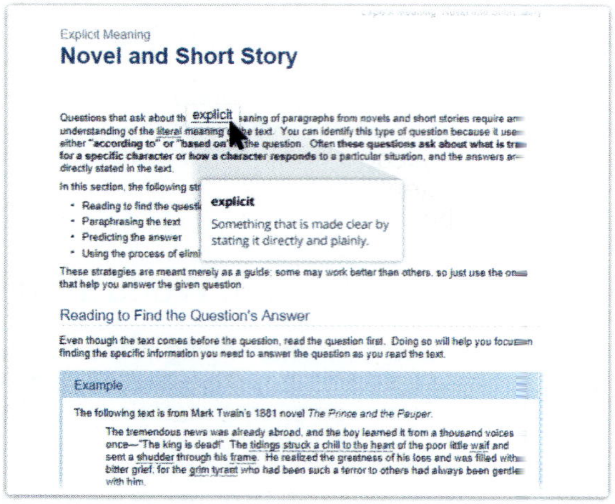

Boost Your Score with the Ultimate SAT QBank

To purchase SAT QBank access or to begin a free trial, visit https://collegeprep.uworld.com/sat/digital-sat/.

Scan for free trial

Why use the UWorld QBank?

- Over a thousand SAT-level questions
- In-depth, visually engaging answer explanations
- Data-driven performance and improvement tracking
- Fully featured mobile app for on-the-go review

Comprehensive SAT Course: Integrating UWorld's Study Guides and QBank

Our SAT course includes both the digital SAT Study Guide and the QBank. This integrated approach includes tools to personalize your SAT learning, get the most out of our detailed explanations, save valuable time, and know when you are ready for exam day.

My Notebook

My Notebook, a personalized note-taking tool, allows you to easily copy and organize content from the digital Study Guide and the online QBank. Simplify your study routine by efficiently recording the SAT content you will encounter on the exam and streamline your review process by quickly retrieving high-yield concepts to boost your study performance.

Digital Flashcards

Our unique flashcard feature makes it easy for you to copy definitions and images from the digital SAT Study Guide and online QBank into digital flashcards. Each card makes use of spaced repetition, a research-supported learning methodology that improves information retention and recall. Our algorithm will display the flashcard more or less frequently based on how you rate your understanding of the content.

Fully Featured Mobile App

Study for your SAT exam anytime, anywhere. Our industry-leading mobile app provides complete access to your SAT prep materials and syncs seamlessly across all devices. With the UWorld College Prep app, you can catch up on reading on the go, flip through flashcards between classes, or take a practice quiz during lunch to make the most of your downtime and keep SAT material top of mind.

Book and QBank Progress Tracking

Track your progress and review content at your own pace while using our digital SAT Study Guides and online QBank. Our learning tools are enhanced by advanced performance analytics that allow you to assess your preparedness over time. Focus on specific topics to study, identify areas where you need improvement, and even compare your results with those of your peers.

DSAT Verbal

Unit 1: Standard English Conventions — 1

1.1 Agreement: Pronouns — 2
1.2 Agreement: Subject-Verb — 7
1.3 Frequently Confused Words: Pronouns — 17
1.4 Parts of Speech: Verb Forms — 22
1.5 Parts of Speech: Verbs — 27
1.6 Punctuation: Apostrophes — 35
1.7 Punctuation: Colons — 39
1.8 Punctuation: Commas — 43
1.9 Punctuation: Comma + Semicolon — 56
1.10 Punctuation: Dashes — 60
1.11 Punctuation: End marks — 63
1.12 Punctuation: Semicolons — 70
1.13 Punctuation: Unnecessary Punctuation — 79
1.14 Sentence Structure: Modifiers — 90
1.15 Sentence Structure: Parallel — 97

Unit 2: Information and Ideas — 101

2.1 Explicit Meaning: Novel and Short Story — 102
2.2 Explicit Meaning: Poem — 109
2.3 Explicit Meaning: Nonfiction — 116
2.4 Main Idea: Novels and Short Stories — 122
2.5 Main Idea: Poem — 129
2.6 Main Idea: Nonfiction — 136
2.7 Evidence: Novel and Short Story — 143
2.8 Evidence: Play — 148
2.9 Evidence: Poem — 153
2.10 Evidence: Nonfiction — 158
2.11 Inference: Completes Text — 164
2.12 Graphic Displays: Bar Graphs — 170

2.13 Graphic Displays: Tables 180
2.14 Graphic Displays: Line Graph 186

Unit 3: Expression of Ideas 195

3.1 Transitions: Conjunctive Adverbs 196
3.2 Synthesis: Notes 205

Unit 4: Craft and Structure 213

4.1 Vocabulary: Logical and Precise 214
4.2 Vocabulary: Most Nearly Means 225
4.3 Purpose: Main 229
4.4 Purpose: Portion 239
4.5 Purpose: Sentence 244
4.6 Purpose: Structure 250
4.7 Connections: Between Texts 257

Unit 1: Standard English Conventions

1.1	Agreement: Pronouns	2
1.2	Agreement: Subject-Verb	7
1.3	Frequently Confused Words: Pronouns	17
1.4	Parts of Speech: Verb Forms	22
1.5	Parts of Speech: Verbs	27
1.6	Punctuation: Apostrophes	35
1.7	Punctuation: Colons	39
1.8	Punctuation: Commas	43
1.9	Punctuation: Commas + Semicolons	56
1.10	Punctuation: Dashes	60
1.11	Punctuation: End Marks	63
1.12	Punctuation: Semicolons	70
1.13	Punctuation: Unnecessary Punctuation	79
1.14	Sentence Structure: Modifiers	90
1.15	Sentence Structure: Parallel	97

Agreement

Pronouns

Pronouns are words that **take the place of nouns** so that the same noun isn't repeated multiple times.

Sentence with repeated noun: Edgar went to the gym, where Edgar lifted weights.

Sentence with pronoun: Edgar went to the gym, where he lifted weights.

The first sentence repeats the noun "Edgar," whereas the second uses the pronoun "he" in place of "Edgar," making it less repetitive. The noun referred to by the pronoun is called an antecedent. In the above example with the pronoun, "Edgar" is the antecedent of "he."

This section will discuss

- pronoun/antecedent agreemen
- reflexive pronouns

Third-Person Pronoun Chart

	Subject pronouns	Object pronouns	Possessive adjectives	Possessive pronouns
Third person (singular female)	she	her	her	hers
Third person (singular male)	he	him	his	his
Third person (singular non-person)	it	it	its	–
Third person (plural)	they	them	their	theirs

Because the third person tends to be used in SAT texts, first- and second-person pronouns are not usually correct answers to questions about agreement.

Pronoun/Antecedent Agreement

***Rule*: Pronouns must match their antecedents—the nouns they refer to—in number (singular or plural), person (first, second, or third), and gender (male or female).**

Number

Singular: The pink bike has streamers on its handlebars.

Plural: The store's registers have scanners on them.

Person

First: I lost my keys.

Second: You need to study for your test.

Third: The company provides health benefits to its employees.

Gender

Female: Juanita signed her name on the bottom of the tax return.

Male: Tyrone took his basketball to the gym.

Examples

✗ When the jet stream around the North Pole pushes southward, they cause the air to be colder than normal in some areas.

✓ When the jet stream around the North Pole pushes southward, it causes the air to be colder than normal in some areas.

To check if the pronoun is used correctly, ask what noun could be substituted for the pronoun. In these examples, what causes the air to be colder? The jet stream. Because "jet stream" is singular, the correct pronoun is "it."

Reflexive Pronouns

Reflexive pronouns end with "-self" or "-selves." They are used in a sentence with a subject and an object that refer to the same person, persons, or things.

Subject Object
Football players protect themselves by wearing various pads.

The subject is who or what is "wear[ing]...pads": football players. The object is who is being protected by the pads: also football players. Because the sentence contains a subject and object that refer to the same people, the reflexive pronoun "themselves" should be used.

Reflexive Pronouns

	Reflexive pronouns
Third person (singular female)	herself
Third person (singular male)	himself
Third person (singular non-person)	itself
Third person (plural)	themselves

Examples

✗ Although they roll around in the dirt, outdoor cats keep their fur clean by licking them.

✓ Although they roll around in the dirt, outdoor cats keep their fur clean by licking themselves.

The subject of the independent clause after the introductory information is "cats," and the verb is "keep." The object of the preposition "by" also refers to cats because they are the ones doing the licking to keep their fur clean. Because the subject and object refer to the same noun, the correct pronoun is the reflexive "themselves."

Practice

1. Scientists use data visualizations to emphasize the significant results of ______ studies, but artist Sarah Nance treats geologic data as expressive and abstract inspiration for her art.

Which choice completes the text so that it conforms to the conventions of Standard English?

A) one's

B) its

C) their

D) her

See Appendix for answer

2. Masting—the overproduction of seeds by a plant in synchronization with other plants—has been historically important for both animals and humans, who depend on these sources to feed ______.

Which choice completes the text so that it conforms to the conventions of Standard English?

A) it

B) themselves

C) them

D) itself

See Appendix for answer

3. Although President Biden's proposed regulatory changes aim to ban logging of old growth and mature forests within the next several years, scientists argue that such logging should stop immediately, so forests can remove carbon from the air and store ______ in the trees, a process that is currently needed to combat climate change.

Which choice completes the text so that it conforms to the conventions of Standard English?

A) itself

B) it

C) them

D) themselves

See Appendix for answer

Things to Remember:

- Pronouns take the place of nouns, typically when a noun is repeated.
- Pronouns should match the nouns they refer to in number (ex. singular noun with singular pronoun; plural noun with plural pronoun).
- Pronouns should match the nouns they refer to in person (ex. first, second, or third)
- SAT texts are generally written in the third person.
- Pronouns should match the nouns they refer to in gender (ex. female noun with female pronoun; male noun with male pronoun; gender-neutral noun with gender-neutral pronoun).
- Use reflexive pronouns (ending in "–self" or "–selves") when a verb's subject and object refer to the same person, persons, or things.

Agreement: Pronouns
Check for Understanding

1. Endangered right whales feed on large, dense patches of zooplankton found at specific water depths, leading regulators to question whether building wind turbines that alter waves, tides, and currents could affect whale feeding or cause these animals to change the foraging habitats ______ frequent.

   Which choice completes the text so that it conforms to the conventions of Standard English?

   A) they

   B) it

   C) one

   D) you

2. The chickadee is a bird that, each autumn, hides thousands of individual food items for ______ throughout the forest—under edges of tree bark or even between pine needles—using specialized spatial memory to retrieve that food during the winter months.

   Which choice completes the text so that it conforms to the conventions of Standard English?

   A) it

   B) themselves

   C) them

   D) itself

3. Recent studies on whether long-term or short-term consequences are more likely to influence health-related choices reveal that immediate effects are a stronger motivator than are results that would take longer to achieve. For instance, study participants who read that consuming an energy drink could cause ______ to experience a sugar crash within a few hours were 25% less likely to choose an energy drink than the participants who read that these drinks had the potential to contribute to the eventual development of diabetes.

   Which choice completes the text so that it conforms to the conventions of Standard English?

   A) them

   B) oneself

   C) it

   D) itself

Agreement

Subject-Verb

For a sentence to be grammatically complete, it must contain a subject and a main verb. Both present tense verbs and some past tense **verbs can be singular or plural**, so their **subjects must agree with verbs in number**: singular subjects must have singular verbs, and plural subjects must have plural verbs.

To locate the verb's subject, ask who or what is doing an action or being discussed in the sentence.

Like sentences, independent clauses and dependent clauses must contain both a subject and a verb that agree in number.

Independent clause — Dependent clause
Subject — Verb — Subject — Verb

Singular: A geologist explains why Iceland experienced a volcanic eruption.

Subject — Verb — Subject — Verb

Plural: Geologists explain how earthquakes in Iceland served as warnings of the volcanic blast.

Independent clause — Dependent clause

Notice how the subject "geologist" is preceded by "a," which indicates that it is singular. Also, the fact that "geologists" ends in "s" indicates that it is plural.

Anytime "a" or "an" precedes a noun, that noun is singular.

✗ A birds fly over an oceans.

✓ A bird flies over an ocean.

However, verbs are different from nouns in this respect. A present tense verb ends in the suffix "s" if it is singular and in the third person (meaning its subject is not "I" or "you"); conversely, the same verb when plural does not end with an "s" suffix.

This section will discuss subject-verb agreement in the context of

- Interrupted subjects and verbs
- Clauses
- Gerunds
- Inverted antecedents and subjects

Interrupted Subjects and Verbs

Often, **subjects and verbs are interrupted** by other words, which can cause confusion when the interruption places a noun other than the subject closer to the verb.

These interruptions can be prepositional phrases, appositives, participle phrases, or dependent clauses.

Interrupting prepositional phrase examples:

✗ The parents at the meeting is concerned with school safety.

✓ The parents at the meeting are concerned with school safety.

The singular "meeting" is the noun closest to the verb, but it is the object of the preposition "at." Also, a meeting is inanimate and can't show concern. Instead, the subject of the verb is the plural noun "parents," which makes sense because "parents" could reasonably be "concerned," so the plural verb "are" is correct.

> An object of the preposition is never the subject of the sentence.

Interrupting appositive phrase examples:

✗ The researcher, a student majoring in social sciences, are gathering data about solar energy costs.

✓ The researcher, a student majoring in social sciences, is gathering data about solar energy costs.

In each of these interrupting appositives—"a student majoring in social sciences"—the noun nearest the verb is not its subject. In fact, because a sentence is still grammatical if a nonessential appositive phrase set off by commas is omitted completely, look for the verb's subject before the appositive phrase.

***Rule*: The title of a book, television show, or movie is always singular even if the title is a plural noun.**

Examples:

✗ *Holes*, a novel by Louis Sachar, were made into a movie.

✓ *Holes*, a novel by Louis Sachar, was made into a movie.

Notice that even though *Holes* is a plural noun, it is considered singular because it is used as the title of the novel, so the matching verb should also be singular, making "was" the correct verb.

Interrupting participle phrase:

The photo depicting her beloved dogs is one of Lizzie's favorites.

In the example above, the noun closest to the verb is the plural "dogs," which is part of the interrupting participle phrase "depicting her beloved dogs." To find the subject of the verb, ask what is one of Lizzie's favorites. The answer is the singular noun "photo." Therefore, the correct verb is the singular "is."

Interrupting dependent clause examples:

The report, which contained over 100 pages, were about worker productivity.

The report, which contained over 100 pages, was about worker productivity.

In both the correct and incorrect examples, the interrupting dependent clause is "which contained over 100 pages." Because the subject is the singular noun "report," the correct verb is the singular "was."

Practice

1. The 1987 comedy film *Planes, Trains, & Automobiles* starring Steve Martin and John Candy ______ the story of a businessman experiencing a variety of obstacles on his quest to get home so that he can spend Thanksgiving with his family.

Which choice completes the text so that it conforms to the conventions of Standard English?

A) tells

B) have told

C) are telling

D) tell

See Appendix for answer

2. In the landscapes he created for his PBS television show *The Joy of Painting*, Bob Ross used a wet-on-wet oil painting technique that enables rapid progress because it doesn't require waiting for the canvas to dry before adding additional brushstrokes. Also, his limited use of equipment meant that an expensive investment in tools ______ not required.

Which choice completes the text so that it conforms to the conventions of Standard English?

A) were

B) have been

C) was

D) are

See Appendix for answer

When both singular and plural verbs are offered as answer choices, locate the subject referred to by the verb to see which answer agrees in number.

Often, the correct third-person verb is the one unlike the others. If there are three plural and one singular choice, the singular one is usually correct, and vice versa.

Subject-Verb Agreement in Clauses

On the SAT, the word **"that" is often used to begin** a clause functioning as **an adjective** to describe the preceding noun or noun phrase. Identify the antecedent of "that" to determine subject-verb agreement for these clauses.

Muriel is worried about her earring that has a loose post.

Independent clause: Muriel is worried about her earring
Clause describing earring: that has a loose post.

In the above example, the adjective clause describes the singular "earring," so the verb is the singular "is."

Ava signed the loan paperwork, documents that were needed to buy the house.

Independent clause: Ava signed the loan paperwork,
Appositive: documents
Adjective clause: that were needed to buy the house.

In the above example, even though "paperwork" is singular, its appositive "documents…house" is plural. The adjective clause describes the plural noun right before it: "documents." Therefore, the correct verb is the plural "were."

Dependent clauses can also begin with other words like "who," "whom," "whose," "which," "where," "when," and "why."

Example:

Jamal is a senior who participates in track and field events.

Practice

3. Water striders—tiny insects that _______ on water and can go their entire lives without touching land—primarily inhabit humid, rainy regions.

Which choice completes the text so that it conforms to the conventions of Standard English?

A) is walking

B) walk

C) walks

D) has walked

See Appendix for answer

4. A researcher who studied infants _______ that an interest in socializing begins even before babies develop language skills.

Which choice completes the text so that it conforms to the conventions of Standard English?

A) were finding

B) have found

C) find

D) has found

See Appendix for answer

Gerund as Subjects

A **gerund** looks like a verb because it **ends with "–ing,"** but it **functions as a singular noun**.

Examples:

✗ Swimming are a fun activity and can be good exercise.

✓ Swimming is a fun activity and can be good exercise.

In these examples, "swimming" functions as the sentence's subject. Notice in the correct example that this gerund is followed by the singular verb "is." Whenever a gerund is a verb's subject, the verb must be singular.

Sometimes, the gerund subject and its verb are separated by other words and phrases.

Subject gerund — Prepositional phrase

In checkers, jumping over opponents' pieces

Singular verb

means that you have captured them.

Here, the gerund subject "jumping" is separated from the verb "means" by the prepositional phrase "over opponents' pieces." Therefore, the singular verb "means" is used to match the singular noun "jumping," not the plural object "pieces."

A gerund might also be part of a dependent clause.

Independent clause

Denise hasn't scheduled any activities with her friends this weekend

Gerund — Singular verb

because studying for finals is time-consuming.

Dependent clause

Here, the gerund is the subject of the dependent clause that begins with "because," so the corresponding verb must be the singular verb "is."

Practice

5. Studies suggest that people's musical preferences correspond to their personalities; for instance, enjoying mellow, sophisticated music ______ people open to new experiences, whereas listening to intense music denotes individuals who are conscientious.

    A) indicates

    B) indicate

    C) are indicating

    D) have indicated

See Appendix for answer

6. Many health systems are starting to emphasize "relational medicine": care that focuses on the patient as a human being, not just on the ailment to be treated. Although this term may be new in the health care industry, the basic idea is not; viewing each person as someone with inherent worth ______ fundamental to numerous faith-based approaches concerning medical ethics.

Which choice completes the text so that it conforms to the conventions of Standard English?

    A) are

    B) is

    C) have been

    D) were

See Appendix for answer

Inverted Subjects and Antecedents

Usually, the subject of a sentence comes before its main verb.

Several students were eating breakfast in the cafeteria.

It's important to recognize an inverted subject so that you can select the appropriate corresponding verb.

When an independent clause begins with a prepositional phrase followed by its main verb and then its subject, the subject is considered to be inverted.

Prepositional phrase | Plural verb | Subject

On the kitchen table sit my dirty dishes from breakfast.

Plural noun

In this case, note that the subject contains the plural noun "dishes." Therefore, the plural "sit" would agree with the subject.

When the pronoun "there" begins a sentence, the antecedent it refers to could be either singular or plural, so that noun determines whether a singular or plural verb is needed.

Examples:

✗ There is several notebooks on the desk.

✓ There are several notebooks on the desk.

In the above examples, the antecedent for "there" is the plural "notebooks," so the correct verb is the plural "are."

Practice

7. Sound baths, typically used in yoga studios, surround listeners with sounds generated from simple instruments, like gongs and tuning forks. Sound baths are purported to lead to a deep sense of peace or harmony, and there ______ evidence showing that this type of aural therapy can decrease tension and fatigue while improving blood pressure and respiratory rate.

Which choice completes the text so that it conforms to the conventions of Standard English?

A) have been

B) are

C) were

D) is

See Appendix for answer

8. Close to 30% of US adults claim to have no religious affiliation, and only half of those associated with a spiritual group attend worship services on a regular basis. Consequently, "secular congregations" have filled people's desire for ritual and community; in fact, among those who attend such assemblies ______ humanists who want to cultivate a sense of belonging and purpose.

Which choice completes the text so that it conforms to the conventions of Standard English?

A) are

B) is

C) was

D) has been

See Appendix for answer

Things to Remember:

- Verbs must agree with their subjects in number (singular or plural).
- Don't be distracted by words that interrupt the subject and verb; locate the subject of the verb by asking who or what is completing an action or being discussed in the sentence.
- If the noun described by an adjective clause functions as a subject, choose the corresponding singular or plural verb offered in the answer choices.
- Gerunds are singular, and their corresponding verbs should be singular as well.
- When prepositional phrases begin a sentence and are immediately followed by a verb, look for the inverted subject after the verb to determine subject-verb agreement.
- When "there" begins an independent clause, determine whether its antecedent is singular or plural and then choose a verb that matches in number.
- Because SAT texts are written in third-person, if three answers are singular, choose the plural answer; if three answers are plural, choose the singular answer.

Agreement: Subject-Verb
Check for Understanding

1. Russian novelist Ivan Turgenev's *Fathers and Sons* (1862), a controversial book when published, ______ the tension not only between generations but also between intellectual and societal values.

   Which choice completes the text so that it conforms to the conventions of Standard English?

   A) have explored

   B) explore

   C) are exploring

   D) explores

2. A variety of approaches have been tried for diverting the flow of lava from erupting volcanoes, and among those deemed somewhat successful ______ the construction of ditches to direct the hot, viscous fluid away from towns.

   Which choice completes the text so that it conforms to the conventions of Standard English?

   A) was

   B) have been

   C) were

   D) are

3. A growing body of research suggests that winter can have a profound effect on people's thoughts, feelings, and behaviors. In fact, according to the American Psychiatric Association, five percent of Americans experience depressive symptoms that ______ known as seasonal affective disorder, or SAD.

   A) is

   B) was

   C) are

   D) has been

4. John Cage composed "Organ2 /ASLSP" (1987) with the tempo marking "as slowly as possible," and most performances have lasted between 20 and 70 minutes. However, a group of organists, artists, scholars, and theologians ____ the directive literally and made a very long performance a reality at the St. Burchardi Church in Halberstadt, Germany, where the piece began playing in 2001 and will continue to play until the year 2640.

   Which choice completes the text so that it conforms to the conventions of Standard English?

   A) are taking

   B) have taken

   C) has taken

   D) were taking

5. According to a national study, American adults tend to sleep less if they do not consume the recommended amount of fruits, vegetables, legumes, and whole grains as compared to those who do. Likewise, a separate study found that increasing fruit and vegetable intake for three months leads to better sleep quality and reductions in insomnia. Therefore, eating healthy foods ______ to correspond with getting a good night's sleep.

   A) seem

   B) seems

   C) have seemed

   D) are seeming

Frequently Confused Words

Pronouns

Words that sound the same but are spelled or punctuated differently are easy to confuse. Therefore, it is important to **recognize frequently confused words** and how to use them correctly.

This section will discuss the proper usage of

- its
- it's
- their
- they're
- there

Its / It's

Rule: "Its" is the possessive form of "it" and is used before a noun that "it" possesses.

Singular noun — Singular possessive pronoun

The guitar needs its strings tightened.

"Its" is a pronoun that refers to the singular "guitar" and shows that this instrument possesses "strings." Because a guitar is not male or female, the correct pronoun is the singular "its."

> "Its" is an exception to the rule that possessives are formed with an apostrophe.

Rule: "It's" is a contraction meaning "it is."

The apostrophe is a placeholder for the missing "i" in "is."

"It's" = It is

It's not too late to study for the test.

"It is" functions as the subject and main verb in the above example. Because "not too late" isn't a noun phrase that can be possessed, "its" would be incorrect.

To check whether "it's" is used correctly, substitute "it is" and see whether the sentence still makes sense.

Examples

✗ Smartphone scanners recognize a fingerprint by identifying it's specific two-dimensional pattern.

✓ Smartphone scanners recognize a fingerprint by identifying its specific two-dimensional pattern.

The pronoun "its" refers to "fingerprint" and possesses a "specific two-dimensional pattern." It would be incorrect to say that "the device identifies it is specific two-dimensional pattern." Because "it is" can't be substituted in the sentence, "its" is correct.

> A possessive noun with apostrophe + "s" may be a correct answer on the SAT, but a contraction rarely is.

Their / They're / There

Rule: "Their" is the possessive pronoun used when referring to a plural noun.

Plural noun — Plural possessive pronoun

Teachers determine the rules of their classrooms

In this example, "their" indicates the teachers' possession of "classrooms."

Rule: "They're" is a contraction for "they are."

The apostrophe is a placeholder for the missing "a" in "are."

Independent clause: **The students are excited for summer** because

Dependent clause: **they're ready for a break from school.**

The dependent clause requires a subject and a verb, which can be accomplished by using "they're" since it means "they are."

To check whether "they're" is used correctly, substitute "they are" and see whether the sentence still makes sense.

***Rule*: "There" can be used at the beginning of a sentence to indicate that something exists and that the main verb and subject of the sentence follow in that order.**

Main verb — Subject

There are three books on the desk.

"There" is the introductory word in this sentence, indicating the existence of "three books." "There" does not possess something in the sentence or serve as a contraction.

***Rule*: "There" can be used to indicate location.**

Put the decorations over there.

This sentence uses "there" to indicate where the decorations should be placed.

"There" is rarely the correct answer on the SAT.

Examples

✗ Pomegranates symbolize the persistence of life because they're time to bloom is during the winter.

✗ Pomegranates symbolize the persistence of life because there time to bloom is during the winter.

✓ Pomegranates symbolize the persistence of life because their time to bloom is during the winter.

Because "*they are* time to bloom is during the winter" doesn't make sense, the first example is incorrect.

In the second example, "there" doesn't begin the sentence or indicate a location, making it wrong.

"Their" indicates pomegranates' possession of "time," making "their" correct in this sentence.

Practice

1. Emerging approaches to cancer treatment include one called adaptive therapy, which uses X-rays to adjust treatment as a patient's tumor and ______ position change.

Which choice completes the text so that it conforms to the conventions of Standard English?

A) there

B) their

C) its

D) it's

See Appendix for answer

2. Research has found that individuals who focus on the immediate benefits rather than the delayed benefits of healthy habits increase ______ motivation.

Which choice completes the text so that it conforms to the conventions of Standard English?

A) their

B) its

C) they're

D) it's

See Appendix for answer

Things to Remember:

- Its = singular possessive referring to nouns that aren't people.
- It's = "it is."
- Their = plural possessive.
- They're = "they are."
- There = (1) indicates a noun's existence when the noun follows a verb, or (2) indicates a location.

Frequently Confused Words: Pronouns
Check for Understanding

1. In 1967, the railroad industry implemented Kartrak, the world's first official bar code system. As the rail cars moved past a scanner, they were automatically identified by their bar codes. ______ varying colors looked more like modern art than today's black bar codes.

   Which choice completes the text so that it conforms to the conventions of Standard English?

   A) There

   B) They're

   C) It's

   D) Their

2. The coastal redwoods that grow in the Pacific Northwest of the United States are the tallest plants on the planet. Beyond their incredible biomass, though, the trees are also home to over a hundred species of lichen and are so interconnected that the ecosystem is greater than the sum of ______ parts.

   Which choice completes the text so that it conforms to the conventions of Standard English?

   A) it's

   B) its

   C) their

   D) they're

Parts of Speech

Verb Forms

Verbs often look the same as, or can be used as, **other parts of speech**, like nouns, adjectives, and adverbs. The SAT tests whether students understand which form is correct in a given sentence.

This lesson will explore the correct usage for the following verb forms:

- Infinitives
- Participles
- Gerunds

Infinitives

Infinitives precede the basic form of the verb with the word "to" (ex. to run, to hope, to think, to be) and often show intent. Infinitives can function as nouns that serve as objects in the sentence.

Carolyn wants to see a movie.

Rule: Infinitives do not function as verbs but rather as nouns, adjectives, or adverbs.

When an infinitive is used as a noun, it can be either a subject or an object.

Subject: To explore the world sounds exciting.

Object: Jun agreed to keep Tasha's secret.

An infinitive can also function as an adjective to describe a noun or pronoun.

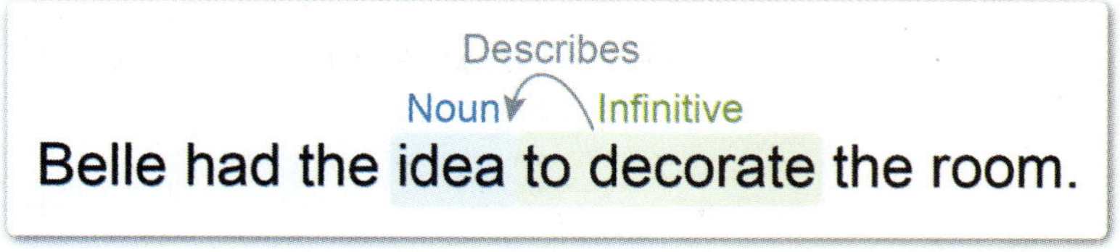

In addition, an infinitive can function as an adverb to describe a verb or verb phrase.

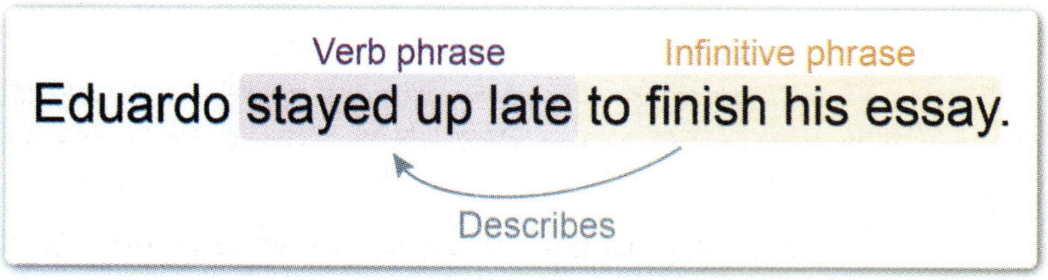

Practice

1. Professor Zachary Knight and graduate student Truong Ly have developed a method of observing the brains of mice while the animals eat. Their observations led the two ______ that the sensation of taste helps pace the speed of eating.

Which choice completes the text so that it conforms to the conventions of Standard English?

A) to discover

B) discovering

C) discovered

D) and discovered

See Appendix for answer

2. The threats people face online range from identity theft to lax security, even in interactions with trusted institutions like banks and government agencies. Media scholars who research the online environment assert that various dangers require computer users ______ differently depending on the situation.

Which choice completes the text so that it conforms to the conventions of Standard English?

A) responding

B) responded

C) and responding

D) to respond

See Appendix for answer

Participles

A participle is a verb form that functions as an adjective and that typically ends with –ing or –ed. Participles often show a quality of the noun they are describing.

–ing participle: The screaming eagle landed on the tree.

–ed participle: The exhausted new mother took a nap.

Participles can be placed not only before the nouns they describe but also afterward. Generally, when directly placed after the noun it describes, the participle is part of a participle phrase.

The person running the show is the school's theater teacher.

Participles describe a noun:
The tired flight attendant sighed.
The boy mowing the yard sneezed.

***Rule*: A comma is used to set off participles or participle phrases when they are not immediately after their noun.**

Examples

✗ Johan played online video games with friends on Saturday enjoying every minute of it.

✓ Johan played online video games with friend on Saturday, enjoying every minute of it.

"Saturday" is the closest noun to the participle "enjoying," but a day of the week can't enjoy anything. The participle phrase instead refers to Johan. Because the participle isn't describing the noun closest to it, a comma is required between "Saturday" and "enjoying."

Rule: **When participle phrases provide introductory information, they are separated from the independent clause with a comma.**

Introductory participle phrase: Dedicated to ensuring the safety of products that people consume, (Comma)

Refers to → Noun phrase

Independent clause: the US Food and Drug Administration also oversees pet products.

The comma shows where the introductory information ends and the independent clause begins.

When two actions occur at the same time and are done by the same person or thing, a present participle can be used as one of the actions that is describing the person or thing.

Driving home from work, Alyssa listened to music.

(For more information on introductory participle phrases, see the Sentence Structure – Modifiers section of the Study Guide.)

Practice

3. According to research, most of New York City is sinking between 1 to 4 centimeters per year due, in part, to the weight of its more than 1 million buildings. This settling, _______ with a predicted sea level rise of between 20 and 75 centimeters by 2025, further increases the city's vulnerability to flooding during coastal storms.

Which choice completes the text so that it conforms to the conventions of Standard English?

A) combines

B) to combine

C) combined

D) is combining

See Appendix for answer

4. In Michigan, the job of drawing election districts has been assigned to a group of citizens with no special qualifications. Although this way of dividing the state may seem like a new concept, it is rooted in a 2,500-year-old practice in which Athenian government officials were chosen from a pool of everyday citizens ______ a lottery system.

Which choice completes the text so that it conforms to the conventions of Standard English?

A) used

B) using

C) to use

D) use

See Appendix for answer

Gerunds

A gerund is a verb form that ends in –ing and functions as a noun. Gerunds can be used as either subjects or objects.

Subject: Walking can be a challenge for some toddlers.

Object of the preposition: Tomás spoke to his son about returning home.

When a gerund functions as the sentence's subject, its corresponding present tense verb is singular.

Examples

✗ Hoping are essential to enthusiasm.

✓ Hoping <u>is</u> essential to enthusiasm.

(For more information about the use of gerunds on the SAT, refer to the Study Guide lesson on subject/verb agreement.)

Things to Remember:

- Infinitives begin with "to" followed by the base form of a verb.
- Infinitives can show intention rather than action and can function as nouns, adjectives, or adverbs.
- When functioning as nouns, infinitives can be either subjects or objects.
- Participles generally end with –ing or –ed.
- Participles function as adjectives and describe the action or qualities of a noun or pronoun.
- Present participles can show actions happening at the same time as the sentence's main verb.
- Gerunds end with –ing and function as nouns—either as subjects or objects.
- A gerund is always singular.

Parts of Speech: Verb Forms
Check for Understanding

1. The original Apple Macintosh was known for more than its personal computing power, storage, and accessibility. This early desktop computer became popular because of its ability ______ a satisfying, simplified user experience for the average person, someone who might not be an expert in computing but who would benefit from this technology.

   Which choice completes the text so that it conforms to the conventions of Standard English?

   A) provide

   B) to provide

   C) and providing

   D) provided

2. According to scientists, when dogs tilt their heads, they may be trying to listen by ______ their ears in a way that helps them determine where a sound originates. Also, those dogs gifted with the ability to easily learn words may move their heads a little to the left when they hear a familiar word, like the name of a toy, as a sign of their increased attention.

   Which choice completes the text so that it conforms to the conventions of Standard English?

   A) to position

   B) position

   C) positioned

   D) positioning

Parts of Speech

Verbs

Both independent and dependent **clauses must contain a subject and a main verb**. The SAT often asks about the correct form of the main verb in sentences.

Verbs show action or states of being.

Action: The children skipped quickly.

State of being: Trina is sick.

"State of Being" Verbs

Present tense	am, are, is, be, being
Past tense	was, were

Main verbs are needed to complete both independent and dependent clauses.

Independent clause — Dependent clause

Hall monitors sweep the high school for late students after the tardy bell rings.

Main verb (sweep) — Main verb (rings)

Verb tense refers to when an action or state occurs: in the past, present, or future.

Past: Carlton went to the mall yesterday.

Present: Kendra needs milk for the recipe.

Future: Hwan will be happy when he gets his license.

This section will explore

- Main verbs in independent clauses
- Main verbs in dependent clauses
- Verb Tense

Main Verbs in Independent Clauses

If the test question provides a variety of **verbs as answer choices** and has a **blank instead of a main verb**, choose the option that can function as a main verb.

***Rule*: "–ing" verbs can't function as main verbs by themselves; they must be used with helping verbs.**

Helping Verbs

Present tense	am, are, is, has, have, do, does
Past tense	was, were, had, did
Future tense	will, will be
Conditional	must, may, might, shall

The process of elimination can be a helpful strategy for determining which verb will work in a sentence.

Examples

✗ We going on vacation next month.

✓ We are going on vacation next month.

"Going" in the first example can't function as a main verb by itself. The correct example adds the helping verb "are," which works because "are going" *can* function as the main verb of the independent clause.

***Rule*: Present tense participles and infinitives can't be main verbs.**

Examples

✗ The birds flying south for the winter.

✗ The birds to fly south for the winter.

✓ The birds fly south for the winter.

In the first incorrect example, "flying" cannot function as a main verb without a helping verb. Likewise, "to fly" in the second incorrect example is an infinitive, which can't function as a main verb. The correct example uses the present tense "fly," which can function as the main verb of an independent clause.

Practice

1. Five thousand years ago, the first known alphabet ______ in ancient Egypt, where the motivation for creating these "hieroglyphs," or "sacred carvings," seems to have been to record religious texts.

Which choice completes the text so that it conforms to the conventions of Standard English?

A) to invent

B) was invented

C) having invented

D) inventing

See Appendix for answer

2. American pikas, small, rabbit-like mammals, ______ bunches of wildflowers, weeds, and grasses into their dens in the summertime, making up to 200 trips a day between the fields and their homes to ensure they have food and insulation when plants are scarce in the winter.

Which choice completes the text so that it conforms to the conventions of Standard English?

A) gather

B) to gather

C) having gathered

D) gathering

See Appendix for answer

Main Verbs in Dependent Clauses

Dependent clauses cannot stand by themselves as grammatical sentences and often begin with words like "that," "which," "because," "although," "since," "if," "when," "though," and "while."

Examples

- that Shelby thought were good
- which the ant carried away
- because she said so
- although Henry wanted the car

***Rule*: Dependent clauses require both subjects and main verbs.**

As in independent clauses, infinitives and present participles can't be the main verbs in dependent clauses.

Examples

✗ Scott needs to train because he wanting to participate in a triathlon.

Scott needs to train because he to want to participate in a triathlon.

✓ Scott needs to train because he <u>wants</u> to participate in a triathlon.

Without a helping verb, "wanting" can't function as the main verb of the dependent clause that begins with "because." Likewise, the infinitive, "to want" can't function as a main verb. However, "wants" can be a main verb.

Practice

3. The first Black staff photographer for *Life* magazine, Gordon Parks is known for his photo essays highlighting social justice issues, which ______ an indelible impression on mid-20th-century readers.

Which choice completes the text so that it conforms to the conventions of Standard English?

A) making

B) having made

C) to make

D) made

See Appendix for answer

4. Recently, scientists discovered abundant fungi in a largely unexplored area of the ocean too deep for sunlight to penetrate that ______ the key for the development of new medicines.

Which choice completes the text so that it conforms to the conventions of Standard English?

A) having held

B) holding

C) could hold

D) to hold

See Appendix for answer

Verb Tense

When trying to determine the correct verb tense, **look for dates and other words in the text that indicate time** like "currently," "previously," and "subsequently." Determining when the action takes place can help you select the correct verb.

***Rule*: Verb tense must match the time of the action described in the sentence—past, present, or future.**

Examples

✗ Yesterday, the infant will receive her first vaccinations.

✗ Yesterday, the infant receives her first vaccinations.

✓ Yesterday, the infant <u>received</u> her first vaccinations.

"Yesterday" is a clue that the vaccinations were given in the past and that the past tense "received"—not the future tense "will receive" or the present tense "receives"—is correct.

Read the entire text to locate context clues to help you determine verb tense.

Practice

5. In 1832, Mexican army officers ______ all the pastries from the Mexico City shop of French National Monsieur Remontel, sparking the first Franco-Mexican War, which was ultimately settled when Great Britain intervened by paying for the stolen treats.

Which choice completes the text so that it conforms to the conventions of Standard English?

A) take

B) have taken

C) took

D) will be taking

See Appendix for answer

6. A recent video of ambidextrous French artist Helena Soubeyrand went viral; in it, she was drawing a portrait on a shop window with both hands simultaneously. Soubeyrand said she was unable to master the skill until she ______ for countless hours over the course of months to master this skill.

Which choice completes the text so that it conforms to the conventions of Standard English?

A) will practice

B) is practicing

C) practices

D) practiced

See Appendix for answer

7. Excavations in the 1700s recovered over 1,000 whole or partial scrolls that were buried when Mount Vesuvius erupted 2,000 years ago. Previously the ink on these charred scrolls could not be read, but CT images and AI algorithms ______ papyrologists to decode the text and gain a better understanding of these ancient documents.

Which choice completes the text so that it conforms to the conventions of Standard English?

A) have allowed

B) had allowed

C) allowed

D) was allowing

See Appendix for answer

Things to Remember:

- Every sentence requires an independent clause (which may be the entire sentence).
- Both independent and dependent clauses require a subject and a main verb.
- Infinitives and present participles can't function as main verbs.
- Look for context clues that indicate whether a past, present, or future tense verb is needed.

Sometimes infinitives and participles *are* the correct answer to test questions. (For more information on when this is the case, see the Parts of Speech – Verb Forms section of the Study Guide.)

Parts of Speech: Verbs
Check for Understanding

1. Glycan structures, networks of individual sugar molecules bonded together, ______ information to help cells recognize and respond to other cells, a process that allows human immune cells to remove harmful bacteria and cancerous cells while leaving healthy cells alone.

   Which choice completes the text so that it conforms to the conventions of Standard English?

   A) had stored

   B) will store

   C) was storing

   D) store

2. At the end of the 19th century, California's Tulare Lake was drained to allow the land underneath it to be farmed; however, heavy rains in 2023 flooded the area and brought the lake back. Environmentalists ______ the lake to remain intact, given its role in attracting native birds and cooling the San Joaquin Valley during hot summers.

   Which choice completes the text so that it conforms to the conventions of Standard English?

   A) wanting

   B) want

   C) having wanted

   D) to want

3. In 1945, Grace Hopper and her colleagues ______ on Mark II, an electromechanical computer, when they encountered a problem that led them to take the machine apart. After discovering a large moth, they started to refer to all the computer problems they encountered as "bugs" that required "debugging."

   Which choice completes the text so that it conforms to the conventions of Standard English?

   A) work

   B) will work

   C) were working

   D) are working

4. In 1989, a NASA study revealed that some common houseplants can purify the air of volatile organic compounds (VOCs) present in certain aerosol household products. The scientists also asserted that the presence of indoor plants ______ stress and blood pressure in humans.

   Which choice completes the text so that it conforms to the conventions of Standard English?

   A) reduced

   B) to reduce

   C) reducing

   D) having reduced

5. The rare St. George's Cross medusa (*Santjordia pagesi*) has only been seen twice, and that was in the Sumisu Caldera, a deep-sea volcanic structure in Japan's Ogasawara Islands. Unlike other larger medusa jellyfish, *S. pagesi* boasts 240 tentacles that probably contain several types of venom, and it ______ prey with the bright red mark on its stomach reminiscent of the cross for which it is named.

   Which choice completes the text so that it conforms to the conventions of Standard English?

   A) had lured

   B) lured

   C) would lure

   D) lures

Punctuation

Apostrophes

An apostrophe (') is used on the SAT only to show possession. A possessive noun is one that indicates ownership or possession of the word that follows (ex. the dog's house).

To determine if a noun is possessive, restate it along with the following noun as a phrase containing the words "of the" (ex. the club's bylaws = bylaws **of the** club). If the "of the" phrasing works, the noun is possessive.

Rule: If a plural noun ends in "s," use an apostrophe after the "s" to make it possessive.

When plural nouns show possession, they usually just end with the apostrophe.

Plural Possessive Noun: cats' food = food of more than one cat

For a plural noun ending in "s," use only an apostrophe to make it possessive (ex. the tires' hubcaps = the hubcaps of the tires).

Note that some plural nouns do not end in "s," such as "mice" (for "mouse") and "children" (for "child"). In these cases, an apostrophe plus "s" is used to indicate possession, as it is for singular nouns not ending in "s" (ex. the children's toys = the toys of the children).

The trick is determining whether the possessive noun is singular or plural and punctuating it accordingly. Some sentences may even include two possessive nouns where one is singular and the other is plural—or where both are singular or both plural.

Sentence includes	Example
Singular + plural possessive	The *fox's* health was damaged by *farmers'* pesticide use.
Two singular possessives	The *novel's* author requested her *editor's* advice.
Two plural possessives	The *boys'* mother asked about their *teachers'* support.

The SAT typically includes two possessive nouns to punctuate correctly in an apostrophe question. Here is a shortened example of what a question might look like on the test:

The teacher was pleased with Samantha because the ______ quality.

Which choice completes the text so that it conforms to the conventions of Standard English?

A) students brilliance was evident in most of her assignment's

B) student's brilliance was evident most of her assignments

C) student's brilliance was evident in most of her assignments'

D) students' brilliance was evident in most of her assignments'

When an apostrophe question includes answer choices with a singular possessive noun AND a plural possessive noun, examine the sentence's context for clues indicating whether the nouns are singular or plural. Then, choose the answer that puts the apostrophes where they belong.

Examples

✗ After cleaning the kitchen with her dad, Veronica ironed her moms blouse.

✗ After cleaning the kitchen with her dad, Veronica ironed her moms' blouse.

✓ After cleaning the kitchen with her dad, Veronica ironed her mom's blouse.

The noun "mom" is singular because Veronica only has one mother. The garment is "the blouse of her mom," which means the blouse belongs to (is possessed by) her mom, so an apostrophe and an "s" are needed to show that possession.

✗ An octopuses tentacles are super cool.

✓ An octopus' tentacles are super cool.

The word "an" indicates that "octopus" is singular even though it ends with an "s." The sentence discusses the tentacles "of the octopus," so octopus is a singular possessive noun.

✗ The mens restroom needs cleaning.

✗ The mens' restroom needs cleaning.

✓ The men's restroom needs cleaning.

The possessive noun "men" is plural without an "s" added. Therefore, an apostrophe and an "s" go after this plural possessive to state that the restroom "of the men" needs cleaning.

✗ In the early morning, several beaches sand dunes revealed the tsunamis fury.

✗ In the early morning, several beach's sand dunes revealed the tsunami's fury.

✓ In the early morning, several beaches' sand dunes revealed the tsunami's fury.

The word "several" indicates that the sentence refers to more than one beach, so the noun should be the plural "beaches." In addition, the sentence is about the "dunes of the beach," meaning that "beaches" is possessive. Meanwhile, the end of the sentence could be rephrased as "the fury of the tsunami," proving that "tsunami" is possessive. Therefore, an apostrophe should be included after the "s" in "beaches" and another apostrophe included before the final "s" in "tsunamis."

Practice

1. The football coach for the University of Alabama encouraged the ______ to lead by example.

Which choice completes the text so that it conforms to the conventions of Standard English?

A) team's veterans

B) teams' veteran's

C) team's veteran's

D) teams veterans'

See Appendix for answer

2. The technology expert scrutinized the ______ and found no viruses.

Which choice completes the text so that it conforms to the conventions of Standard English?

A) salesmens account's

B) salesmen's accounts

C) salesmens accounts

D) salesmen's account's

See Appendix for answer

Things to Remember:

- Singular possessive nouns generally end with an apostrophe plus "s" (cat's).
- An apostrophe without an "s" afterward is used for singular nouns ending in "s" (walrus').
- Plural possessive nouns generally end with only an apostrophe after the plural suffix "s" (cars').
- An apostrophe plus "s" is used for irregular plural nouns when they are possessive (men's).

Punctuation: Apostrophes
Check for Understanding

1. Although a storm was expected last night, several automobiles remained parked outside. Damage to the ______ hail was quite large.

   Which choice completes the text so that it conforms to the conventions of Standard English?

   A) cars hoods revealed that the storm's

   B) car's hoods revealed that the storms

   C) cars' hoods revealed that the storm's

   D) cars' hoods revealed that the storms'

2. As a Halloween tradition, generations of our family have read a book with tales of horror by Edgar Allen Poe. The ______ are now worn and faded, but the tradition lives on.

   Which choice completes the text so that it conforms to the conventions of Standard English?

   A) book's pages

   B) books' pages

   C) book's page's

   D) books pages'

3. Cinderella's coach was painted white with exquisite gold accents. Many marveled at its beauty, but the ______ widened in amazement when they saw the magnificent white horses that would pull it.

   A) peoples eyes

   B) people's eye's

   C) peoples eye's

   D) people's eyes

Punctuation

Colons

A colon (:) is used in the middle of a sentence to introduce new information. The information can be an explanation or elaboration of what was just stated.

***Rule*: Use a colon after an independent clause to indicate that additional, related information follows.**

Colons may be used between two statements: the first is often a general idea, while the second adds clarity and detail about that general idea.

> Adds clarity
> General idea — Related details
>
> Roberto changed: he was irresponsible as a freshman, but he became more dependable in his sophomore year.
>
> Colon

The first independent clause indicates that Roberto changed, but it doesn't tell how. The information after the colon provides specific details about how he changed—from irresponsible to dependable.

Colons with Conjunctive Adverbs

Some SAT questions require you to choose between placing a colon before or after a conjunctive adverb. A conjunctive adverb describes the relationship between an idea stated in a previous independent clause or sentence and a second idea that follows the adverb.

> A conjunctive adverb always points back to a preceding idea.

When an idea explains a preceding statement, the conjunctive adverb should be part of the second idea's independent clause because the second idea points back to the first, even if they are in different sentences.

Typically, a conjunctive adverb (plus a comma) follows the colon.

> Explains
> First idea — Second idea
>
> Ilsa saw Dieter at a party. At first, she was worried: however, instead of Dieter becoming angry about their breakup, he greeted her with kind understanding.
>
> Colon — Comma

The conjunctive adverb "however" is used to indicate a contrast that follows, with Dieter's kind response contrasting with the previous idea about what Ilsa expected—Dieter becoming angry.

A colon is therefore placed *before*—not after—the conjunctive adverb because "however" belongs with the second idea about how Dieter greeted Ilsa.

Sometimes a colon is placed after the conjunctive adverb.

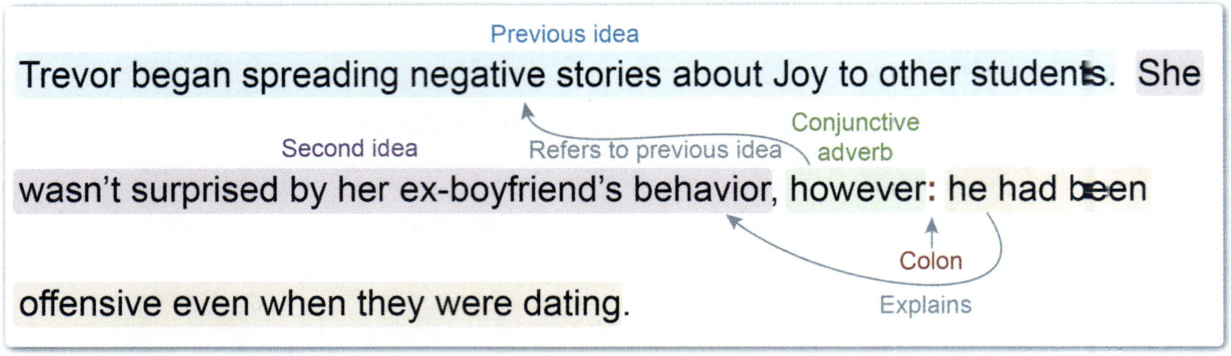

In the second sentence (She wasn't...behavior), a colon is placed between a general idea about Joy not being surprised and a second idea explaining why. Notice that the colon is placed after the conjunctive adverb—not before it—because "however" refers to the previous idea expressed in the first sentence about Trevor gossiping (Trevor...students).

Examples

✗ The picture amazed Sylvia, she had no idea her aunt was a talented artist.

✓ The picture amazed Sylvia: she had no idea her aunt was a talented artist.

A comma after "Sylvia" creates a comma splice. The first independent clause ("The picture...Sylvia") is followed by another independent clause ("she...artist") explaining why Sylvia was amazed. However, the two clauses aren't joined by a FANBOYS conjunction or semicolon.

In the correct example, a colon joins the independent clauses and properly indicates that the second idea provides details that explain the previous statement.

✗ John was caught plagiarizing his research paper. The response of his English teacher surprised him: though, Mrs. Jones taught him how to avoid plagiarism instead of punishing him.

✓ John was caught plagiarizing his research paper. The response of his English teacher surprised him, though: Mrs. Jones taught him how to avoid plagiarism instead of punishing him..

The conjunctive adverb "though" indicates a contrast to something stated previously. In this case, the previous sentence expresses the idea that John plagiarized and expected to be punished, but Mrs. Jones' response of giving him helpful instruction contrasts with what he imagined would happen. The sentence with a comma after "though" is incorrect because a sentence can't begin with "though" if it's followed by a comma.

> A colon is placed after the first independent clause when the information that follows it explains the previously stated idea.

Practice

1. Savannah and Beau made a big decision when they ______ for richer or poorer, they promised to love each other for life and got married during their sophomore year.

Which choice completes the text so that it conforms to the conventions of Standard English?

A) were still in college:

B) were still in college,

C) were still in college

D) were: still in college

See Appendix for answer

2. During the football game's halftime, Coach Stevenson defined champions as those who played with "teamwork, tenacity, and total ______ that these were the three keys to victory.

Which choice completes the text so that it conforms to the conventions of Standard English?

A) effort": claiming

B) effort," claiming

C) effort"; claiming

D) effort." Claiming

See Appendix for answer

3. Maya led the student council, participated in club soccer, and played for her high school soccer team too. She didn't have much free______ meetings, practices, games, and tournaments took up most of her evenings and weekends.

Which choice completes the text so that it conforms to the conventions of Standard English?

A) time, consequently

B) time, consequently,

C) time consequently:

D) time. Consequently,

See Appendix for answer

Things to Remember:

- Colons join related information.
- A colon must have an independent clause before it.
- The information after the colon explains the idea expressed before it.
- A conjunctive adverb can precede or follow a colon. The adverb should be in the same clause as the idea that describes or relates to a previous idea.

Punctuation: Colons
Check for Understanding

1. At the beach, people on vacation sometimes ______ in addition to high prices, they experience changing weather and water conditions that make desirable activities unavailable.

   Which choice completes the text so that it conforms to the conventions of Standard English?

   A) are: disappointed,

   B) are disappointed,

   C) are disappointed

   D) are disappointed:

2. Dominic organized a baking contest for the town. He was surprised to see a selection of pies that was so ______ some were sweet pies that he thought perfectly suitable for dessert, but others were savory pies he considered preferable as a main course.

   Which choice completes the text so that it conforms to the conventions of Standard English?

   A) diverse:

   B) diverse,

   C) diverse, though

   D) diverse though

3. When Invincible Corporation acquires Strategic Solutions, the number of employees will be reduced significantly. The acquisition will create new ______ within each department, several positions will become available to those interested in applying.

   Which choice completes the text so that it conforms to the conventions of Standard English?

   A) opportunities, though,

   B) opportunities, though:

   C) opportunities. Though,

   D) opportunities though

Punctuation

Commas

A comma (,) separates parts of a sentence to make the meaning of the sentence clear. Use commas when a grammar rule dictates that they are needed. In this section, you will learn the rules that tell you how to use commas correctly to choose the right answer on the SAT.

Commas with FANBOYS Conjunctions

***Rule*: Two independent clauses joined by a FANBOYS conjunction require a comma placed between the first independent clause and the conjunction.**

Tony asked for a raise, but his boss refused to give him one.

Notice that the comma is correctly placed after the first independent clause ("Tom…raise") and before the FANBOYS "but" that joins the first independent clause with the second ("his boss…one").

When a question about punctuation includes a long sentence, identify one or more independent clauses by locating the subject and main verb of each clause.

A question on the SAT can include a sentence with elements that make the sentence longer and the independent clauses harder to identify. For example, a question might include a participle phrase or a nonessential appositive.

Independent clause 1 — Participle phrase

The old building scheduled to be demolished next month is in the downtown

Describes — Independent clause 2

area, **and** people are planning to watch it fall.

Independent clause 1 — Appositive

My grandmother, a great cook who specializes in Italian cuisine, said we could

Describes — Independent clause 2

go to her home for dinner, **or** she could bring dinner to us.

In addition, an SAT question may include a dependent clause and participle phrase in the same sentence with an independent clause.

Locate the subjects and main verbs of clauses in long sentences to see whether a clause can stand on its own as a grammatical sentence (an independent clause) or cannot stand alone as a grammatical sentence (a dependent clause). After identifying multiple independent clauses joined by a FANBOYS conjunction, select the answer that has a comma before that conjunction.

Subject | Main verb
Adithya **seems** confident about his college plans, claiming that engineering is his best career option, **but** his **friends** from high school **had** doubts because he had always been interested in teaching.

Independent clause: "Adithya seems confident about his college plans, claiming that engineering is his best career option"
Subject: "friends" | Main verb: "had"
Independent clause: "his friends from high school had doubts"
Dependent clause: "because he had always been interested in teaching."

Example

✗ Ishmael, a participant in soccer and marching band, usually performed well in his math classes but during the fall semester, he was too busy to excel in AP Calculus.

✓ Ishmael, a participant in soccer and marching band, usually performed well in his math classes, but during the fall semester, he was too busy to excel in AP Calculus.

The correct example includes a comma before the FANBOYS conjunction joining two independent clauses. The subject of the first independent clause ("Ishmael…classes") is "Ishmael," which is followed by a descriptive phrase ("a participant…band") and then the main verb "performed." The second independent clause ("during…Calculus") is introduced by a prepositional phrase ("during…semester") and has the subject "he" and the verb "was."

Practice

1. Students in the theater program raised money to attend a competition in ______ they sold enough merchandise to cover all their expenses.

Which choice completes the text so that it conforms to the conventions of Standard English?

A) Indianapolis, and

B) Indianapolis,

C) Indianapolis: whereas

D) Indianapolis, meanwhile

See Appendix for answer

2. The volleyball team promised to communicate better on the ______ when they played their next opponent, they didn't talk to each other enough, which resulted in costly mistakes.

Which choice completes the text so that it conforms to the conventions of Standard English?

A) court

B) court,

C) court, but

D) court, but,

See Appendix for answer

Commas with Mid-Sentence Transitions

***Rule*: A transition in the middle of an independent clause should be set off with commas.**

A transition can be a word or a phrase that logically connects one idea to the next. When a transition is placed in the middle of an independent clause and interrupts the flow of thought, it should have a comma before and after it.

April enjoyed rack of lamb for dinner. Jenny, however, had a tuna sandwich.

Common Transitions on the SAT

accordingly	consequently	furthermore	indeed	second
actually	currently	however	instead	similarly
additionally	currently	in addition	in turn	specifically
afterward	evidently	in comparison	meanwhile	still
alternatively	finally	in contrast	moreover	subsequently
as a result	for example	in fact	nevertheless	therefore
besides	for instance	in other words	nonetheless	though
by contrast	for this reason	increasingly	regardless	to conclude

Conjunctive adverbs are words or phrases that often follow a semicolon as a mid-sentence transition that shows the relationship between independent clauses separated by a semicolon. In this situation, the semicolon is typically placed before the conjunctive adverb, followed by a comma.

Independent clause 1

Shigero Yokoi and his friends played Mario Bros. on Nintendo Switch late into

Conjunctive adverb — Independent clause 2

the night; as a result, they had difficulty staying awake in class the next day.

Semicolon

Examples

✗ The journalist didn't like her easy assignment, though thinking that if women were given the same type of assignments as men, greater equality with men would be achieved for reporters.

✗ The journalist didn't like her easy assignment; though, thinking that if women were given the same type of assignments as men, greater equality with men would be achieved for reporters.

✓ The journalist didn't like her easy assignment, though, thinking that if women were given the same type of assignments as men, greater equality with men would be achieved for reporters.

The first example has a comma before the transition ("though"), but there should be a second comma after it. The second example has a semicolon and transition that is followed by a comma, but the words after the semicolon cannot stand alone as a grammatical sentence, making it incorrect.

The correct example includes a comma before and after the transition that interrupts the independent clause.

✗ Sean Paul didn't like mushrooms, nevertheless, he loved eating pho that includes Shiitake mushrooms because the soup tasted so good.

✓ Sean Paul didn't like mushrooms; nevertheless, he loved eating pho that includes Shiitake mushrooms because the soup tasted so good.

The first example places commas before and after the mid-sentence conjunctive adverb "nevertheless," but this results in a run-on sentence because the two independent clauses, "Sean Paul...mushrooms" and "he loved...good," aren't joined by a FANBOYS conjunction or separated by a semicolon

The second example correctly separates the independent clauses with a semicolon before "nevertheless" and a comma after it.

Practice

3. Some students completed a semester of student teaching and became certified by the state to _______ most certified instructors were better prepared for the classroom than uncertified educators.

Which choice completes the text so that it conforms to the conventions of Standard English?

A) teach, consequently

B) teach; consequently,

C) teach, consequently,

D) teach; consequently

See Appendix for answer

4. It was an uncomfortably cold and rainy week. Salvation Army workers decided to ring bells and collect charitable _______ believing that funds for the poor were more important than their own discomfort.

Which choice completes the text so that it conforms to the conventions of Standard English?

A) donations, however

B) donations, however;

C) donations, however,

D) donations; however,

See Appendix for answer

Commas with Appositives

***Rule*: A mid-sentence appositive that isn't needed for the sentence to be grammatical should have a comma before it and after it.**

Appositive phrases are considered nonessential if they only provide extra information but are not needed for the noun they describe to be correctly identified. When an SAT question includes only one comma before or after a mid-sentence appositive phrase, a second comma will be needed to separate it from the rest of the sentence.

Last night we climbed over the fence to enter the old Radley

Renames
Noun Appositive phrase

house, 1313 Mockingbird Lane, and saw it was filled with

eerie shadows, scary noises, and creepy cobwebs.

***Rule*: A nonessential appositive at the end of a sentence should have a comma before it.**

Sometimes a nonessential appositive comes at the end of the sentence. In that case, a comma should set it apart from the previous information and a period should end the sentence.

Examples

✗ The squire knelt before the queen the most powerful leader in Rigel, and asked to serve in her court.

✓ The squire knelt before the queen, the most powerful leader in Rigel, and asked to serve in her court.

The sentence includes a mid-sentence appositive phrase that describes the queen as "the most powerful leader in Rigel." The first example lacks the comma needed before this appositive. The second example correctly includes commas before and after the nonessential appositive.

✗ We waited patiently as the photographer adjusted her camera an expensive Canon EOS R5.

✓ We waited patiently as the photographer adjusted her camera, an expensive Canon EOS R5.

The nonessential appositive "an expensive Canon EOS R5" comes at the end of the sentence and describes "camera." The correct example includes a comma before the appositive that the incorrect example lacks.

Practice

5. John watched his boss, a ______ harshly criticize another worker in his department.

Which choice completes the text so that it conforms to the conventions of Standard English?

A) micromanager,

B) micromanager; and

C) micromanager and

D) micromanager;

See Appendix for answer

6. When taking a walk, my neighbors used a leash to restrain their energetic ______ an Irish Wolfhound with fur the color of charcoal.

Which choice completes the text so that it conforms to the conventions of Standard English?

A) dog; or

B) dog or

C) dog,

D) dog

See Appendix for answer

Commas with Participles

***Rule:* If a participle phrase immediately follows the noun it describes, don't use a comma to separate the two.**

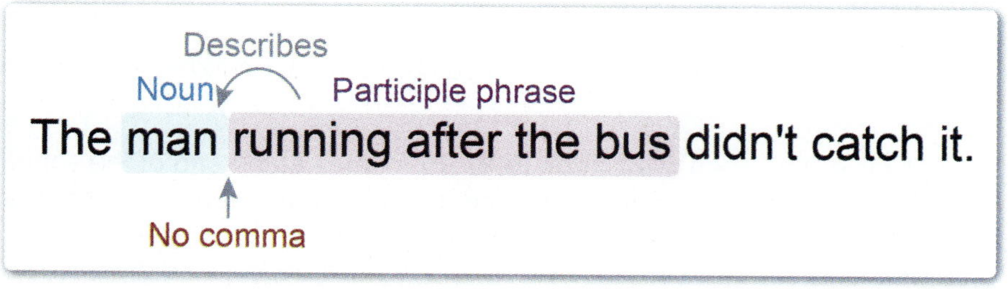

Because the participle "running" describes the noun "man" and immediately follows this noun, no comma is needed before "running."

***Rule:* If a participle does NOT immediately follow the noun it describes, place a comma before the participle to indicate that the noun is somewhere else in the sentence.**

Describes
Noun — Noun — Participle phrase

Amberlee auditioned for the lead role in the play, hoping to get cast.

Because it isn't the play that hopes to get cast, but rather Amberlee who hopes for the lead part, the participle phrase "hoping to get cast" is describing a noun earlier in the sentence, not the noun immediately before it. Therefore, a comma is needed between "play" and "hoping."

Examples

✗ The neighbors told the police about an elderly man, wandering from his home, and volunteered to help with the search.

✓ The neighbors told the police about the elderly man wandering from his home and volunteered to help with the search.

The participle phrase "wandering from his home" is immediately after the noun it describes ("man"). Therefore, no commas should be placed before or after the participle phrase to set it apart. In the correct example, "wandering from his home" is immediately after the noun "man," so no commas are placed before or after the participle phrase.

✗ After two weeks, Shareeka and Jermaine broke off their relationship tired of the constant bickering.

✓ After two weeks, Shareeka and Jermaine broke off their relationship, tired of the constant bickering.

The participle phrase "tired...bickering" describes the couple who broke up. Because the participle does not immediately follow the nouns "Shareeka and Jermaine" that it describes, a comma before the participle phrase is needed.

Practice

7. The teacher split the students into several ______ each a different part of the unit to present to the class.

Which choice completes the text so that it conforms to the conventions of Standard English?

A) groups assigning
B) groups; assigning
C) groups, assigning
D) groups: assigning

See Appendix for answer

8. The competition required physics students to create a ______ raw eggs from breaking after a 25-foot drop.

Which choice completes the text so that it conforms to the conventions of Standard English?

A) container, protecting
B) container protecting
C) container; protecting
D) container: protecting

See Appendix for answer

Commas with Introductory Information

Rule: **Use a comma to separate introductory phrases or clauses from an independent clause that follows.**

Introductory information before an independent clause can be a phrase, such as a participle phrase, or a dependent clause. A comma should come immediately after these introductory elements.

Comforted by her mom, the girl felt happy and grateful.

The participle phrase "Comforted...mom" comes before "the girl," which is the noun it describes.

When an introductory dependent clause precedes the independent clause, a comma should separate it from the independent clause.

Dependent clause | Independent clause

Because my sister is sick, she stayed home from school.

Comma

Examples

✗ Attacked by angry bees Samir dove into the river.

✓ Attacked by angry bees, Samir dove into the river.

The participle phrase ("Attacked...bees") comes before the independent clause ("Samir...river") that follows it. Because the phrase describes Samir, a comma is needed between the participle phrase and the noun "Samir."

✗ When Kurt got home he prepared dinner.

✓ When Kurt got home, he prepared dinner.

The introductory dependent clause "When...home" has a subject "Kurt" and a verb "got", but it cannot stand by itself as a sentence because it begins with "When." A comma should be included after the introductory dependent clause because the clause describes the subject "he" of the independent clause.

Practice

9. When Carlota and Juan compared their semester ______ discovered that they had three classes together.

Which choice completes the text so that it conforms to the conventions of Standard English?

A) schedules they

B) schedules; they

C) schedules. They

D) schedules, they

See Appendix for answer

10. Escaping the violence in their home ______ refugees were relieved to be welcomed by the Red Cross team.

Which choice completes the text so that it conforms to the conventions of Standard English?

A) country; the

B) country. The

C) country the

D) country, the

See Appendix for answer

Commas with Concluding Information

Unlike an introductory dependent clause, which requires a comma to separate it from the independent clause that follows, a dependent clause at the *end* of a sentence *may or may not* require a comma to separate it from the preceding independent clause.

In most such cases, a comma between an independent clause and a concluding dependent clause is not required. However, the SAT will test students only on sentences where this comma is used.

Ex: The dog ran outside when Juan left the door open.

(Sentences without a comma before a concluding dependent clause are NOT on the SAT.)

Ex: The cat stayed inside, whereas the dog ran outside.

(Sentences with a comma before a concluding dependent clause *are* on the SAT.)

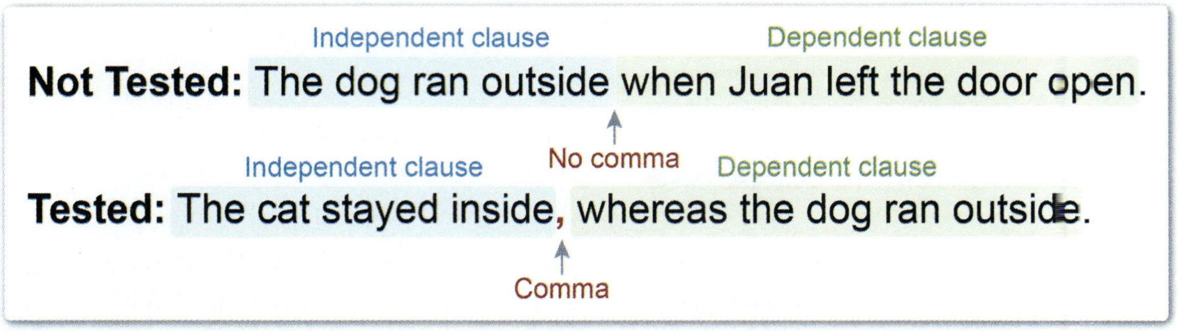

To determine whether a comma is needed, you should first locate the subjects and **main verbs** of clauses to see whether a clause can stand on its own as a grammatical sentence (an independent clause) or cannot stand alone as a grammatical sentence (a dependent clause). Clauses can be identified by locating subject nouns and main verbs—these are needed in every clause.

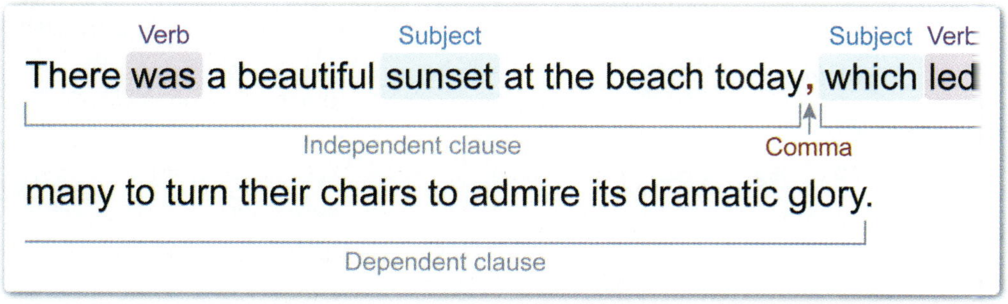

Rule: Separate an appositive phrase at the end of the sentence from the independent clause before it with a comma.

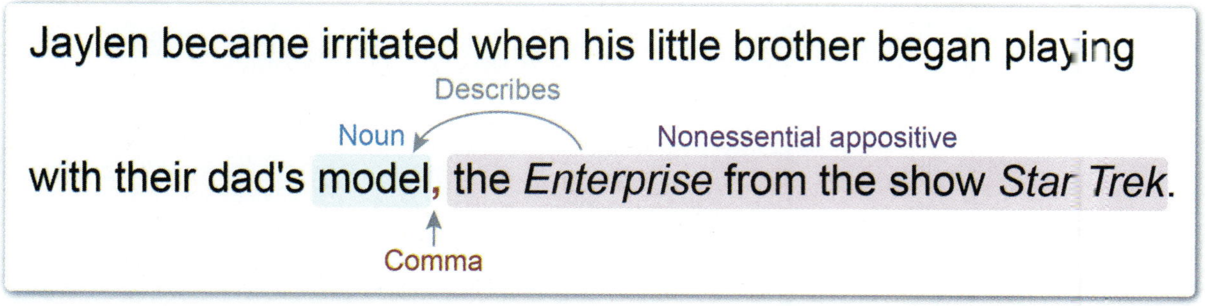

The concluding information ("*the Enterprise…Star Trek*") is an appositive that describes the noun "model." Therefore, a comma should be placed before this concluding phrase.

Examples

✗ I enjoy hiking in the forest whereas my sister prefers reading in her room.

✓ I enjoy hiking in the forest, whereas my sister prefers reading in her room.

The independent clause is "I...forest." Because the subordinating conjunction "whereas" begins a concluding dependent clause ("whereas...room"), a comma is needed before it.

Practice

11. The candy shop was well organized. For example, the chocolates and soft candy were all displayed in a long glass ______ the hard candy was displayed in racks on another wall.

Which choice completes the text so that it conforms to the conventions of Standard English?

A) case, while

B) case; while

C) case while

D) case. While

See Appendix for answer

Things to Remember:

- Two independent clauses joined by a FANBOYS conjunction require a comma before the conjunction.
- Set off a transition word or phrase in the middle of an independent clause with commas.
- Nonessential appositives require a comma or commas to set them apart.
- A participle phrase that doesn't describe the noun right next to it should be set off with a comma.
- A comma is used to separate introductory information from the sentence's independent clause.
- On the SAT, include a comma before a concluding dependent clause in punctuation questions.

Punctuation: Commas
Check for Understanding

1. The manufacturer's car models, constructed with materials from many countries around the world, included costly new features this year to meet ______ the car's price increased so much that auto sales declined.

   Which choice completes the text so that it conforms to the conventions of Standard English?

   A) expectations but

   B) expectations, but

   C) expectations

   D) expectations,

2. Despite the setbacks to his career goals, Joel was ______ keeping a healthy perspective and remaining persistent in efforts to accomplish his aims.

   Which choice completes the text so that it conforms to the conventions of Standard English?

   A) happy, though

   B) happy; though

   C) happy, though;

   D) happy, though,

3. From growing and observing plants, Pedro perceived that learning about "green life" had become his greatest ______ a singular interest that led him to study botany at the university.

   Which choice completes the text so that it conforms to the conventions of Standard English?

   A) passion,

   B) passion; and

   C) passion and

   D) passion

4. Based on his anthropological studies at Harvard, the young man wrote that "different languages, cultures, and animal husbandry practices have much in ______ that despite wide cultural differences, people are more similar to each other than is generally understood.

   Which choice completes the text so that it conforms to the conventions of Standard English?

   A) common": arguing

   B) common," arguing

   C) common"; arguing

   D) common." Arguing

5. A poetic ______ Macbeth was much easier to read than the Shakespeare sonnets that we had studied previously.

   Which choice completes the text so that it conforms to the conventions of Standard English?

   A) drama written, in blank verse, during the Elizabethan age

   B) drama written in blank verse during the Elizabethan age,

   C) drama written in blank verse during the Elizabethan age

   D) drama, written in blank verse during the Elizabethan age,

6. In the Neoclassical and Romantic periods, paintings had a finished appearance. When the Impressionist period began, however, critics thought the artists were displaying unfinished ______ slapdash sketches an artist might create complete later but not to sell.

   Which choice completes the text so that it conforms to the conventions of Standard English?

   A) paintings, and the

   B) paintings; the

   C) paintings. The

   D) paintings, the

Punctuation

Commas + Semicolons

A semicolon (;) has the force of a period but is used in the middle of a sentence to join independent clauses.

A transition word—typically, a conjunctive adverb—is often used between the clauses to indicate how the information in one relates to the information in the other. For example, a conjunctive adverb may indicate that related information is to follow (ex. "additionally"), or it may signal a difference in meaning (ex. "however").

When a transition word is included before or after the semicolon, a comma (,) is required to set it apart.

Common Conjunctive Adverbs on the SAT

accordingly	consequently	however	instead	similarly
actually	currently	in addition	in turn	specifically
additionally	evidently	in comparison	meanwhile	still
afterward	finally	indeed	moreover	subsequently
alternatively	for example	in contrast	nevertheless	therefore
as a result	for instance	in fact	nonetheless	though
besides	for this reason	in other words	regardless	thus
by contrast	furthermore	increasingly	second	to conclude

Conjunctive Adverbs with Semicolons

Rule: **A conjunctive adverb preceded by a semicolon must have a comma after it.**

When a conjunctive adverb is preceded by a semicolon joining two independent clauses, a comma is placed after it, indicating that the conjunctive adverb introduces the second clause.

Independent clause 1 — Conjunctive adverb

Casimir Jaworski is a man, not a god; therefore,

Independent clause 2 — Semicolon — Comma

he has limitations and makes mistakes.

"Casimir…god" and "he…mistakes" are independent clauses joined by a semicolon. The conjunctive adverb "therefore" indicates how the information in the second clause logically concludes from the preceding information before the semicolon—Casimir's limitations and mistakes result from being human. Conjunctive adverbs show that a second idea refers to a previous idea. Because it is not part of the clause itself, the adverb must be set off with a comma.

Rule: **A conjunctive adverb followed by a semicolon must have a comma before it.**

When a semicolon joins two independent clauses and the conjunctive adverb applies only to information stated in a previous sentence, a semicolon is placed after the conjunctive adverb, and a comma precedes it.

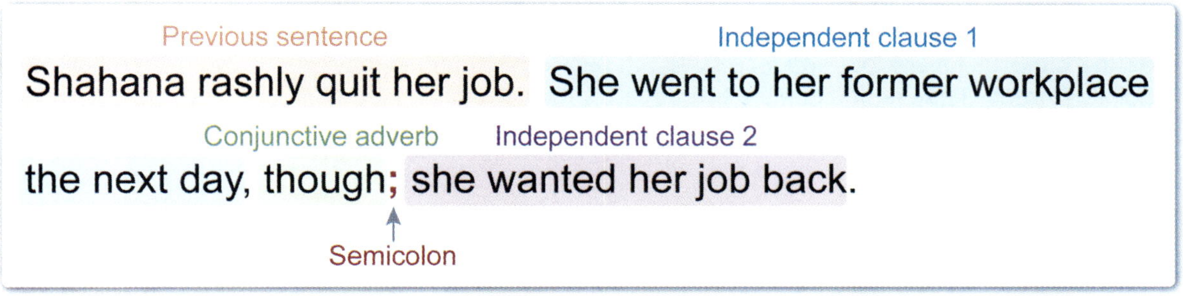

Rule: **A conjunctive adverb points back to a previous clause; therefore, it must appear in the clause that *follows* the clause it refers to.**

Remember that the conjunctive adverb indicates a relationship between one clause and another. That means that in a sentence with two independent clauses separated by a semicolon, the adverb can't go in the same clause it refers to. If it refers to a clause in a previous sentence, then the adverb goes *before* the semicolon because it must refer to that previous sentence. However, if the adverb refers to the first clause in the two-clause sentence, it must appear in the second clause, *after* the semicolon.

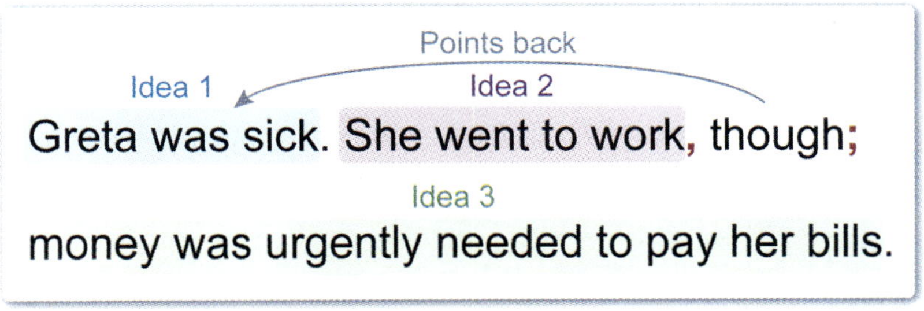

After the first idea stated in the opening sentence, the independent clauses "She...work" and "money...bills" are joined by a semicolon. The word "though" points back to the first statement about Greta being ill, so the conjunctive adverb belongs with "She...work."

Examples

✗ The Lone Ranger rode a white stallion named Silver, in contrast; Tonto rode Scout, a brown and white pinto.

✓ The Lone Ranger rode a white stallion named Silver; in contrast, Tonto rode Scout, a brown and white pinto.

The conjunctive adverb "in contrast" belongs with the second idea about the horse Tonto rides because his pinto contrasts with the Lone Ranger's white stallion that is described in the previous clause. A semicolon is correctly placed before "in contrast," which is then followed by a comma. This placement of the punctuation correctly includes the conjunctive adverb in the second clause that points back to the first idea.

✗ Roy Rogers had a Palomino stallion that was very quick, and he named his horse Trigger; consequently, the name suggests Trigger is as fast as a speeding bullet.

✓ Roy Rogers had a Palomino stallion that was very quick, and he named his horse Trigger, consequently; the name suggests Trigger is as fast as a speeding bullet.

The name of the horse is inspired by its quickness. The first idea is that the horse is "very quick." The conjunctive adverb "consequently" belongs with the second idea about the stallion's name, which points back to the previous idea about Trigger's speed. Therefore, "consequently" should be placed before the semicolon, correctly keeping the conjunctive adverb with the second idea.

Practice

1. The band teacher enjoyed jazz the ______ he had a large record collection that included his favorites—recordings by Jelly Roll Morton, Ella Fitzgerald, Duke Ellington, and Louis Armstrong.

Which choice completes the text so that it conforms to the conventions of Standard English?

A) most as a result

B) most, as a result,

C) most; as a result,

D) most, as a result;

See Appendix for answer

2. Lei Lei smiled and laughed during the party yesterday, happy to socialize with everyone. Her pleasure didn't last ______ Corey, the boy she was attracted to, arrived late and ignored her throughout the evening.

Which choice completes the text so that it conforms to the conventions of Standard English?

A) long; though,

B) long, though,

C) long though

D) long, though;

See Appendix for answer

Things to Remember:

- A conjunctive adverb preceded by a semicolon must have a comma after it.
- A conjunctive adverb followed by a semicolon must have a comma before it.
- A conjunctive adverb must appear in the clause that *follows* the clause it refers to.

Punctuation: Commas + Semicolons
Check for Understanding

1. In 1975, Massachusetts created the Boston Landmarks Commission (BLC) to preserve historic places in one of the oldest cities in the US. Its jurisdiction includes several important ______ the BLC identifies and preserves properties that are historic and reviews development and demolition activities proposed by the city.

   Which choice completes the text so that it conforms to the conventions of Standard English?

   A) functions; for example,

   B) functions for example

   C) functions, for example;

   D) functions, for example,

2. In 2021, Michael S. Regan became the 16th administrator of the US Environmental Protection Agency (EPA), responsible for protecting the environment and ensuring that citizens have clean air, land, and water. The Endangered Species Act is not under his ______ endangered species are primarily managed by the US Fish and Wildlife Service.

   Which choice completes the text so that it conforms to the conventions of Standard English?

   A) supervision; however,

   B) supervision however

   C) supervision, however,

   D) supervision, however;

Punctuation

Dashes

A dash (—) can be used once or twice in a sentence to set off interrupting information. When used in pairs, dashes are similar to offsetting commas or parentheses, which may also be used to set apart a mid-sentence interruption.

Generally, dashes are preferred when the writer wants to indicate a more abrupt interruption than one offset by commas but surrounding more important information than typically used between parentheses.

Unlike offsetting commas and parentheses, however, a dash can appear only once in a sentence. In that sense, a solitary dash is like a solitary comma in a sentence—each is not pairing with another instance of the same punctuation.

Grammar is my least favorite subject—but you knew that already.

It is so confusing, but for some reason we still have to learn it.

Note, however, that the SAT tends to ask questions about sentences that use two dashes, not one.

Interrupting information between dashes can be a word or phrase. It can even be a clause that could stand alone as a grammatically complete sentence. You can think of these interruptions as "mid-sentence interruptions" because that is where they appear.

One particular holiday—Thanksgiving—is my favorite.

Joshua—along with his furry friend—camped in the Rocky Mountains.

The teacher said that studying the vocabulary words would be Sam's best preparation—in the end, it was his only preparation—for success on the test.

***Rule*: A mid-sentence interruption should have the same punctuation before and after it—either two commas, two dashes, or a pair of parentheses.**

Don't mix and match dashes with commas or parentheses when a mid-sentence interruption calls for paired punctuation. The information that is set apart must have the same punctuation before and after it.

My brother, an irritating little boy, mockingly repeated what I said.

Chidike—the best friend ever—planned an amazing celebration for my birthday.

> A sentence with information between two dashes should still be a grammatical sentence *without* the interrupting information. (Ex. The cat—a calico—licked its paws. Grammatical sentence: The cat licked its paws.)

Examples

✗ Pedro completed the test—an easy set of multiple-choice questions, but the teacher decided it wouldn't count.

✓ Pedro completed the test—an easy set of multiple-choice questions—but the teacher decided it wouldn't count.

The first example sets apart the interruption ("an easy set of...questions") with mixed punctuation because it has a dash before it and a comma after it, which is incorrect. In the correct example, the interruption is set apart with paired, matching punctuation: two dashes.

Practice

1. There were two wild ______ that were often on our property.

Which choice completes the text so that it conforms to the conventions of Standard English?

A) animals, a coyote and a bobcat—

B) animals—a coyote and a bobcat,

C) animals, a coyote and a bobcat,

D) animals; a coyote and a bobcat,

See Appendix for answer

2. Winston loved his new ______ and wouldn't allow any food or drink inside it.

Which choice completes the text so that it conforms to the conventions of Standard English?

A) car—a fully loaded green Jaguar—

B) car—a fully loaded green Jaguar,

C) car, a fully loaded green Jaguar—

D) car: a fully loaded green Jaguar;

See Appendix for answer

Things to Remember:

- A pair of dashes sets off information that interrupts the sentence.
- The same punctuation is used before and after a mid-sentence interruption.

Punctuation: Dashes
Check for Understanding

1. In 2022, Alan decided to spend less time on *The Long* ______ a first-person survival game set in the frigid Canadian wilderness after a geomagnetic storm—and more on his studies.

   Which choice completes the text so that it conforms to the conventions of Standard English?

   A) *Dark*,

   B) *Dark*—

   C) *Dark*:

   D) *Dark*

2. Okra is preserved for a couple of months through a process known as pickling, in which the vegetable is placed in a jar along with five ingredients, including water and ______ that are boiled and poured into the jar after cooling.

   Which choice completes the text so that it conforms to the conventions of Standard English?

   A) vinegar:

   B) vinegar—

   C) vinegar

   D) vinegar,

Punctuation

End Marks

End punctuation refers to marks used at the end of a sentence. There are three punctuation marks used to end sentences—the question mark (?), exclamation point (!) and period (.). Only the question mark and period are tested on the SAT.

This section explains how to choose the right answers to questions about end punctuation.

Question Marks

Rule: Question marks are used at the end of direct questions.

Direct questions usually begin with helping verbs or with question words such as ***Where, Why, How, What***, or ***When***.

Can you help me?

Why won't you talk to him?

Word order can help you to distinguish between statements and direct questions. In statements, the subject typically comes *before* the verb. However, with direct questions, the subject is placed *after* the verb.

Subject — Verb

Statement: His gamer name is MetalNailGun.

Verb — Subject

Direct Question: Is his gamer name MetalNailGun?

Sometimes a dependent clause comes before a direct question. Because a comma is placed after an introductory clause, readers can easily spot a direct question that follows an introductory dependent clause.

Dependent clause — Direct question

If you have time today, can we talk?

Dependent clause — Direct question

When I finish my homework, can I play video games?

Example

✗ If I want to become rich, should I invest in the stock market. I decided to research the answer.

✓ If I want to become rich, should I invest in the stock market? I decided to research the answer.

In the "Correct" and "Incorrect" examples above, the word order of the verb phrase "should invest" is altered and inserts the subject "I" between "should" and "invest." The helping verb "should" comes *before* the subject and *before* the main verb "invest" in the independent clause "should I...market." This alteration indicates that a direct question has possibly been asked and, therefore, that a question mark may belong at the end of the sentence.

Practice

1. When you sleep, ___________ We want to know if earplugs will be needed.

Which choice completes the text so that it conforms to the conventions of Standard English?

A) do you snore?

B) you do snore.

C) you do snore?

D) do you snore.

See Appendix for answer

2. If we have the cash to fund it, ___________ The CEO wants to know if we have an effective plan.

Which choice completes the text so that it conforms to the conventions of Standard English?

A) this proposal will solve the problem?

B) will this proposal solve the problem?

C) this proposal will solve the problem.

D) will this proposal solve the problem.

See Appendix for answer

Periods

***Rule*: Periods separate independent clauses.**

An independent clause can stand by itself as a sentence, but a dependent clause cannot. Identify a clause—a group of words having a subject AND a verb—in a sentence by finding the subject, which is usually a noun, and identifying the verb. Sometimes a pronoun replaces a noun as the subject.

Subject 1 (noun) Verb 1 Subject 2 (pronoun) Verb 2

Joey loves pasta. He also enjoys other Italian dishes, such as chicken parmesan.

After finding clauses, determine whether each clause could be a sentence by itself; if it can stand alone, it's independent. If it can't stand alone, it's a dependent clause.

Independent clause 1 Independent clause 2

Joey loves pasta. He also enjoys other Italian dishes, such as chicken parmesan.

Period Period

All sentences that are NOT direct questions end in a period. In sentence statements, the subject typically precedes the verb.

In the example, finding the subjects and verbs in the sentences helps reveal the two independent clauses. The period between the independent clauses correctly separates them to create two sentences.

Sometimes independent clauses express a question that is indirect, meaning that a question is implied but is written in statement form, which means the clause makes a statement instead of directly asking a question:

Direct Question: Do you understand me?

Indirect Question: I wonder if you understand me.

Because an indirect question is a statement, it must end with a period, not a question mark.

Like other statements, indirect questions typically place the subject *before* the helping verb, whereas direct questions reverse that order, placing the subject *after* the helping verb.

Examples

✗ The bear wanted to protect her cub hastily she confronted the wild dogs threatening it.

✓ The bear wanted to protect her cub. She hastily confronted the wild dogs threatening it.

Identifying the independent clauses helps students determine that a period should be used between the clauses. The first independent clause is "The bear…cub," which is followed by a second independent clause, "She hastily…it."

✗ The detective was examining the crime scene when a noise caught his attention, without hesitation or fear, he opened the closet door and found a man bound and gagged but unharmed.

✓ The detective was examining the crime scene when a noise caught his attention. Without hesitation or fear, he opened the closet door and found a man bound and gagged but unharmed.

Sometimes it is more challenging to determine where a period is needed. For example, a prepositional phrase could appear at the end of one sentence or at the beginning of the next one.

In this case, "The detective...attention" is followed by a prepositional phrase "without...fear." This prepositional phrase describes how the detective ("he") opened the door, so it belongs with the clause "he opened...unharmed." Therefore, the period correctly separates the two independent clauses

✗ Yusef watched Rebecca's reaction to his marriage proposal, startled by the unexpected request, she was speechless for some time.

✓ Yusef watched Rebecca's reaction to his marriage proposal. Startled by the unexpected request, she was speechless for some time.

The same challenge can occur when a participle phrase appears between two independent clauses. Determine if the participle phrase describes the subject *before* it or the subject *after* it.

In this case, context tells us that it was "she" (Rebecca) who was "startled," not Yusef. Therefore, the period correctly belongs before the participle phrase.

Sometimes the SAT inserts a dash to interrupt a sentence as part of the answer choices. In this situation, determine if the word or words after the dash belong with the first sentence—despite the interruption—or with the second sentence.

> On the SAT a single dash is used for emphasis, NOT for interrupting.

✗ Megan played—masterfully during one of the nation's premier piano competitions, she won first place.

✓ Megan played—masterfully. At the awards ceremony for one of the nation's premier piano competitions, she won first place.

"Megan played" is the first independent clause, which is followed by a dash to emphasize "masterfully." A single dash is either paired with another dash, or it is followed by a period, which is provided in the second example. The incorrect example has neither another dash or a period. The prepositional phrase "At...competitions" describes when Megan ("she") won, so it belongs with the second independent clause.

Practice

3. Would the topic meet the professor's ______ needed to find out.

Which choice completes the text so that it conforms to the conventions of Standard English?

A) criteria, the students

B) criteria. The students

C) criteria? The students

D) criteria and the students

See Appendix for answer

4. Carmen drove up in her 2023 ______ with a powerful engine, the car went from 0 to 60 mph in 2.6 seconds.

Which choice completes the text so that it conforms to the conventions of Standard English?

A) Chevy Corvette Z06 and equipped

B) Chevy Corvette Z06, equipped

C) Chevy Corvette Z06 equipped

D) Chevy Corvette Z06. Equipped

See Appendix for answer

5. Dominka's interrogation was rude and ______ the interview, Gregorij was surprised at her disrespect and refused to respond to any more questions.

Which choice completes the text so that it conforms to the conventions of Standard English?

A) intrusive during

B) intrusive. During

C) intrusive, during

D) intrusive so during

See Appendix for answer

Things to Remember:

- Direct questions end with question marks.
- Direct questions often include question words (ex. "How") or a helping verb before the subject.
- Periods separate independent clauses.
- Periods go after indirect questions and other complete grammatical statements.

Punctuation: End Marks
Check for Understanding

1. If we watered the yard only once a week, ______ We were set on finding out.

   Which choice completes the text so that it conforms to the conventions of Standard English?

   A) would the grass remain green.

   B) the grass would remain green.

   C) the grass would remain green?

   D) would the grass remain green?

2. Scientists were intrigued by the previously hidden dinosaur ______ in Texas during a 2022 drought that dried up much of the Paluxy River in the Glen Rose area.

   Which choice completes the text so that it conforms to the conventions of Standard English?

   A) tracks discovered

   B) tracks; discovered

   C) tracks. Discovered

   D) tracks and

3. The suburban streets have not had heavy traffic ______ the downtown area, construction work has led to unexpected delays and frustrated drivers.

   Which choice completes the text so that it conforms to the conventions of Standard English?

   A) congestion, in

   B) congestion in

   C) congestion; but in

   D) congestion. In

4. The design for the beach condo ______ a few years after the building's construction, balconies were collapsing.

   Which choice completes the text so that it conforms to the conventions of Standard English?

   A) failed—completely, within

   B) failed—completely. Within

   C) failed—completely within

   D) failed—completely—within

5. With night's arrival, tourists anxiously walked through the foggy ______ rows of tall buildings beside its narrow walkways, the dark streets caused the pedestrians to feel increased fear of danger hidden by the darkness.

   Which choice completes the text so that it conforms to the conventions of Standard English?

   A) city having

   B) city and having

   C) city. Having

   D) city, having

Punctuation

Semicolons

A semicolon (;) can be used to separate two consecutive independent clauses that are in the same sentence.

Semicolons Joining Independent Clauses

***Rule*: Use a semicolons to separate consecutive independent clauses in the same sentence.**

Because semicolons are used between independent clauses, first learn to identify an independent clause by locating its subject and verb.

Subject 1 Verb 1 Subject 2
Some people think social media promotes greater division and hatred; others
Independent clause 1 Semicolon
Verb 2
believe that it helps us find unity and understanding.
Independent clause 2

If a group of words includes a subject and verb and can stand by itself as a grammatical sentence, it's an independent clause. Two independent clauses can be joined by a FANBOYS conjunction or by a semicolon, but not both. In the example sentence above, the independent clauses "Some…hatred" and "others…understanding" form a compound sentence joined by a semicolon.

If a period can replace the semicolon and create two complete grammatical sentences, the semicolon between two independent clauses is correct.

Examples

✗ Seamus Heaney has written great poetry, some have compared him to Robert Frost.

✗ Seamus Heaney has written great poetry; because some have compared him to Robert Frost.

✓ Seamus Heaney has written great poetry; some have compared him to Robert Frost.

"Seamus Heaney" is the first subject and "has written" is the first verb. The second subject is "some," followed by the second verb, "have compared." Both clauses are independent because "Seamus…poetry" and "some…Frost" can each stand alone as a grammatical sentence.

In the first (incorrect) example, a comma between the independent clauses creates a run-on sentence; in the second (also incorrect) example, a subordinating conjunction, "because," would begin a dependent clause—"because…Frost"—not a second independent clause. Only the third example is correct, using a semicolon to join two independent clauses.

Practice

1. Dagobert and Reginald walked through the ______ to search for leprechauns, ogres, and trolls.

   A. forest;

   B. forest; and

   C. forest,

   D. forest

See Appendix for answer

2. My twin brothers care for each other and seem ______ I wish I had a twin.

   A. inseparable;

   B. inseparable,

   C. inseparable; so

   D. inseparable

See Appendix for answer

Semicolons with FANBOYS Conjunctions

***Rule*: Do not use a FANBOYS conjunction after a semicolon that joins two independent clauses.**

A FANBOYS conjunction at the beginning of an independent clause changes the clause so that it can no longer stand alone as a grammatical sentence: it becomes a dependent clause. Therefore, a semicolon can't be used before a FANBOYS conjunction because semicolons don't belong between independent and dependent clauses.

Independent clause 1

Teaching careers generally offer a lower salary than other careers;

No FANBOYS

Independent clause 2

many people won't pursue a career in education due to its low pay.

Examples

✗ The flowers in the backyard were wilting; but the flowers in the front were flourishing.

✓ The flowers in the backyard were wilting; the flowers in the front were flourishing.

A semicolon is placed between the two independent clauses that describe flowers in the backyard and flowers in the front. Because the semicolon joins the independent clauses, the FANBOYS conjunction "but" should not be used.

> A FANBOYS conjunction should not immediately follow a semicolon that joins two independent clauses.

Practice

3. Jimmy said the movie had puzzling challenges and an intriguing ______ Jonathan and Tim decided to watch something else.

   A) plot; but

   B) plot but

   C) plot;

   D) plot,

See Appendix for answer

4. In 2022, Graciela and Pedro were married in the city's ______ in 2023, they celebrated the birth of their first child, Horacio.

Which choice completes the text so that it conforms to the conventions of Standard English?

   A) cathedral; and

   B) cathedral

   C) cathedral;

   D) cathedral,

See Appendix for answer

Conjunctive Adverbs Following Semicolons

***Rule*: When a conjunctive adverb separates two independent clauses, place a semicolon before the adverb and a comma after it.**

A conjunctive adverb after a semicolon serves as a transition between the related independent clauses.

Independent clause 1	Conjunctive adverb	Independent clause 2
I ate the entire box of donuts;	consequently,	I felt uncomfortably full and hyperactive.

Conjunctive adverbs describe the relationship between two ideas that appear in consecutive independent clauses. Because a conjunctive adverb always refers to the preceding idea or previous sentence, it should be attached to the second clause, not the first clause.

In the example sentence above, the conjunctive adverb ("consequently") describes the resulting discomfort from eating too many donuts, an idea stated in the preceding independent clause, "I ate...donuts." Therefore, "consequently" belongs with the second independent clause, "I felt...hyperactive."

Examples

✗ The wild mustangs didn't approach our ranch, instead; they roamed miles away from us in unsettled territory.

✓ The wild mustangs didn't approach our ranch; instead, they roamed miles away from us in unsettled territory.

"The wild...ranch" is an idea stated as an independent clause about what the mustangs did not do. It is followed by another idea describing what the mustangs *did* do: "they...territory." The conjunctive adverb "instead" indicates that what the mustangs did not do was an alternative to what they did: mustangs roamed far away rather than approached the ranch.

Therefore, "instead" belongs with the second independent clause because it describes how the second clause differs from the first clause. A semicolon is placed before the adverb to indicate that the adverb belongs with the second clause. A comma, which is weaker than a semicolon, is placed after the conjunctive adverb.

Common Conjunctive Adverbs on the SAT

accordingly	consequently	however	instead	similarly
actually	currently	in addition	in turn	specifically
additionally	evidently	in comparison	meanwhile	still
afterward	finally	indeed	moreover	subsequently
alternatively	for example	in contrast	nevertheless	therefore
as a result	for instance	in fact	nonetheless	though
besides	for this reason	in other words	regardless	thus
by contrast	furthermore	increasingly	second	to conclude

Practice

5. Aaron and Sue reduced the number of organized activities chosen by their nine-year-old ______ the whole family found the free time added to their new schedule delightfully liberating.

Which choice completes the text so that it conforms to the conventions of Standard English?

A) daughter, consequently,

B) daughter, consequently

C) daughter, consequently;

D) daughter; consequently,

See Appendix for answer

6. The restaurant's food was bland, and service wasn't the best. Xavier will eat there ______ his parents own it, and he works with them as part of the family business.

Which choice completes the text so that it conforms to the conventions of Standard English?

A) again, though,

B) again, though

C) again, though;

D) again though;

See Appendix for answer

Another type of question might require you to decide whether the semicolon between two independent clauses goes *before* or *after* the conjunctive adverb.

A conjunctive adverb indicates a relationship between one clause and another. That means that in a sentence with two independent clauses separated by a semicolon, the adverb can't go in the same clause it refers to.

If it refers to a clause in a previous sentence, then the adverb goes before the semicolon because it must refer to that previous sentence. However, if the adverb refers to the first clause in a two-clause sentence, it must appear in the second clause, after the semicolon.

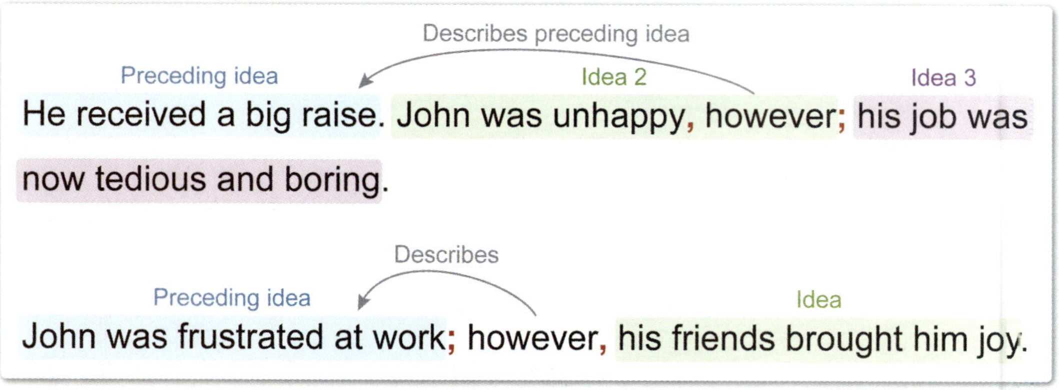

No Semicolon Between an Independent and Dependent Clause

***Rule*: When an independent clause is followed by a subordinating conjunction that begins a dependent clause, no punctuation is used before the conjunction.**

Independent clause | Subordinating conjunction | Dependent clause

The volleyball team was successful in games when the team communicated more effectively.

No punctuation

An incorrect answer choice might place a semicolon between an independent clause and a dependent clause, which is wrong because the dependent clause cannot stand by itself after the semicolon.

Independent clause (can stand on its own)

The tribe thought the warrior's blazing wrath would lead her to victory;

Dependent clause (cannot stand on its own)

because they believed nothing could match the fury of a woman.

Incorrect

Examples

✗ The teacher was happy with Shakira's effort; when her academic performance showed her amazing work ethic.

✓ The teacher was happy with Shakira's effort; her academic performance showed her amazing work ethic.

"The teacher...effort" is an independent clause, but "when...work ethic" is a dependent clause, so it is incorrect to separate them with a semicolon.

The subordinating conjunction "when" that begins the second clause makes it a grammatically incomplete sentence. However, in the correct example, a semicolon separates two independent clauses: "The teacher...effort" and "her...ethic."

Practice

7. The elderly military veteran respectfully placed his hand on his ______ when the national anthem was sung.

Which choice completes the text so that it conforms to the conventions of Standard English?

A) heart;

B) heart

C) heart,

D) heart.

See Appendix for answer

8. Blanche seemed unable to control her buying ______ she went to the store for a blouse but came home with 4 large bags of new clothes.

    A) impulses; for example,

    B) impulses, for example

    C) impulses, for example,

    D) impulses, for example;

See Appendix for answer

Semicolons and Complex Lists

Rule: Semicolons separate items within a complex series.

Until now, we have looked at the semicolon that has the force of a period in the middle of a sentence. However, there is also another type of semicolon, which can be thought of as a stronger comma. It is used instead of a comma to separate items in a complex list.

Whereas a simple list typically contains short items, a complex list is a series of multiword items that may include their own comma:

Item 1 | Item 2 | Item 3

The building was designed by John, an engineer; Lakshmi, an architect; **and** Ernesto, a green builder.

Comma | Comma | And | Comma

The sentence includes a list of three items—the people responsible for designing the building—that each have a comma before an appositive. Because the listed items include commas, a semicolon is placed between the items to avoid confusion.

Examples

✗ In 2011, Rashod traveled to the Eternal City, Rome, in 2015, to the City of Light, Paris, and in 2020, to the Big Apple, New York.

✓ In 2011, Rashod traveled to the Eternal City, Rome; in 2015, to the City of Light, Paris; and in 2020, to the Big Apple, New York.

Here, a complex list describes three places that Rashod visited in different years. Each city is identified by its nickname, followed by the city's name.

A semicolon is the correct punctuation to separate the three items in the list—the cities of Rome, Paris, and New York—to make it clear which year Rashod traveled to which city.

Practice

9. Batman fought crimes perpetrated by the ______ Poison Ivy, who was capable of mind control; and Scarecrow, who released fear toxin in Gotham.

Which choice completes the text so that it conforms to the conventions of Standard English?

A. Riddler, who planned a bank heist;

B. Riddler, who planned a bank heist,

C. Riddler; who planned a bank heist;

D. Riddler who planned a bank heist;

See Appendix for answer

10. Ignacio decided on a road trip to visit several places on his bucket list, including Santa Fe, New Mexico, in 2020; ______ and Gulf Shores, Alabama, in 2023.

Which choice completes the text so that it conforms to the conventions of Standard English?

A. Dallas, Texas, in 2021,

B. Dallas, Texas, in 2021;

C. Dallas, Texas in 2021,

D. Dallas; Texas, in 2021,

See Appendix for answer

Things to Remember:

- A semicolon can join two independent clauses within a sentence.
- When a semicolon joins two independent clauses, a FANBOYS conjunction after the semicolon is incorrect.
- Conjunctive adverbs describe the relationship between an idea and a preceding idea.
- A conjunctive adverb belongs in the clause after the idea it refers to.
- When a conjunctive adverb follows a semicolon, a comma is used after the adverb.
- A semicolon can separate listed items that already include commas.

Punctuation: Semicolons
Check for Understanding

1. One side of my 1965 US quarter features an image of ______ the other side shows an eagle and laurel branches.

   Which choice completes the text so that it conforms to the conventions of Standard English?

   A) George Washington,

   B) George Washington; and,

   C) George Washington;

   D) George Washington

2. Bellingrath Gardens and Mobile Botanical Gardens are two of many beautiful gardens in Alabama dedicated to promoting ______ educating people about plants; and fostering an appreciation of plants.

   Which choice completes the text so that it conforms to the conventions of Standard English?

   A) research, both locally and worldwide,

   B) research, both locally and worldwide;

   C) research; both locally and worldwide,

   D) research both locally and worldwide,

3. Rahul's collection of over 140 Steam computer games included older classics such as *Wingspan*, a digitized boardgame where players attract birds to their ______ a collaborative multiplayer game where players destroy zombies while seeking rescue; and *Half-Life*, a single player shooter game involving combat and puzzle-solving.

   Which choice completes the text so that it conforms to the conventions of Standard English?

   A) habitats, *Left for Dead* 2,

   B) habitats; *Left for Dead* 2,

   C) habitats, *Left for Dead* 2:

   D) habitats; *Left for Dead* 2

4. To her friends, Yukina seemed cold and distant as she sat at a table by ______ she was exhausted and emotionally drained after breaking up with her boyfriend.

   Which choice completes the text so that it conforms to the conventions of Standard English?

   A) herself, however,

   B) herself however,

   C) herself, however;

   D) herself; however,

Punctuation

Unnecessary Punctuation

Punctuation errors involving periods, commas, semicolons, dashes, and apostrophes fall into two categories: the correct punctuation not being used where it is required, and punctuation being used where it doesn't belong. To understand the difference, you need to know about parts of speech and sentence structure.

Possessive Nouns

Rule: A possessive noun must include an apostrophe, usually followed by "s" at the end of the word.

Possession is typically indicated by placing the possessor noun (ex. a person) immediately before the noun that is being possessed (ex. an object). For most singular possessive nouns, use an apostrophe and an "s" at the end.

Singular Possessive: The child's dog frequently escapes the backyard.

Some nouns, however, are singular but end with an "s." When a singular noun ends with an "s," simply add an apostrophe at the end to make it possessive.

Singular: The octopus' tentacles wrapped around its prey.

A plural possessive noun requires an apostrophe *after* the "s."

Plural Possessive: At Sasha's college, the dormitories' entrances are locked at 10 p.m.

In spoken English, a plural noun can be mistaken for a possessive noun because both usually end with "s." In written English, if the possessive's apostrophe is omitted by mistake, you can still spot a possessive noun because it must be followed by another noun or by a noun phrase. In contrast, plural nouns are not immediately followed by other nouns.

Sometimes there are other clues indicating whether a noun is singular or plural. For example, "a" is singular and is often used before a singular noun, while plural specifiers like "many" may precede a plural noun.

Note that there are some plural nouns that don't end with "s," such as "men," "children," or "teeth." When a plural noun doesn't end with an "s," add an apostrophe and an "s" at the end, as with a singular possessive noun.

The women's bathroom had a longer line than the men's bathroom.

Examples

✗ That books chapters were all short, and its stories plots were intriguing.

✓ That book's chapters were all short, and its stories' plots were intriguing.

The singular "That" and "its" reveal that the chapters and stories belong to the singular possessive noun "book," so an apostrophe and an "s" are needed at the end of "book" because "book" must be possessive. In the second part of the sentence, "plots" and "stories" are both plural, ending with "s" and

"–ies," respectively. The plural noun "plots" belongs to the preceding plural possessive noun "stories," so an apostrophe is needed at the end of "stories."

✗ The boys' are playing on the computer.

✓ The boys are playing on the computer.

A possessive noun must have another noun immediately after it, but in the example above, the noun "boys" is followed by the verb "are playing," which indicates that "boys" isn't possessive. Nouns don't possess verbs—they possess other nouns. Therefore, "boys" is plural but not possessive, so an apostrophe shouldn't be used.

Practice

1. In her popular book *The House on Mango Street*, Sandra Cisneros includes a series of short, descriptive sketches that reveal the significant ______, a 12-year-old Mexican American girl, over the course of a year.
   A) experience's of Esperanza Cordero
   B) experience's of Esperanza Cordero'
   C) experiences of Esperanza Cordero
   D) experiences' of Esperanza Cordero's

See Appendix for answer

2. On Gordon Ramsay's television show *Hell's Kitchen*, when two or three ______ are spotted, the famous chef often responds with explosive outbursts.
   A) contestant's mistakes'
   B) contestants' mistake's
   C) contestant's mistakes
   D) contestants' mistakes

See Appendix for answer

Preposition and Object

Rule: Punctuation shouldn't be inserted between a preposition and its object.

A preposition typically shows the spatial relationship between two nouns in a sentence. For example, in "The plane flew over the mountain," the preposition "over" describes the spatial relationship between the plane and the mountain: the plane flew over, not around or into, the mountain.

A preposition always begins a prepositional phrase, which ends with the first noun or pronoun after the preposition. The noun or pronoun concluding the prepositional phrase is called the object of the preposition.

Giovanni ran from the dog that chased him.

The prepositional phrase here is "from the dog" because it begins with the preposition "from" and ends with the first noun after it, "dog."

A prepositional phrase consisting of only a preposition and a noun never includes punctuation between the preposition and its object.

> On the SAT, answers with a colon, dash, or comma between a preposition and its object are always wrong.

Most prepositions are single words. However, there are some multi-word prepositions (ex. such as, except for, in addition to).

Because the definition of a preposition is so broad, learning common prepositions will help you to identify them during the test.

Common Prepositions

under	to	into	like
around	between	through	after
among	out	over	during
of	against	at	from
for	near	before	by
with	about	as	below
without	in	down	toward
within	through	behind	among
on	in addition to	instead of	in front of
across	inside of	except for	as well as

Examples

✗ Sally went to: the concert while Tiffany went shopping

✗ Sally went to—the concert while Tiffany went shopping.

✗ Sally went to, the concert while Tiffany went shopping.

✓ Sally went to the concert while Tiffany went shopping.

The prepositional phrase "to the concert" begins with the preposition "to" and ends with the noun "concert." Because no punctuation can be placed between a preposition and its object, the first three examples are incorrect.

Even when a preposition is located immediately before a quotation, no comma is used between the preposition and its object.

✗ Hans wrote a play about, "the inspiration of the muse through birds."

✓ Hans wrote a play about "the inspiration of the muse through birds."

Sometimes a preposition is followed not by only one object but by two or more objects joined by a FANBOYS conjunction, such as "and." In that case, the prepositional phrase ends with the final noun instead of the first noun after the preposition.

The donations were distributed by my sister and me.

The prepositional phrase is "by my sister and me." Although "sister" is the first object noun after the preposition "by," the phrase has a second object that ends with the pronoun "me." The sentence includes the FANBOYS conjunction "and" to indicate that the donations were distributed by two people, and both are objects of the preposition "by."

I found dust on my brother's shelves, furniture, and keyboard.

Here, the preposition "on" is followed by three nouns that are its objects, joined by the FANBOYS conjunction "and." Therefore, when the objects of a preposition are a list of items, commas are placed between each item—but not immediately after the preposition.

Practice

3. On Wolfgang's final exams ______ English, Spanish, and Introduction to Philosophy, he performed better than others in class by focusing intently on taking good notes and reviewing them each day.

   A) in

   B) in,

   C) in—

   D) in:

See Appendix for answer

4. After finishing dinner and washing the family's dishes, Cletis expressed his concern ______ "strolling to the cave," which is how he describes walking down the rickety steps to his basement office.

   A) about—

   B) about,

   C) about

   D) about:

See Appendix for answer

Dependent Clause after Independent Clause

***Rule:* Punctuation should not separate a necessary dependent clause that directly follows an independent clause.**

Incorrect: Sam started exercising, because he wanted to lose weight.

Correct: Sam started exercising because he wanted to lose weight.

Groups of words are either phrases or clauses. Clauses have both a subject and verb, but phrases never have both.

There are two main types of clauses: An independent clause can stand by itself as a grammatical sentence, but a dependent clause cannot stand alone as a sentence. In fact, dependent clauses must be joined to an independent clause to be part of a grammatical sentence.

Independent clause | Dependent clause

Members of our student council were upset because they weren't supported.

↑ No punctuation

This sentence begins with an independent clause—"Members of our student council were upset"—that could stand alone as a grammatical sentence; its subject is "members" and its verb is "were." It is followed by a dependent clause—"because they weren't supported"—that cannot stand alone as a grammatical sentence even though it has a subject ("they") and a verb ("were"). The difference is that the subordinating conjunction "because" weakens the clause, requiring an independent clause in the same sentence.

Dependent clauses typically begin with a subordinating conjunction or a relative pronoun, and they may come before or after an independent clause. However, when an independent clause precedes a dependent clause, no punctuation should be placed between them.

Common Subordinating Conjunctions

after	although	as	as if
as long as	as much as	as soon as	as though
because	before	by the time	even if
even though	if	in case	in order that
in the event that	now that	once	provided that
since	than	that	though
unless	until	when	whenever
where	wherever	whether	while

Common Relative Pronouns

that	which	who	whom

Examples

✗ Camille drives recklessly, when she is upset.

✗ Camille drives recklessly: when she is upset.

✗ Camille drives recklessly; when she is upset.

✓ Camille drives recklessly when she is upset.

Because the dependent clause (when…upset) follows the independent clause (Camille drives recklessly), no punctuation should be placed before the relative pronoun "that."

Practice

5. As Eunice helped to organize the small home, she put things her mom used frequently in accessible ______ they might be easily found, and anything not used in the last year was donated or thrown out.

   A) places, where

   B) places where

   C) places; where

   D) places: where

See Appendix for answer

6. Both Jack Brown, an attorney for the husband seeking divorce, and Gladys Knight, an attorney for the wife, objected to the judge's decision. Together they filed a Motion for ______ encouraged the judge to take a second look at the decision.

   A) Reconsideration,

   B) Reconsideration that

   C) Reconsideration, that

   D) Reconsideration

See Appendix for answer

Subject and Verb

Rule: **A single comma may NOT be used between a subject noun and its verb or between a verb and its direct object.**

Two commas may be used around an appositive that comes between a noun and its verb, but not a single comma.

Incorrect: Joe, a friend of mine ran to the store because he wanted supplies for the party.

Correct: Joe, a friend of mine, ran to the store because he wanted supplies for the party.

A clause has a noun (or pronoun) as its subject and a main verb; the verb usually follows the subject. Because the subject and verb work together to express an idea, they shouldn't be separated by any punctuation.

Subject noun — Main verb

Samir's essay about the influence of literature on the imagination became a model for the class.

No punctuation

Sometimes other punctuation in the sentence can mistakenly be taken as a sign that punctuation is needed between the subject and the verb. This might occur when commas are placed around an interrupting phrase. Don't let other punctuation trick you into separating a subject and verb with a comma.

Examples

✗ Some teens still write their own poems. At fourteen, Enrique wrote a poem "Heat," for instance, that was posted on a blog, while a poem by fifteen-year-old Theresa called "Black Rain," was published in a magazine.

✓ Some teens still write their own poems. At fourteen, Enrique wrote a poem "Heat," for instance, that was posted on a blog, while a poem by fifteen-year-old Theresa called "Black Rain" was published in a magazine.

There is a comma after "Heat" because the interrupting transition "for instance" requires commas to set it apart from the rest of the sentence. This might make you think that a comma should also be placed after "Black Rain," but that would be INCORRECT because a single comma there would separate the subject "Black Rain" from its verb, "was published."

Practice

7. *Craving the Cold*, a psychological thriller, creates an intense, "edge of your seat" movie experience, whereas *Escaping the* ______ a slow-paced drama about prison life.

   A) *Heat—*

   B) *Heat,* offers

   C) *Heat:* offers

   D) *Heat* offers

See Appendix for answer

Restrictive Appositives

Rule: Essential appositives should not be separated from the rest of the sentence with one or more commas.

Appositives are nouns or noun phrases placed beside another noun to identify or describe it further. Sometimes the information in the appositive is essential (necessary) for the sentence's meaning to be clear. No commas are placed before or after essential appositives.

A capitalized proper noun appositive following an uncapitalized common noun expresses information that is needed.

Identifies
Noun ← Appositive

Celebrity chef Anthony Bourdain graduated from The Culinary Institute of America in 1978.

↑ No comma (between "chef" and "Anthony") ↑ No comma (between "Bourdain" and "graduated")

In the example above, the common noun "celebrity chef" is followed by the capitalized proper noun "Anthony Bourdain." The sentence requires the appositive "Anthony Bourdain" to make it clear which celebrity chef graduated in 1978. Therefore, it is an essential appositive that should not have commas around it.

However, if the proper noun comes first, then the common noun's information that follows it is unnecessary (nonessential).

Describes

Proper noun → Appositive

Anthony Bourdain, a celebrity chef, graduated from the The Culinary Institute of America in 1978.

In the second example, "Anthony Bourdain" is a proper noun that makes it clear who is being discussed. It is placed before the common noun "celebrity chef" that adds unnecessary information in a nonessential appositive, which should always be set apart by commas.

> On the test, when an appositive is a capitalized noun needed to identify the person being discussed, the appositive is not set apart with commas.

Practice

8. Last year, sophomore Cameron Mackery, who had never performed in a theater production before, earned a supporting role in the school ______ and received high praise for his acting, increasing his confidence that he might be given a starring role this year.

   A) play *Our Town,*

   B) play *Our Town,*

   C) play, *Our Town*

   D) play *Our Town*

See Appendix for answer

9. In 1971, Mexican American singer Selena Quintanilla was born in ______ and later became so successful that she was called the Queen of Tejana Music.

   A) Texas, a state known for producing talented musicians,

   B) Texas a state known for producing talented musicians

   C) Texas, a state known for producing talented musicians

   D) Texas, a state, known for producing talented musicians

See Appendix for answer

Things to Remember:

- A possessive noun must include an apostrophe, usually followed by "s" at the end of the word.
- Prepositions should not be separated from their objects with a comma.
- No punctuation should be placed between an independent clause immediately followed by a dependent clause that is essential.
- Never separate a subject from its verb with a single comma.
- Don't place commas around restrictive appositives.

Punctuation: Unnecessary
Check for Understanding

1. In his fascinating book *Why Immigrants Come to America: Braceros, Indocumentados, and the Migra*, Robert Joe Stout includes personal encounters, newspaper articles, interviews, and conversations to present ______, explaining why they risk their lives to get to the US and why they continue to come despite the measures taken to stop them.

   A) account's of undocumented workers

   B) account's of undocumented workers'

   C) accounts of undocumented workers

   D) accounts' of undocumented worker's

2. When technology company Floober Bloofer Dynamics surveyed its employees about their contentment at work, the majority responded that having a flexible schedule would help them ______ "finding a work-life balance that was less stressful," said manager Humphrey Dumphrey, fondly referred to by his employees as Mr. Pocket Protector.

   A) with,

   B) with

   C) with:

   D) with—

3. Glycans, cell surface sugars that are made by all living organisms, have been poorly understood until recently. In 2022, American ______ won the Nobel Prize in chemistry and was recognized as the founder of biorthogonal chemistry, which involves chemical reactions that allow scientists to study the interaction of molecules in living things without interference to their natural biological processes.

   A) chemist, Carolyn Ruth Bertozzi,

   B) chemist, Carolyn Ruth Bertozzi

   C) chemist Carolyn Ruth Bertozzi

   D) chemist Carolyn Ruth Bertozzi,

4. As evolutionary geneticist Marina Ascunce stated recently, "We can think of human lice as heirlooms of our past." She provides evidence that the DNA of head lice seems to have recorded the large migration of humans over the Bering Strait Land Bridge to inhabit North and South America. Specifically, lice are parasites that survive on human blood, and they were gripping the hair of ______ they migrated to the Americas to settle and colonize.

   A) humans when

   B) humans; when

   C) humans, when

   D) humans. When

5. In her nonfiction books, English-born Lynne Truss has been inspired by her deep concern about correct punctuation. Her 2003 book *Eats, Shoots, and Leaves: A Zero Tolerance Approach to Punctuation*, for example, is a witty explanation about comma usage, while her 2007 book ______ focuses on proper apostrophe use.

   A) *The Girl's Like Spaghetti*

   B) *The Girl's Like Spaghetti—*

   C) *The Girl's Like Spaghetti:*

   D) *The Girl's Like Spaghetti,*

Sentence Structure

Modifiers

Sentence structure is how words fit together in a sentence. The structure of a sentence involves the sequence of its parts, which should be placed in an order that results in clear, coherent writing. Common sequences include placing an adjective before the noun it describes, a subject before its predicate, and an adverb before a verb.

Placing an adjective or adverb next to what they describe improves clarity. Placing descriptive words farther from what they modify may confuse the reader rather than clarify your meaning.

On the SAT, questions about correct word placement often require you to choose the best word so the first step is to identify both the words *being described* and the words that *describe* them.

Introductory Phrases and Misplaced Nouns

Rule: A noun described by an introductory descriptive phrase should immediately follow that phrase.

In SAT questions about misplaced modifiers, the sentence always begins with a descriptive phrase followed by a comma. Most of these introductory phrases begin with a preposition and include an –ing verb form after a preposition. That –ing verb form can be a clue to which noun is being described, so evaluate the word ending with "ing" and other words in the introductory phrase to determine which noun should immediately follow that phrase.

Describes

Descriptive phrase

By completing all homework carefully and on time, Raul achieved better grades in every class.

The preposition "By" begins the phrase, and the –ing verb form "completing" follows it. These two words provide clues as to which noun should follow the introductory phrase: "completing all homework" refers to an action by Raul, so the phrase "By…time" should immediately be followed by "Raul." This sentence correctly includes the described noun immediately after the introductory phrase describing it.

The introductory phrase might begin with a participle, a verb form that functions as an adjective. PRESENT participles end in –ing, but PAST participles end with "–ed," "–d," "–t," "–en," or "–n," as shown by these words: heat**ed**, creat**ed**, knel**t**, eat**en**, rise**n**).

When a descriptive phrase begins a sentence, evaluate which noun it describes.

Describes

Introductory phrase Noun

Praised by her family and friends at the gathering, Ahnika blushed while her mother smiled with pride.

The introductory descriptive phrase "Praised...gathering" includes the pronoun "her," and "Ahnika," not her mother, is the person being praised. Therefore, the noun "Ahnika" should immediately follow the introductory phrase for clarity.

> The descriptive phrase that begins the sentence will have a comma separating it from the rest of the sentence, which makes it easy to identify.

Rule: The words "there are" and "it is" should NOT be placed immediately after an introductory phrase.

An introductory descriptive phrase adds details about a noun. However, the words "there is/are/was were" and "It is/are/was/were" do not include nouns—they can be thought of as filler words that delay the introduction of the noun that follows.

Introductory filler — Noun

There is a toy **train** on the shelf in my bedroom.

Subject noun

A toy **train** is on the shelf in my bedroom.

The sentences in the above image express the same idea, but the first sentence begins with "There is," delaying the introduction of the noun "train." The second sentence uses that noun as the subject at the beginning of the sentence.

Words like "there is" cannot follow an introductory descriptive phrase because the subject following "There were" or "It was" clauses would be distanced from the descriptive phrase, causing confusion. In the example below, "Showing...ship" describes "the movie *Titanic*," which is expressed more clearly when it is next to that title.

Incorrect: Showing frightened people on the ship, there was a group of musicians who in the movie *Titanic* had continued to play while the vessel sank.

Correct: Showing frightened people on the ship, the movie *Titanic* tells the story of musicians continuing to play while the vessel sank.

On misplaced noun questions, don't choose answers beginning with wording like "there is" or "it was." Instead, the correct answer will begin with the noun described by the introductory descriptive phrase.

Incorrect: Impressed by the students' performance on the test, there was a teacher who organized a party to celebrate their success.

The introductory phrase "Impressed...test" doesn't describe "there." It refers to the noun "teacher" later in the sentence, so beginning the independent clause with "there was" results in confusion because "impressed" doesn't describe "there."

Instead, include the noun being described immediately after the introductory phrase describing it.

Correct: Impressed by the students' performance on the test, a teacher organized a party to celebrate their success.

The modified noun "teacher" immediately follows the phrase "Impressed...test," which correctly describes the teacher as the person who was impressed.

> Eliminate answers beginning with "there" or "it" after an introductory descriptive phrase.

Rule: An introductory descriptive phrase can't describe a possessive noun.

An apostrophe and sometimes an "s" are added to a noun to make it possessive. A word in its possessive form is an adjective describing ownership of another noun after it. Therefore, it's not the word with the apostrophe that is being described by the introductory information but the noun that follows—whatever is possessed.

The first noun after the introductory descriptive phrase must be able to do the action that the description expresses. Because the apostrophe plus "s" makes "Jasmine" a possessive, "Walking...thicket" incorrectly describes the noun immediately after it, which is "jacket." However, "walking" can't describe the noun "jacket" because clothing isn't able to walk.

The correct version would include a noun that isn't possessive after the introductory phrase describing it.

Here, after the introductory description, the first noun is "Jasmine," a person who is able do the action of walking. This version correctly places a noun that isn't possessive—"Jasmine"—immediately after the introductory phrase that describes her as "walking through a thicket."

> Eliminate answers that include a possessive word immediately after an introductory modifier.

Rule: An introductory phrase can't describe a prepositional phrase.

As mentioned, when a sentence begins with a descriptive phrase, the noun it describes should be placed immediately after it, but a prepositional phrase never functions as a noun. Therefore, an introductory descriptive phrase shouldn't be immediately followed by a prepositional phrase.

Sometimes a test question on misplaced nouns will have a sentence that begins with a descriptive phrase and include an answer choice that begins with a prepositional phrase, but this will always be an incorrect answer that can be eliminated.

Incorrect: Assigned to a new military base in Pensacola, in 2023 Major Joseph Bolton enjoyed fishing in the Gulf of Mexico.

The introductory phrase "Assigned...Pensacola" describes a person who can be "assigned" to a military base. This descriptive phrase is followed by the prepositional phrase "in 2023," but the year 2023 wasn't assigned—"Major Joseph Bolton" was. The phrase "in 2023" refers to "enjoyed."

Correct: Assigned to a new military base in Pensacola, Major Joseph Bolton enjoyed fishing in the Gulf of Mexico in 2023.

Because the noun described by the introductory phrase immediately follows it, this sentence places the modifier and noun closer together, which avoids misplacing the described noun.

Eliminate answers that include a prepositional phrase immediately after an introductory modifier.

Examples

✗ After becoming a celebrated actress, Arthur Miller, a famous American writer who wrote plays such as *The Crucible,* married Marilyn Monroe.

✓ After becoming a celebrated actress, Marilyn Monroe married Arthur Miller, a famous American writer who wrote plays such as *The Crucible*.

The introductory information describes an actress, which refers to a female. "Marilyn" is a female name; "Arthur" is a male name. Therefore, "actress" indicates that the introductory phrase is meant to describe "Marilyn Monroe," not "Arthur Miller." The second example is correct because it places the name of the actress immediately after the introductory information.

✗ Referred to as the class clown by her fellow students, the teacher was always upset by Elena.

✓ Referred to as the class clown by her fellow students, Elena was always upsetting the teacher.

The word "referred" begins a phrase about someone being a "class clown," and "fellow students" indicates that the phrase is meant to refer to a student. Because the word described by "Referred to...students" is the noun "Elena," her name should be placed immediately after the descriptive phrase. The first example incorrectly suggests that the teacher is the class clown, which isn't what the writer meant.

✗ Before applauding the actors, there were people who waited to be sure the performance had ended.

✓ Before applauding the actors, people waited to be sure the performance had ended.

"Before...actors" describes people who can applaud, not the words "there were." Therefore, the described noun "people" should be placed immediately after the introductory phrase.

✗ After thinking about the difficulties, Samir's belief that he had a chance for success was crushed.

✓ After thinking about the difficulties, Samir believed that his chance for success was crushed.

An introductory descriptive phrase doesn't describe a possessive noun. The incorrect example has the possessive form for "Samir," making "belief" the noun described by the introductory phrase, but that doesn't make sense because a belief can't think. The word "thinking" describes what a person can do, so the first noun after the introductory information should be "Samir." By placing "Samir" immediately after the introductory description, the correct example clearly indicates that it was Samir who experienced difficulties.

✗ Considered by many the greatest leader of a fledgling nation, in 1789 George Washington became the first president the United States.

✓ Considered by many the greatest leader of a fledgling nation, George Washington became the first president the United States in 1789.

On the test, an introductory descriptive phrase doesn't refer to a prepositional phrase, so placing "in 1789" immediately after it is incorrect. In this example, the introductory phrase describes the first US president, so "George Washington" is the noun that should immediately follow it.

Practice

1. Performing before an audience caused many students to be nervous and concerned about mistakes. Despite the positive feedback from his parents, ______ would be needed for his next concert.

   A) Stefon Washington claimed that more practice

   B) Stefon Washington's claim revealed that more practice

   C) it was more practice, claimed Stefon Washington, that

   D) the statement made by Stefon Washington claimed that more practice

See Appendix for answer

2. Enemies for the last twenty years, the villagers and the elves continued fighting despite both sides losing many great warriors and suffering deprivation caused by the ongoing clashes. After defeating the ogres in the winter, ______ against the elves.

   A) Finnegan's fight was resumed

   B) it was Finnegan who resumed his fight

   C) the resumption of Finnegan's fight began

   D) Finnegan resumed his fight

See Appendix for answer

3. Mexican American Ignacio Rodriguez was a popular student at his high school in Corpus Christi, Texas. Voted as Most Likely to Succeed by his senior class, ______ inspired his peers to like, respect, and admire him.

   A) Ignacio's willingness to help others with homework and difficult concepts in math

   B) others who were struggling with homework and difficult concepts in math were helped by Ignacio and

   C) Ignacio willingly helped others with homework and difficult math concepts, which

   D) in homework and difficult concepts in math, Ignacio willingly helped others; it

See Appendix for answer

4. *Hamilton* is a highly acclaimed musical created by Lin-Manuel Miranda that premiered Off-Broadway in 2015. Based on the biography by Ron Chernow, ______ fought in the American Revolutionary War and died after being shot in a duel with Aaron Burr.

   A) *Hamilton* covers the life of Alexander Hamilton, a founding father of the United States who

   B) Alexander Hamilton, a founding father of the United States in the musical *Hamilton*,

   C) there was a founding father of the United States, Alexander Hamilton, who in *Hamilton*

   D) a founding father of the United States whose life is covered in the musical, Alexander Hamilton

See Appendix for answer

Things to Remember:

- Introductory phrases should have the noun they describe placed immediately after them.
- An introductory descriptive phrase should not be followed by wording such as "there is" or "there are."
- An introductory descriptive phrase should not be immediately followed by a possessive noun.

Sentence Structure: Modifiers
Check for Understanding

1. *10,909* is a Chinese dance drama that premiered in Wuxi, Jiangsu province, in 2023. Depicting the people on a deep-sea manned submersible, ______ had set a record by diving to a depth of 10,909 meters in 2010.

   A) there was a team of brave Chinese researchers who in *10,909*

   B) brave Chinese researchers, a team of scientists in *10,909*

   C) *10,909* tells the story of brave Chinese researchers, a team of scientists who

   D) the team of scientists whose success is celebrated in*10,909*, brave Chinese researchers

2. In 2018, Alabama quarterback Jalen Hurts was taken out of the college football championship game against Georgia at halftime. Subsequently, freshman quarterback Tua Tagovailoa replaced him and led Alabama to victory. Although he had been benched by his coach, ______ enjoying success that led to the Philadelphia Eagles selecting him in the first round of the NFL draft.

   A) the career of quarterback Hurts continued with the Oklahoma Sooners,

   B) Hurts continued his career as the quarterback of the Oklahoma Sooners,

   C) Hurts' career as quarterback continued with the Oklahoma Sooners,

   D) it was Hurts who continued as a quarterback with the Oklahoma Sooners,

3. In evaluating the immersive film *Avatar* that was directed by James Cameron in 2009, ______ may have overlooked the potential offensiveness of a plot suggesting that a foreign savior is needed to lead people to freedom.

   A) Cameron's use of incredible special effects has amazed many viewers, who

   B) there are many viewers who have focused on Cameron's use of incredible special effects, but they

   C) the focus of many viewers is on Cameron's use of incredible special effects; they

   D) many viewers have been amazed by Cameron's addition of incredible special effects, but they

4. African American neurosurgeon Alexa Canady has helped thousands of young patients at Children's Hospital of Michigan. Distinguished in 1984 as the first female certified by the American Board of Neurological Surgery, ______ successfully elevated her neurosurgery team into one of the best in the country.

   A) from 1987 until 2001 Canady led the hospital's neurosurgery department; it

   B) Canady's leadership of the hospital's neurosurgery department from 1987 to 2001

   C) Canady led the hospital's neurosurgery department from 1987 until 2001, which

   D) the hospital's neurosurgery department was led by Canady from 1987 until 2001 and

Sentence Structure

Parallel

Sentence structure refers to how words, phrases, and clauses fit together to form a grammatical sentence.

A rule of sentence structure is that words joined with a conjunction must be of the same part of speech. Similarly, phrases or clauses connected with a conjunction must be of the same type.

When the same types of words, phrases, or clauses are used with a conjunction, the sentence is said to be of parallel structure.

Examples of Parallelism

Rule: Use the same part of speech for items before and after a FANBOYS conjunction.

FANBOYS are coordinating conjunctions that require parallel structure because they join words that are grammatical equivalents. For example, FANBOYS conjunctions can join words that are all nouns:

Noun 1 Noun 2 Noun 3

My friend Leeroy wanted ham, grits, **and** eggs for breakfast.

Parallel

This example makes use of parallel structure by listing three nouns that detail what Leeroy wanted for breakfast.

FANBOYS conjunctions can also join similar items that are more than a single word:

Verb Prepositional phrase Verb Prepositional phrase

At daycare, one child was **running around the house**, **tripping on toys**,

Verb Prepositional phrase

and **getting into trouble**.

The repeated pattern of an –ing verb followed by a prepositional phrase is used to describe three things children did at daycare. Therefore, the above sentence is parallel because three verb phrases are joined with a FANBOYS conjunction.

Similarly, independent clauses must be parallel with each other when joined by a FANBOYS conjunction:

> Caesar came, he saw, and he conquered.

In this way, a FANBOYS conjunction is different from a subordinating conjunction, which joins unlike elements—a dependent clause and an independent clause.

***Rule*: When two verbs are joined by a FANBOYS conjunction and the first verb is preceded by a helping verb, that helping verb may be understood as also applying to the second verb.**

To improve his health, Joe would exercise at the gym and eat healthy foods.

In the example above, the helping verb "would" is before the main verb "exercise," so "would" applies to the second verb "eat" as well.

Parallel Grammar Structures

Types	Example
Nouns	Sue took care of the **dog**, **cat**, **and** **chicken**.
Verbs	Waking up late, Sally **ran** outside **but** **missed** the bus.
Verb Phrases	The security guard patrol**led** the area, watch**ed** the security video, **and** plann**ed** his report.
Prepositional Phrases	**In the forest** **and** **far from home**, the hikers enjoyed being away from the city.
Independent Clauses	**I searched upstairs**, **my sister searched downstairs**, **yet** **Tom wasn't there**.
Infinitives	Renee wanted **to play**, **to eat**, **and** **to sleep**.
Gerunds	I want a friend who enjoys hik**ing**, swimm**ing**, **or** fish**ing**.

Examples

✗ In 1966, Minnesota would reintroduce the Trumpeter Swan to Three Rivers Park District and adds this magnificent bird to its list of Endangered and Threatened Species in 2013.

✓ In 1966, Minnesota would reintroduce the Trumpeter Swan to Three Rivers Park District and add this magnificent bird to its list of Endangered and Threatened Species in 2013.

In the sentence, "reintroduce" and "add" are connected by the FANBOYS conjunction "and." The verb "reintroduce" is preceded by the helping verb "would," so "would" is understood to apply to the second verb phrase "(would) add." The first example violates parallel structure because "add" should follow the helping verb "would," but "would adds" is incorrect. The second example uses parallel structure by including two verb forms that follow "would."

Practice

1. In addition to teaching history at Central High School during the academic year, Anne would also volunteer at a soup kitchen and ______ to learn Spanish.

    A) attempting

    B) attempt

    C) attempted

    D) attempts

See Appendix for answer

2. When I travel to England, I plan on attending a professional soccer match at the stadium or ______ a soccer game on television with the local people because I don't want to spend the entire time visiting museums and monuments.

    A) viewing

    B) view

    C) views

    D) viewed

See Appendix for answer

Things to Remember:

- Parallel structure requires using the same parts of speech (or types of phrases or clauses) when they are joined with a FANBOYS conjunction.
- When two verbs are joined by a FANBOYS conjunction and the first verb is preceded by a helping verb, that helping verb may be understood as also applying to the second verb.

Sentence Structure: Parallel
Check for Understanding

1. In his effort to fight crime in the city of Los Angeles, Chief Michael Moore has been responsible for improving the police department's effectiveness. He has promoted community engagement that would assist the police and ____ the community a stronger role in deterring criminal behavior.

   A) gives

   B) giving

   C) gave

   D) give

2. Holidays sometimes bring out the generosity and kindness of people. Moved by the holiday spirit, Coeli became interested in working for charitable organizations that feed the poor or by ______ money to others that she knew needed financial assistance.

   A) to provide

   B) providing

   C) provided

   D) provide

Unit 2: Information and Ideas

2.1	Explicit Meaning: Novel and Short Story	102
2.2	Explicit Meaning: Poem	109
2.3	Explicit Meaning: Nonfiction	116
2.4	Main Idea: Novel and Short Story	122
2.5	Main Idea: Poem	129
2.6	Main Idea: Nonfiction	136
2.7	Evidence: Novel and Short Story	143
2.8	Evidence: Play	148
2.9	Evidence: Poem	153
2.10	Evidence: Nonfiction	158
2.11	Inference: Completes Text	164
2.12	Graphic Displays: Bar Graphs	170
2.13	Graphic Displays: Tables	180
2.14	Graphic Displays: Line Graphs	186

Explicit Meaning

Novel and Short Story

Questions that ask about the explicit meaning of paragraphs from novels and short stories require an understanding of the literal meaning of the text. You can identify this type of question because it uses either **"according to" or "based on"** in the question. Often **these questions ask about what is true for a specific character or how a character responds** to a particular situation, and the answers are directly stated in the text.

In this section, the following strategies will be discussed:

- Reading to find the question's answer
- Paraphrasing the text
- Predicting the answer
- Using the process of elimination

These strategies are meant merely as a guide; some may work better than others, so just use the ones that help you answer the given question.

Reading to Find the Question's Answer

Even though the text comes before the question, read the question first. Doing so will help you focus on finding the specific information you need to answer the question as you read the text.

Example

The following text is from Mark Twain's 1881 novel *The Prince and the Pauper*.

> The tremendous news was already abroad, and the boy learned it from a thousand voices at once—"The king is dead!" The tidings struck a chill to the heart of the poor little waif and sent a shudder through his frame. He realized the greatness of his loss and was filled with a bitter grief; for the grim tyrant who had been such a terror to others had always been gentle with him.

Based on the text, how does the boy react to the news of the king's death?

Given the question, you know you are reading the text to find out the feelings of the boy in response to his hearing about the king's death. Is he happy, sad, angry, confused? Look for specific words and phrases like "the greatness of his loss" and "filled with bitter grief" that specifically reveal how the boy is feeling.

Paraphrasing the Text

Often the SAT chooses complex texts that can be challenging to understand. Paraphrasing (restating in your own words) each sentence can help you better comprehend difficult texts.

Paraphrase

S1	The boy learned the news about the king's death by hearing many people talk about it at once.
S2	The news made this homeless boy physically shiver.
S3	The boy was saddened because the king who had been mean to others had been nice to him.

Given this paraphrase, it's easy to see how the boy feels when he hears the news that the king is dead.

Predicting the Answer

After you have read the question and the text, it can be helpful to come up with your own answer to the question before looking at any of the choices. Then you can match your idea to the answer that seems closest.

This strategy works best when the question asks about a specific detail in the text such as how a character responds to a situation rather than a general question about what is true for a character.

In *The Prince and the Pauper* text, it's clear that the boy feels sad that the king is dead. Therefore, when you look at the answers, you can choose the one with a similar meaning.

Suppose these are the answer choices provided:

A) He is surprised to hear so many strangers announcing the death.

B) He becomes fearful about being alone in the world without his father.

C) He experiences a wide range of emotions that he has trouble identifying.

D) He feels distressed over the loss of one who had treated him kindly.

Given these answers, the one that best matches the idea that the boy is sad is Choice D because being distressed is similar to being sad.

Using the Process of Elimination

Using the process of elimination can be helpful to get rid of incorrect answers. Often the wrong answers will contain ideas that aren't supported by the information in the text. Also, it is possible that some part of an incorrect answer is accurate, but the rest of it lacks text support. If any part of the answer cannot be found in the text, then the entire answer is wrong.

✗ **Choice A:** Although the text mentions lots of people announcing the king's death, it doesn't indicate that the boy is surprised by this fact.

✗ **Choice B:** "Terror" is mentioned regarding how the king treats people, not with how the boy feels. Also, the text doesn't specify that the king is the boy's father.

✗ **Choice C:** The text identifies that the boy feels "grief," and no other emotions are discussed regarding his reaction to the king's death.

✓ **Choice D:** The text states that the king was kind to the boy and the boy feels grief, which is a kind of distress, when he hears about the ruler's death.

Example

The following text is from Herman Melville's 1853 short story "Bartleby, the Scrivener: A Story of Wall Street." The narrator, who is Bartleby's employer, has asked him to examine a paper.

> Imagine my surprise, nay my consternation, when without moving from his privacy, Bartleby in a singularly mild, firm voice, replied, "I would prefer not to."
>
> I sat awhile in perfect silence, rallying my stunned faculties. Immediately it occurred to me that my ears had deceived me, or Bartleby had entirely misunderstood my meaning. I repeated my request in the clearest tone I could assume.

Based on the text, how does the narrator respond to Bartleby's refusal of his request?

A) He considers Bartleby's response, contemplating whether his request is an unreasonable demand for an employer to make.

B) He is startled, believing that either he hasn't heard Bartleby correctly or that Bartleby has failed to comprehend the request.

C) He overlooks it and does not take immediate action in order to consider the best discipline for Bartleby.

D) He judges Bartleby to be an unusual individual who is unfamiliar with social conventions

Question: Asks how the narrator reacts when his employee prefers not to do what is asked of him.

Text Paraphrase: The narrator is surprised and confused when Bartleby stays put and politely declines to do what has been requested. The narrator silently tries to gather himself after this unexpected response and then thinks he hasn't heard correctly or that his employee hasn't understood what he asked. Therefore, the narrator repeats the request as clearly as possible.

Answer Prediction: The answer will have something to do with the narrator being surprised or confused about Bartleby's refusal.

Process of Elimination

✗ **Choice A:** The text says that the narrator sits "awhile in perfect silence," but it doesn't give the reason for doing so as being to consider whether the demand was reasonable.

✓ **Choice B:** The text says that the narrator experiences surprise and then thinks that either he misheard or that Bartleby didn't understand what was being asked. Because this answer choice accurately reflects the text's information, it is correct.

✗ **Choice C:** Although the text indicates that the narrator paused, it says the reason is because he is surprised, not because he is considering a way to discipline Bartleby.

✗ **Choice D:** The word "singularly" can mean strange, but this word is used to describe Bartleby's reply, not Bartleby himself. Also, there is no mention in the text of the narrator questioning Bartleby's familiarity with social conventions.

Practice

1. The following text is from Ivan Turgenev's 1862 novel *Fathers and Sons*. Arkady is Kirsanov's son.

> In 1847 Kirsanov's wife died and the blow all but crushed him. His hair turned grey in a few weeks: he was on the point of going abroad, for the sake of distraction, when the year 1848 intervened. He was obliged to return to the village and, after a rather prolonged period of idleness, devoted himself to improving his estate. In 1855 he took his son to the university in St. Petersburg, where he spent the winters with him, hardly ever going out and trying to make friends with Arkady's young chums.

According to the text, what is true about Kirsanov?

A) Kirsanov goes overseas to distract himself from signs that he is getting older.

B) Kirsanov is saddened by his wife's death and tries to divert his attention from it.

C) Kirsanov decides to work on his property so that it will be valuable to his son.

D) Kirsanov prioritizes his son's education more than he does his own career.

See Appendix for answer

2. The following text is from Stephen Crane's 1898 short story "The Blue Hotel." The cowboy and Johnny are partners in a card game playing against the Swede and the Easterner.

> The cowboy was a board-whacker. Each time that he held superior cards he whanged them, one by one, with exceeding force, down upon the improvised table, and took the tricks with a glowing air of prowess and pride that sent thrills of indignation into the hearts of his opponents. A game with a board-whacker in it is sure to become intense. The countenances of the Easterner and the Swede were miserable whenever the cowboy thundered down his aces and kings, while Johnnie, his eyes gleaming with joy, chuckled and chuckled.

According to the text, what is true about the cowboy?

A) He wins card games by tricking his opponents.

B) Playing cards is his preferred method of entertainment.

C) His most important priority is winning the card game.

D) He takes great pride in revealing his winning cards.

See Appendix for answer

3. The following text is from Charles Dickens's 1854 novel *Hard Times*. Cecilia (Sissy) Jupe's father has deserted her, and schoolmaster Mr. Gradgrind is talking with her while his friend Mr. Bounderby observes the exchange.

> "I understand you have been in the habit of reading to your father?"
>
> "Oh yes, sir, thousands of times. They were the happiest—Oh, of all the happy times we had together, sir!"
>
> ... "And what," asked Mr. Gradgrind, in a still lower voice, "did you read to your father, Jupe?"
>
> "About the Fairies, sir, and the Dwarf, and the Hunchback, and the Genies," she sobbed out, "and about—"
>
> "Hush!" said Mr. Gradgrind, "that is enough. Never breathe a word of such destructive nonsense any more. Bounderby, this is a case for rigid training, and I shall observe it with interest."

Based on the text, how does Mr. Gradgrind respond to Sissy's memory of reading to her father?

A) He interrupts her and asks her not to speak again about books with imaginary characters in them.

B) He asks her to remember only the happy times with her father and forget her sadness.

C) He disapproves of her upbringing because he realizes she has not had a proper education.

D) He acknowledges her reading abilities but questions her competency in other academic subjects.

See Appendix for answer

Make sure to read the introductory information before the text as it often contains useful details about the characters that will help you better understand who they are when they are referenced.

Things to Remember

- Read to find the question's answer.
- Paraphrase the text to better understand what is being discussed.
- Formulate your own answer before reading the choices.
- Eliminate answers not supported by the text.

Explicit Meaning: Novel and Short Story
Check for Understanding

1. The following text is from Louisa May Alcott's 1869 novel *An Old-Fashioned Girl*. Fanny is frustrated with her brother after arguing with him.

    "If I was the President, I'd make a law to shut up all boys till they were grown; for they certainly are the most provoking toads in the world," said Fanny, as she watched the slouchy figure of her brother strolling down the street. She might have changed her mind, however, if she had followed him, for as soon as he turned the corner, his whole aspect altered; his hands came out of his pockets, he stopped whistling, buttoned his jacket, gave his cap a pull, and went off at a great pace.

    According to the text, what is true about Fanny's brother?

    A) He purposely behaves in ways that he knows will irritate his sister.

    B) He cares about his appearance only when adults are present.

    C) He hopes to one day be a lawmaker who can dress however he wants.

    D) He acts differently in his sister's presence than when he is out of her sight.

2. The following text is an adaptation from Kate Chopin's 1899 novel *The Awakening*. Mrs. Pontellier, Madame Ratignolle, and Robert are vacationing at a popular holiday resort.

    Mrs. Pontellier had brought her sketching materials, which she sometimes dabbled with in an unprofessional way. She liked the dabbling. She felt in it satisfaction of a kind which no other employment afforded her.

    She had long wished to try [sketching] Madame Ratignolle. Never had that lady seemed a more tempting subject than at that moment, seated there like some sensuous Madonna, with the gleam of the fading day enriching her splendid color.

    Robert crossed over and seated himself upon the step below Mrs. Pontellier, that he might watch her work. She handled her brushes with a certain ease and freedom which came, not from long and close acquaintance with them, but from a natural aptitude.

    According to the text, what is true about Mrs. Pontellier?

    A) Mrs. Pontellier is a talented amateur artist.

    B) Mrs. Pontellier makes a living drawing people.

    C) Mrs. Pontellier often draws attractive women.

    D) Mrs. Pontellier enjoys spending time with friends.

3. The following text is from Thomas Hardy's 1874 novel *Far from the Madding Crowd*. Gabriel Oak is a sheep farmer in rural England who is checking on his farm at night.

   > Being a man not without frequent consciousness that there was some charm in the life he led, he stood still after looking at the sky as a useful instrument and regarded it in an appreciative spirit, as a work of art superlatively beautiful. For a moment he seemed impressed with the speaking loneliness of the scene, or rather with the complete abstraction from all its compass from the sights and sounds of man.

   Based on the text, how does Gabriel Oak respond to his surroundings?

   A) He feels unhappy about being isolated from others.

   B) He has a spiritual feeling when experiencing nature's music.

   C) He is thankful for the loveliness of nature.

   D) He likes to travel but gets lost without directions.

Explicit Meaning

Poem

Questions that ask about the explicit meaning of a poem require understanding of what is communicated by its words, images, and figurative language. Poems will have both literal and figurative meanings, but these kinds of questions focus on what is stated literally.

In this section, the following strategies for answering questions about the meaning of poems will be discussed:

- Analyzing the question
- Reading to locate relevant information
- Paraphrasing the stanzas
- Predicting the answer
- Using the process of elimination

These strategies are intended to be a guide; some may work better for you than others, so use whichever ones help you the most to answer any given question.

Analyzing the Question

A question that begins with the phrase **"based on the text"** is asking about the literal meaning or some stated detail in the text. To answer this type of question about a poem, determine what is being asked and then read the text to find that answer.

Example

The following text is an excerpt from the William Wordsworth 1807 poem "My Heart Leaps Up."

My heart leaps up when I behold
A rainbow in the sky:
So was it when my life began;
So is it now I am a man;
So be it when I shall grow old,
Or let me die!

Based on the text, what makes the narrator joyful?

Because the question begins with "based on the text," you know that you are looking for an explicit statement in the poem about what brings joy to the narrator.

Reading to Locate Relevant Information

As you read the poem, look for details related to the question being asked. The previous question asks what "makes the narrator joyful." Therefore, when reading the poem, focus on any details that are related to that idea.

> My heart leaps up when I behold
> A rainbow in the sky:
> So was it when my life began;
> So is it now I am a man;
> So be it when I shall grow old,
> Or let me die!

Based on the text, what makes the narrator joyful?

In the poem's first two lines, the narrator states that "my heart leaps up when I behold / A rainbow in the sky." In other words, this beautiful sight makes the narrator happy. Look for an answer that refers to seeing a rainbow. If no answer mentions a rainbow specifically, look for something in the choices that might describe a rainbow, like "nature's beauty."

Paraphrasing the Stanzas

Sometimes a poem is difficult to understand because of its wording or sentence structure. To better understand a poem, it can be helpful to put each of its stanzas into your own words.

Example

The following text is from Henry Howland's 1914 poem "When You Are Safe."

> It's easy to be boasting when all your ventures pay;
> It's easy to be cheerful when good things come your way;
> It's easy to speak proudly to every one you meet,
> Except when you are feeling the bruises of defeat.
>
> It's easy to talk bravely when danger is not near;
> It's easy to have courage when there is naught to fear;
> It's easy to be boasting when you are safe ashore,
> That you hear only music when angry billows roar.
>
> It's easy to cry, "Coward"—when you have not been tried—
> At him who runs from danger, forgetting manly pride;
> It's easy to be telling how fearless you would be
> When all is peaceful round you, as far as you can see.

Based on the text, when is it easiest to accuse another person of not being brave?

Paraphrase

Stanza 1	It's easy to brag when you are successful and to be happy when things are going well but not so easy when you experience failure.
Stanza 2	Being brave is easy when you're not in danger and don't have anything to fear. Then, you can tell others that rough seas might as well be music.
Stanza 3	It's easy to call someone a coward when you haven't experienced the same problems. You tell yourself you would be brave in the same situation, but you don't know because everything around you is peaceful.

Once you have paraphrased the stanzas, consider the poet's overall message. In the above poem, that message might be something like "when everything is going well, it's easy to be confident."

Based on the paraphrase, the third stanza mentions calling someone a coward. Given the text in that stanza, the answer to the question about when to accuse someone of not being brave would be something like "when everything around you is peaceful."

Predicting the Answer

Along with understanding the question, reading to find the answer, and paraphrasing the poem, it's helpful to formulate your own answer before looking at the choices.

Example

The following text is from Emily Dickinson's 1891 poem "Hope Is the Thing with Feathers."

"Hope" is the thing with feathers -
That perches in the soul -
And sings the tune without the words -
And never stops - at all -

And sweetest - in the Gale - is heard -
And sore must be the storm -
That could abash the little Bird
That kept so many warm -

I've heard it in the chilliest land -
And on the strangest Sea -
Yet – never - in extremity,
It asked a crumb - of me.

Based on the text, how is hope characterized?

To answer this question, determine how hope is described.

Stanza 1	Hope is like a bird that never stops singing.
Stanza 2	Both continue despite difficulties.
Stanza 3	Neither asks for anything in return.

Given this description of a persistent, little bird, the answer that characterizes hope could have something to do with overcoming challenges or giving without an expectation of anything in return. Look for an answer with a similar idea and eliminate answers that discuss something else.

Using the Process of Elimination

Eliminate any of the quotations with information unrelated to the claim or that lack support in the poem.

For the example poem "Hope Is the Thing with Feathers," here are the possible answer choices:

A) It gains courage with every passing year.

B) It is the most helpful when faced with storms.

C) It keeps a person warm despite low temperatures.

D) It continues on no matter the difficulties encountered.

Now, compare these answers with the information in the poem and the claim.

✗ Because the poem doesn't mention the passage of time, **Choice A** can be eliminated.

✗ Although storms are mentioned, the poem doesn't say the bird or hope is most helpful during hard times, so **Choice B** can be discarded.

✗ The "chilliest land" is mentioned in the last stanza, but no corresponding warmth gained is discussed, ruling out **Choice C**.

✓ Because the idea of continuing on despite problems is supported by the poem's information and is also closest to the predicted answer, **Choice D** is correct.

Practice

1. The following text is an excerpt from Edgar Allan Poe's 1875 poem "Alone."

From childhood's hour I have not been
As others were—I have not seen
As others saw—I could not bring
My passions from a common spring—
From the same source I have not taken
My sorrow—I could not awaken
My heart to joy at the same tone—
And all I lov'd—I lov'd alone—

Based on the text, why does the narrator feel isolated?

A) He has a disability that prevents him from seeing clearly.

B) He is shamed for expressing his emotions more openly than others.

C) He doesn't view the world in the same way as others.

D) He experiences sadness over a loss that he cannot explain.

See Appendix for answer

2. The following text is from Ezra Pound's 1915 poem "Taking Leave of a Friend."

Blue mountains to the north of the walls,
White river winding about them;
Here we must make separation
And go out through a thousand miles of dead grass.

Mind like a floating white cloud,
Sunset like the parting of old acquaintances
Who bow over their clasped hands at a distance.
Our horses neigh to each other
as we are departing.

Based on the text, in what way is the sunset like saying goodbye to a friend?

A) It depicts an agreed-upon gesture of farewell.

B) It brings comfort due to its consistency.

C) It is a beautiful expression of connection.

D) It represents a natural and inevitable occurrence.

See Appendix for answer

Things to Remember

- Determine what the question is asking.
- Read the poem to find the answer to the question.
- Paraphrase the poem's text to better understand what is being discussed.
- Come up with your own possible answer before reading the choices.
- Eliminate incorrect answers unsupported by the text.

Explicit Meaning: Poetry
Check for Understanding

1. The following text is an excerpt from Elizabeth Barrett Browning's 1843 poem "The Cry of the Children," which depicts child labor in mines and factories.

   Go out, children, from the mine and from the city—

   Sing out, children, as the little thrushes do—

   Pluck your handfuls of meadow-cowslips pretty

   Laugh aloud, to feel your fingers let them through!

   But they answer, "Are your cowslips of the meadows

   Like our weeds anear the mine?

   Leave us quiet in the dark of the coal-shadows,

   From your pleasures fair and fine!

   "For oh," say the children, "we are weary,

   And we cannot run or leap—

   If we cared for any meadows, it were merely

   To drop down in them and sleep."

   Based on the text, what is the children's reaction to the suggestion that they pick flowers?

   A) They refuse to leave the factory where they feel safe.

   B) They would like to have a day off to laugh and have fun.

   C) They do not want to travel to do something they could do at work.

   D) They are too tired to do so and would rather rest than play.

2. The following text is from T. S. Eliot's 1911 poem "Preludes," which highlights the beginning of an evening in the city.

The winter evening settles down

With smell of steaks in passageways.

Six o'clock.

The burnt-out ends of smoky days.

And now a gusty shower wraps

The grimy scraps

Of withered leaves about your feet

And newspapers from vacant lots;

The showers beat

On broken blinds and chimney-pots,

And at the corner of the street

A lonely cab-horse steams and stamps.

And then the lighting of the lamps.

Based on the text, what does the speaker observe outside?

A) People are searching for a restaurant to have dinner.

B) The streets are mostly deserted due to the inclement weather.

C) The streetlights reveal that the sidewalks are flooded.

D) Newspapers are used for umbrellas as people walk in the rain.

Explicit Meaning

Nonfiction

The SAT expects students to understand the explicit meaning of nonfiction texts covering a wide range of topics. Luckily, **no SAT question requires specific knowledge about the subject** because all the information can be found in the text.

In this section, the following strategies for answering SAT questions about the meaning of a nonfiction text will be discussed:

- Locating the question's criteria
- Paraphrasing the text and locating the answer
- Predicting the answer
- Using the process of elimination

Locating the Question's Criteria

You can identify explicit meaning questions by their use of the phrase "according to the text." To locate the question's criteria, look to see what information you are being asked to find.

Consider the following question:

> A recent study identified specific biomarkers present in the blood of centenarians. The results of the study indicate a potential link between metabolic health, nutrition, and longevity. For example, low levels of iron and cholesterol in the blood are biomarkers for people who are less likely to live to the age of 100.
>
> According to the text, which common biomarkers are important for understanding longevity?

The criteria needed to answer this question are the important biomarkers needed to better understand why some people live a long time and others do not.

> Reading the question first can help you determine what information from the text is needed.

Paraphrasing the Text and Locating the Answer

To better understand SAT nonfiction texts, it's helpful to put each sentence into your own words.

Once you have paraphrased each sentence, locate the one that contains the answer to the question.

Consider the following text:

> Approximately 116 million US adults have high blood pressure, but only 25% of them have this condition under control. Current treatments include exercise, healthy eating, and medication for reducing hypertension, but these measures are not always successful. Researchers at Columbia University and the University of Paris have another potential solution: an ultrasound device that consistently reduces blood pressure in middle-aged test subjects.

According to the text, what alternative means of reducing hypertension have researchers discovered?

The information that is needed to answer the question is highlighted above. What follows is a possible paraphrase of the text discussing US adults with high blood pressure:

S1	Only 1/4 of Americans with high blood pressure have it under control.
S2	The treatments usually used to lower blood pressure don't always work.
S3	Researchers have found an ultrasound device that can lower blood pressure.

The third sentence mentions the ultrasound device, which is something researchers discovered could lower blood pressure. This device is given as an alternative to the current treatments of "exercise, healthy eating, and medication" discussed in the second sentence. Therefore, the correct answer would likely mention this device or describe it in some way.

The answer to explicit meaning nonfiction questions can be found directly stated in the text, but the answer will often use different words that mean the same thing.

Predicting the Answer

It's helpful to formulate your own idea about the answer before looking at the choices because it's then much easier to eliminate choices that contain information unrelated to the text's discussion or that don't answer the question being asked.

Think about how you would answer the explicit meaning question associated with this nonfiction text:

> About 9,700 years ago, one female and two male teenage hunter-gatherers were chewing resin after eating. Researchers analyzed 100 pieces of this black gummy resin and found food remnants stuck to the gum, which helped them determine that the diet of these three young people consisted of deer, duck, fox, trout, and hazelnuts.

According to the text, how does ancient chewing gum show what Stone Age teens were eating?

Because the question asks "how" the gum reveals the food the teenagers ate, that is the criteria you need to locate. Based on the text, the bits of food that the teens had eaten stuck to the resin they were chewing, allowing researchers to identify the foods. Therefore, the answer will probably have something to do with the ancient chewing gum capturing food particles.

Using the Process of Elimination

Carefully examine each answer choice and get rid of the ones that don't contain accurate information that is supported by the text. Also, even if information is supported by the text, it won't be the correct answer if it doesn't meet the criteria asked for in the question.

You might find it helpful to strike through the answer choices you have eliminated so that you can more clearly see the answers you still have to consider.

Let's use the process of elimination on the question about the hunter-gatherer teenagers mentioned in the previous section.

> About 9,700 years ago, one female and two male teenage hunter-gatherers were chewing resin after eating. Researchers analyzed 100 pieces of this black gummy resin and found food remnants stuck to the gum, which helped them determine that the diet of these three young people consisted of deer, duck, fox, hazelnuts, and trout.

According to the text, how does ancient chewing gum show what Stone Age teens were eating?

A) It is made from a material that does not decay for over ten thousand years.

B) It is formed from a substance that allows food particles to adhere to it.

C) It consists of a black resin that makes food particles easy to identify.

D) It is effective at trapping protein sources but not carbohydrates like fruits.

Choice A ✗ Whether the material decays doesn't guarantee it would reveal what people were eating unless food also sticks to the resin.

Choice B ✓ This answer is very close to the information discussed in the text and to the answer we predicted about the gum capturing food particles, making it the correct choice.

Choice C ✗ Nothing in the text says that the resin's color made the pieces of food that were stuck to it easy to identify.

Choice D ✓ Although what stuck to the resin were protein sources, the text doesn't mention that carbohydrates like fruits could not be trapped by the resin.

Example

Accomplished mathematicians, ancient Mayan scribes recorded their observations of the stars, Sun, and planets. They tracked solstices, equinoxes, and zenith days in a book called the *Dresden Codex*, which dates to the eleventh century. This book provides evidence that the Maya could predict solar eclipses based on tables divided into 177-day solar eclipse seasons. According to some scholars, the Maya tracked the sky so their priests could know which rituals to perform to guarantee that the cycles of destruction, rebirth, and renewal, which they associated with celestial events, would continue.

According to the text, what do some scholars suggest about Maya culture?

A) The Maya accurately made notations about their observations of the solar system for future generations.

B) The Maya predicted the exact time that solar eclipses would occur based on information in a book.

C) The Maya recorded celestial events to provide spiritual leaders with information about the timing of ceremonies.

D) The Maya tracked the sky to ensure that their mathematical calculations were consistent with celestial movements.

Question's Criteria: The question asks, "What do scholars suggest?" The scholars are mentioned in the last sentence of the paragraph. That sentence gives the scholars' explanation for why Mayans tracked the sky.

Possible Answer: To help religious leaders know when to perform specific practices related to the cycle of life mirrored by happenings in the sky.

Text Paraphrase:

S1 states that the Maya were good at math, which helped them keep track of the movement of the moon, Sun, and stars.

S2 gives the name and date of a book in which the Maya kept track of celestial occurrences.

S3 provides evidence that the Maya kept track of solar eclipses.

S4 provides the scholars' reasoning as to why the Maya kept track of what was going on in the sky: to help religious leaders know when to conduct ceremonies associated with celestial events.

Process of Elimination:

Choice A ✗ Although the text states that the Maya recorded their observations of the sky, it doesn't say that the reason they did so was to leave this information for their descendants.

Choice B ✗ The text says that the Maya kept track of solar eclipses in the *Dresden Codex*, but it doesn't indicate that the reason they did this was to predict when the next one would occur.

Choice C ✓ The last sentence in the text makes a similar statement as this answer choice about religious leaders using celestial information to plan their rituals, making this the correct answer.

Choice D ✗ The text mentions that the Maya were good at math and that they tracked the movements they saw in the sky. However, consistency isn't mentioned by the scholars as the reason the Maya did so.

Practice

1. Baleen whales have unique mechanisms in their voice boxes that enable low-frequency vocalizations. In a study led by Coen Elemans, researchers examined the larynx of three different baleen whale species (a minke, humpback, and sei) and found each one had long cylinders that are fused to form a large U-shaped structure that pushes against a fatty cushion inside the whale's voice box. They created computer models that simulated certain aspects of the whales' voice boxes, ultimately leading the researchers to determine that when whales move air from their lungs past the cushion, a vibration begins that generates very low frequency sounds underwater, creating the distinctive songs these whales are known for making.

According to the text, what did the research reveal about how baleen whales create underwater sounds?

A) They create different low frequency vibrations based on the specific species.

B) They make unique noises to communicate their location with other whales.

C) They have developed a special apparatus that creates vibrations detectable in water.

D) They use a U-shaped larynx to reverse air flow from the lungs and turn it into sound.

See Appendix for answer

2. Groundwater supplies drinking water to half the people on Earth and is the source of half of the water used to irrigate crops. This valuable resource is renewable, but, according to water specialists, once groundwater has been depleted, it can take hundreds of years to restore the shortfall. Though groundwater levels are falling in many locations worldwide, specialists say some societies have been proactive in halting the drain on these water supplies.

According to the text, why are water specialists concerned about groundwater?

A) Groundwater reserves cannot recover after they have fallen below a certain level.

B) Groundwater use could cause a shortage that will not be restored for many years.

C) Groundwater takes so long to renew itself that a mass extinction may occur.

D) Groundwater will no longer be available as a resource for human use.

See Appendix for answer

Things to Remember

- Determine what the "according to" question is asking.
- Paraphrase the text to better understand what is being discussed.
- Come up with your own possible answer before reading the choices.
- Eliminate answers that aren't supported by the text.

Explicit Meaning: Nonfiction
Check for Understanding

1. It is widely understood that although there are dozens of blood types, most people have one that belongs to one of four groups: A, B, AB, and O with either positive or negative Rh factor designations. However, in a discovery that can help doctors treat blood incompatibility issues resulting from transfusions, scientist Tim Satchwell and others have discovered a new blood group called Er, the 44th known blood system, which contains the Piezo1 protein.

   According to the text, why is Satchwell and his team's discovery of Er significant?

   A) The new blood group system surprised scientists who thought that the Piezo1 protein was limited to certain blood types.

   B) The new blood group system is the only one that goes beyond traditional blood types and Rh factor designations.

   C) The new blood group system has helped scientists realize that there are many more undiscovered blood groups systems.

   D) The new blood group system could prevent physicians from using blood that would harm a patient receiving it.

2. Neuroengineer Solaiman Shokur and his team at the Swiss Federal Institute of Technology in Lausanne want to help patients "feel" the sensation of temperature in the prosthetic replacements for their amputated limbs. Because prosthetics do not have nerves that register heat and cold, a limb replacement cannot transmit these sensory signals. In a 2023 study, the researchers attempted to transmit sensations from a part of a patient's body that could still feel these sensations to their artificial limb by attaching thermal electrodes to the arm with an amputated hand. When a patch of skin was stimulated with either hot or cold stimuli, participants reported feeling those sensations in their prosthetic hand.

   According to the text, why can't individuals with amputated limbs feel a sensation like heat or cold in their prosthetic?

   A) Because an artificial limb doesn't have a way to communicate with the body about what is being experienced.

   B) Because it is challenging to create hot and cold sensations that are the correct temperatures to be detected by a prosthetic.

   C) Because using electrodes to detect the body's temperature changes is dependent on finding the correct nerves.

   D) Because there is no way to determine the extent of the nerve damage that occurred as a result of amputation.

Main Idea

Novels and Short Stories

In a question about the main idea in a paragraph of fiction, the text typically focuses on a **character**. The task is to identify what the character description reveals and find the answer that states that idea in different words. Pay attention to the statement introducing the text because this information provides helpful context.

This section presents several strategies for evaluating a text to see what it reveals about a fictional character. One or more may be helpful; use what works best for you on any given question.

Strategies for Finding the Main Idea

- Paraphrase each sentence in the text.
- Examine words describing a character and evaluate what that description reveals.
- Predict the main idea.
- Look for the answer with a meaning similar to yours.

Summarizing Each Sentence in the Text

Paraphrasing the text's sentences can make its main idea apparent because putting those ideas in your own words improves comprehension. A fiction paragraph's main idea is found by considering what *all* its sentences express.

Example

The following text is about a young cook named John who recently accepted a job at a café.

> John discovered work that he found fascinating, and he was very contented indeed. In the café's kitchen each day, he labored zealously; at home, he enjoyed studying the techniques of experienced chefs. John felt like an artist when he was creating delicious food that he beautifully plated, and he dreamed of becoming a great chef.

Sentence Summary

S1	John is content in his new job.
S2	John enthusiastically cooks and enjoys studying other chefs.
S3	Cooking makes John feel like an artist and inspires him to master the craft.

Evaluating What a Character's Actions, Thoughts, or Feelings Reveal

When a text is about a character, identify what that person **does**, **thinks**, or **feels**, and note any adjectives or verbs that describe the individual.

Instead of focusing on details in only one sentence, examine the character description throughout the entire text.

Example

In this part, we are looking at the same text for descriptions of the character.

The following text is about a young cook named John who recently accepted a job at a café.

> John discovered work that he found fascinating, and he was very contented indeed. In the café's kitchen each day, he labored zealously; at home, he enjoyed studying the techniques of experienced chefs. John felt like an artist when he was creating delicious food that he beautifully plated, and he dreamed of becoming a great chef.

Text	Description Type	What It Reveals
"fascinating"	Thoughts	The work at the café held his interest entirely in a positive way.
"labored zealously"	Actions	He worked hard but with an enthusiastic passion.
"felt like an artist"	Feelings	He had an elevated sense of purpose and felt like he created a thing of beauty when he prepared food.

Predicting the Main Idea

After examining the details throughout the text, it is often possible to predict the main idea, which can help in identifying the correct answer. First, paraphrase the paragraph's sentences; then summarize in a brief line what all of them are discussing. Predict the main idea based on your summary.

Example

In this part, we are looking at the same text to predict the main idea.

The following text is about a young cook named John who recently accepted a job at a café.

> John discovered work that he found fascinating, and he was very contented indeed. In the café's kitchen each day, he labored zealously; at home, he enjoyed studying the techniques of experienced chefs. John felt like an artist when he was creating delicious food that he beautifully plated, and he dreamed of becoming a great chef.

To be effective, a prediction should be based on details from all the sentences in the paragraph:

- John finds cooking at a café "fascinating."
- John cooks with enthusiasm.
- John feels "like an artist" when he cooks.
- John dreams of "becoming a great chef."

Prediction: The correct answer should express something about the joy of cooking that John experiences.

Looking for an Answer Like Yours

Use the **process of elimination** as you evaluate which answer includes an idea linked to your analysis. Words and phrases in an answer will differ from the language in the text, but the correct answer will describe the character in a similar way.

Example

Consider again the same text as you examine the process of elimination.

The following text is about a young cook named John who recently accepted a job at a café.

> John discovered work that he found fascinating, and he was very contented indeed. In the café's kitchen each day, he labored zealously; at home, he enjoyed studying the techniques of experienced chefs. John felt like an artist when he was creating delicious food that he beautifully plated, and he dreamed of becoming a great chef.

Which choice best expresses the main idea in the text?

A) John cooks at a café to avoid his responsibilities at home.

B) John is tired from his daily work and evening studies.

C) John is cooking at a café to provide for his family.

D) John discovers the joy of cooking while working at a café.

✗ **Choice A:** The text doesn't discuss John's responsibilities at home or whether he cooks to avoid them.

✗ **Choice B:** Although John works and studies throughout the day, the text doesn't mention whether he is tired because of these activities.

✗ **Choice C:** Many people work to provide for their families, but the text doesn't discuss whether John has a family of his own to support.

✓ **Choice D:** The text mentions John's fascination with cooking and describes how he "labored zealously," "enjoyed studying," and became "very contented." These details indicate the joy he finds in cooking at the café.

Practice

1. The following text is from W. Somerset Maugham's 1925 novel *The Painted Veil*. Mrs. Garstin hosts a dinner party.

> In twenty-five years Mrs. Garstin never invited any one to dine at her house because she liked him. She gave large dinner parties at regular intervals. But parsimony was as strong in her as ambition. She hated to spend money. She flattered herself that she could make as much show as any one else at half the price. Her dinners were long and elaborate, but thrifty, and she could never persuade herself that people when they were eating and talking knew what they drank. She wrapped sparkling Moselle in a napkin and thought her guests took it for champagne.

Which choice best states the main idea of the text?

A) Mrs. Garstin doesn't generously spend to entertain dinner guests that she hosts.

B) Mrs. Garstin hosts parties to escape the emptiness of being alone.

C) Mrs. Garstin is embarrassed because she deceived guests about their drinks.

D) Mrs. Garstin is upset after hosting dinner parties that she can't afford.

See Appendix for answer

2. The following text is adapted from Kate Chopin's 1897 short story "The Locket." Edmond remembers how becoming a soldier affected a relationship.

> [Edmond] could see her as she unclasped from her neck the locket which she fastened about his own. It was an old-fashioned golden locket bearing miniatures of her father and mother with their names and the date of their marriage. It was her most precious earthly possession. Edmond could feel again the folds of the girl's soft white gown, and see the droop of the angel-sleeves as she circled her fair arms about his neck. Her sweet face, appealing, pathetic, tormented by the pain of parting, appeared before him as vividly as life.

Which choice best states the main idea of the text?

A) The girl in Edmond's dream looks like an angel.

B) The girl and Edmond's separation contrasts with her parents' togetherness.

C) The girl loves Edmond even though the war will separate them.

D) The girl is returning Edmond's locket to end their relationship.

See Appendix for answer

3. The following text is from Guy de Maupassant's 1884 story "The Diamond Necklace." Mathilde is a pretty girl who married a clerk with little wealth.

> Mathilde suffered ceaselessly, feeling herself born to enjoy all delicacies and all luxuries. She was distressed at the poverty of her dwelling, at the bareness of the walls, at the shabby chairs, the ugliness of the curtains. All those things, of which another woman of her rank would never even have been conscious, tortured her and made her angry.

Which choice best states the main idea of the text?

A) Mathilde considers leaving her husband to escape their distressing poverty.

B) Mathilde feels unhappy about not having what she thinks she deserves.

C) Mathilde plans to remove the ugly furnishings and make her home beautiful.

D) Mathilde is angry that her husband doesn't help with housekeeping chores.

See Appendix for answer

Things to Remember

- Locate words in the text that describe a character's actions, thoughts, and feelings.
- Evaluate what those words reveal.
- Predict the main idea.
- Choose the answer that agrees with what is shown by the text's description.

Main Idea: Novel and Short Story
Check for Understanding

1. The following text is adapted from Virginia Woolf's 1919 novel *Night and Day*. Mr. Clacton plans business meetings at his office.

   [Mr. Clacton] loved the jargon of committee-rooms; he loved the way in which the door kept opening as the clock struck the hour, in obedience to a few strokes of his pen on a piece of paper; and when it had opened sufficiently often, he loved to issue from his inner chamber with documents in his hands, visibly important, with a preoccupied expression on his face that might have suited a Prime Minister advancing to meet his Cabinet.

   Which choice best states the main idea of the text?

   A) Mr. Clacton has become happier since he began working at the office.

   B) Mr. Clacton dislikes the disruption caused by employees who arrive late to meetings.

   C) Mr. Clacton has been pleased by the rooms used for committee meetings.

   D) Mr. Clacton enjoys his role as the leader of office meetings.

2. The following text is adapted from Kate Chopin's 1895 short story "The Kiss." Nathalie thinks about a man who has been courting her.

   [Nathalie and Brantain] were talking low, of indifferent things which plainly were not the things that occupied their thoughts. She knew that he loved her—a frank, blustering fellow without guile enough to conceal his feelings, and no desire to do so. For two weeks past he had sought her society eagerly and persistently. She was confidently waiting for him to declare himself and she meant to accept him. The rather insignificant and unattractive Brantain was enormously rich; and she liked and required the entourage which wealth could give her.

   Which choice best states the main idea of the text?

   A) Nathalie feels appreciated by Brantain after realizing that he loves her.

   B) Nathalie dislikes Brantain's inability to hide what he feels and desires.

   C) Nathalie regards wealth as more important in a marriage than love.

   D) Nathalie has become more desirous of riches since Brantain began courting her.

3. The following text is from Khaled Hosseini's 2003 novel *The Kite Runner*. Amir describes his father who brought them to America.

   Baba was like the widower who remarries but can't let go of his dead wife. He keenly missed the sugarcane fields of Jalalabad and the gardens of Paghman. He keenly missed people milling in and out of his house, missed walking down the bustling aisles of Shor Bazaar and greeting people who knew him and his father, knew his grandfather, people who shared ancestors with him, whose pasts intertwined with his.

   Which choice best states the main idea of the text?

   A) Baba mourns the loss of experiences he previously enjoyed.

   B) Baba is saddened by his previous wife's death despite having remarried.

   C) Baba is living in America to give his son Amir a better life.

   D) Baba escapes his present sorrow by remembering pleasant past experiences.

4. The following text is from Kate Chopin's 1897 short story "A Pair of Silk Stockings." Mrs. Sommers has always been careful with money but now treats herself to a show.

   There were many others who were there solely for the play and acting. It is safe to say there was no one present who bore quite the attitude which Mrs. Sommers did to her surroundings. She gathered in the whole—stage and players and people in one wide impression, and absorbed it and enjoyed it. She laughed at the comedy and wept—she and the gaudy woman next to her wept over the tragedy. And they talked a little together over it.

   Which choice best states the main idea of the text?

   A) Mrs. Sommers watched a play to escape her responsibilities.

   B) Mrs. Sommers was distracted from the play by the gaudy woman.

   C) Mrs. Sommers was attending the play to meet new people.

   D) Mrs. Sommers attentively views several elements of a theatrical performance.

Main Idea

Poem

A question asking about a poem's main idea requires understanding what is conveyed by that poem's **words**, **images**, and **figurative language** like metaphors or similes. Pay attention to the information introducing the poem because those sentences provide helpful context.

This section presents several strategies for evaluating a poem to find its main idea. One or more may be helpful; use what works best for you on any given question.

Strategies for Finding the Main Idea

- Identify punctuation that separates complete thoughts in the poem.
- Paraphrase those complete thoughts and identify any comparisons or contrasts.
- Evaluate what meaning specific words and images add.
- Predict the main idea.
- Use the process of elimination to select an answer with a meaning similar to your predicted idea.

Noting the Punctuation in the Poem

A poem is generally written in sentences to express its ideas. Sometimes a single line of a poem expresses a complete idea, but at other times, a single line only *begins* an idea that is completed in subsequent lines.

Look for ideas by focusing on a poem sentence by sentence instead of expecting each line to express a complete idea. Keep in mind that a single sentence may express several ideas.

> Traditional poems often capitalize the letter at the beginning of each line, but that doesn't mean the line expresses a complete idea.

The following text is from Edmund Spenser's 1595 poem "Amoretti 30." The poem expresses a person's thoughts about a beloved. Notice how the poem's punctuation separates five different ideas.

> My Love is like to ice, and I to fire:
> How comes it then that this her cold so great
> Is not dissolved through my so hot desire,
> But harder grows the more I her entreat?
> Or how comes it that my exceeding heat
> Is not allayed by her heart-frozen cold,

Complete Idea	Punctuation
My Love is like to ice	,
and I to fire	:
How comes it then that this her cold so great Is not dissolved through my so hot desire,	,
But harder grows the more I her entreat?	?
Or how comes it that my exceeding heat Is not allayed by her heart-frozen cold,	,

Poets often use **commas** to separate ideas, and they include **periods** and **question marks** to signal the end of an idea. They may insert a semicolon or colon to join complete ideas placed on each side of the punctuation.

Paraphrasing a Poem's Ideas and Identifying Comparisons or Contrasts

Paraphrasing is restating something in your own words, which can help you better understand what the poem's speaker is saying.

Original Wording	Paraphrase
My Love is like to ice	My beloved is cold like ice
and I to fire	And I'm like fire
How comes it then that this her cold so great Is not dissolved through my so hot desire,	Why doesn't her icy coldness melt because of my hot desire
But harder grows the more I her entreat?	But increases the more I beg of her?
Or how comes it that my exceeding heat Is not allayed by her heart-frozen cold,	Or how come my heat doesn't decrease because of her cold heart?

In the example above, the speaker describes a **contrast** between himself and his beloved that is like the opposite natures of fire and ice.

However, it puzzles him: unlike fire and ice that together would reduce the fire's heat or the ice's coldness, his heat is surprisingly not lessened, and her coldness only intensifies.

Examining the Poem's Words and Images

Poets use imagery—mental pictures created by words—to add meaning. Evaluate the reason the poet uses the images in the poem.

My Love is like to ice, and I to fire:
How comes it then that this her cold so great
Is not dissolved through my so hot desire,
But harder grows the more I her entreat?
Or how comes it that my exceeding heat
Is not allayed by her heart-frozen cold,

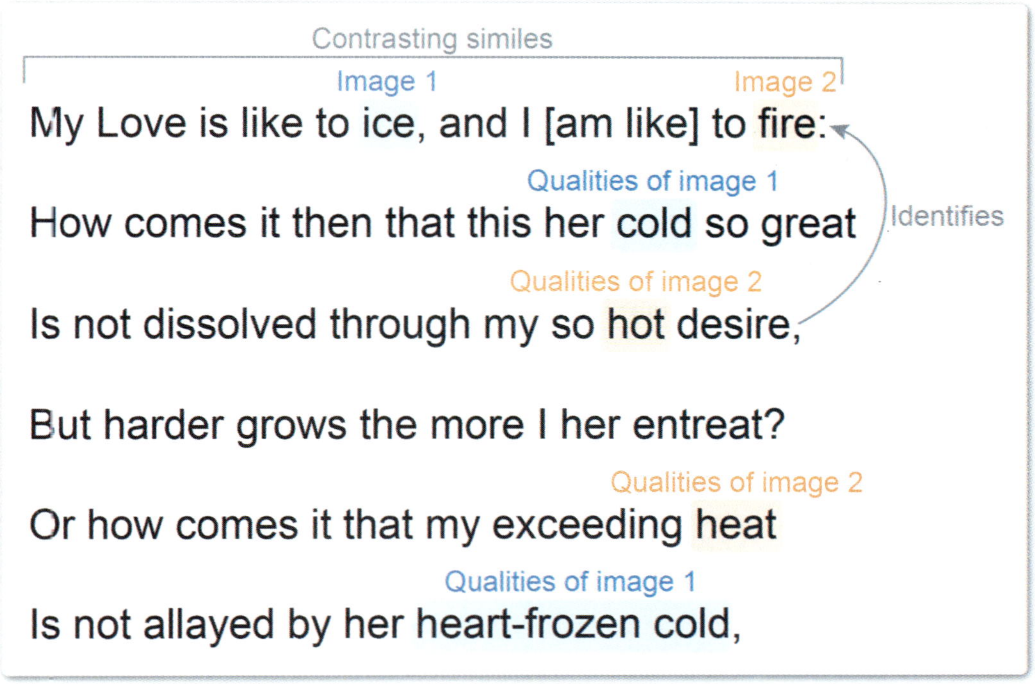

A contrast between the speaker and the beloved is described in a simile with opposite **images** of fire and ice, natural elements that diminish each other because fire can evaporate water, and water can put out a fire.

The speaker's hot desire contrasts with his beloved's cold refusal. When ice and fire meet, one usually gives way to the other; however, the speaker's beloved doesn't respond by becoming less cold like he anticipated, and his desire is not lessened by her disinterest.

Predicting a Poem's Main Idea

Use your understanding of the poem's words and imagery to predict its main idea.

To be effective, a prediction should be based on ALL of the ideas in a poem. For example:

- The beloved is like ice, but the speaker, like fire.
- Either coldness should reduce heat, or warmth should reduce coldness, but that's not what happens between the speaker and his beloved.
- The speaker questions why the normal effect doesn't occur.

Prediction: The correct answer should describe the speaker's puzzled expression about how his hot fire and the beloved's cold ice don't affect each other as expected.

Using the Process of Elimination

The following text is adapted from Edmund Spenser's 1595 poem "Amoretti 30." The poem expresses a person's thoughts about a beloved.

> My Love is like to ice, and I to fire:
> How comes it then that this her cold so great
> Is not dissolved through my so hot desire,
> But harder grows the more I her entreat?
> Or how comes it that my exceeding heat

Is not allayed by her heart-frozen cold,

What is the main idea of the poem?

✗ **Choice A:** The speaker is thinking that his feelings for his beloved are fading.

✗ **Choice B:** The speaker is planning to end his relationship with the beloved.

✓ **Choice C:** The speaker is puzzled by his and his beloved's reactions to each other.

✗ **Choice D:** The speaker is too upset to continue speaking with his beloved.

Choice C most closely matches the prediction about the speaker being puzzled by how his passionate heat and his beloved's icy coldness don't have the same effects that fire and ice should have on each other.

> Read poetry on your own to practice finding a poem's main idea. Check your understanding by searching online for information about the poem's meaning.

Example

The following text is from John Keats 1817 poem "O Solitude! if I must with thee dwell." The poem is addressed to Solitude as if it were a person physically present.

O Solitude! if I must with thee dwell,
Let it not be among the jumbled heap
Of murky buildings; climb with me the steep,—
Nature's observatory—whence the dell,
Its flowery slopes, its river's crystal swell,
May seem a span; let me thy vigils keep
'Mongst boughs pavillion'd, where the deer's swift leap
Startles the wild bee from the fox-glove bell.

What is the main idea of the text?

A) The speaker prefers being alone to having the company of others.

B) The speaker identifies a preferable place to experience being alone.

C) The speaker must be alone to enjoy the beauty of nature.

D) The speaker is uncomfortable with living in a crowded city.

O Solitude! if I must with thee dwell,
Let it not be among the jumbled heap
Of murky buildings; climb with me the steep,—
Nature's observatory—whence the dell,
Its flowery slopes, its river's crystal swell,
May seem a span; let me thy vigils keep
'Mongst boughs pavillion'd, where the deer's swift leap
Startles the wild bee from the fox-glove bell.

Paraphrase

If I have to experience solitude, I'd prefer to be alone in nature rather than in a city darkened by buildings; I invite Solitude to join me in climbing a steep slope—a place to observe nature—where the valley with flowers and a crystal-clear river can be viewed; I would rather be alone where deer and bees can be seen among tree boughs.

Prediction

The main idea should describe the speaker's preference to be alone in nature instead of in the city.

Process of Elimination

✗ **Choice A:** The text doesn't explain whether the speaker prefers solitude over the company of others. The speaker compares solitude in the city with being alone in nature.

✓ **Choice B:** If solitude is necessary, the speaker would prefer to experience it in nature where flowers, a valley, a river, deer, and bees can be seen rather than where "jumbled buildings" block such a view.

✗ **Choice C:** The poem doesn't discuss whether the speaker can enjoy nature's beauty with others or if solitude is necessary.

✗ **Choice D:** The poem doesn't describe how the speaker feels about living in a city. The speaker focuses on where solitude is best experienced without mentioning comfort.

Practice

1. The following text is from William Wordsworth's 1801 poem "I Travelled Among Unknown Men." The poem is addressed to England as if it were a person.

I travelled among unknown men,
In lands beyond the sea;
Nor, England! did I know till then
What love I bore to thee.

'Tis past, that melancholy dream!
Nor will I quit thy shore
A second time; for still I seem
To love thee more and more.

What is the main idea of the text?

A) The speaker is asleep and having a dream about returning to England.

B) The speaker prefers a foreign land and has decided not to return to England.

C) The speaker experiences increased love for England when he travels abroad.

D) The speaker plans to continue traveling to other places but misses England.

See Appendix for answer

Things to Remember

- Identify punctuation marks that separate complete thoughts in the poem.
- Paraphrase the poem's complete thoughts.
- Evaluate the meaning added by specific words and images.
- Predict the main idea.
- Use the process of elimination to find the answer with a meaning like your prediction.

Main Idea: Poetry
Check for Understanding

1. The following poem is from William Shakespeare's 1590 poem "Sonnet 71." The poem is addressed to a good friend as if he were physically present.

   No longer mourn for me when I am dead
   Than you shall hear the surly sullen bell
   Give warning to the world that I am fled
   From this vile world, with vilest worms to dwell;
   Nay, if you read this line, remember not
   The hand that writ it; for I love you so,
   That I in your sweet thoughts would be forgot,
   If thinking on me then should make you woe.

   What is the main idea of the text?

   A) The speaker is hearing a church bell ringing that signals death.

   B) The speaker is realizing how friendship is more important than writing.

   C) The speaker is too discouraged by the horrible world to continue living.

   D) The speaker is preferring that the friend forget him rather than suffer.

2. The following text is from Michael Drayton's 1619 poem "Sonnet 37." The poem is addressed to a beloved as if that person were physically present.

   Dear, why should you command me to my rest
   When now the night doth summon all to sleep?
   Methinks this time becometh lovers best;
   Night was ordain'd together friends to keep.
   How happy are all other living things
   Which though the day disjoin by sev'ral flight,
   The quiet ev'ning yet together brings,
   And each returns unto his love at night!

   What is the main idea of the poem?

   A) The speaker is thinking nighttime should bring lovers closer to each other.

   B) The speaker is offended by his beloved ordering him to sleep.

   C) The speaker is planning to leave his beloved the next day.

   D) The speaker is claiming that sleep during the night separates people.

Main Idea

Nonfiction

In nonfiction, the main idea **summarizes what a text states** about a topic. This section presents several strategies for evaluating a nonfiction text to determine its main idea. One or more may be helpful; use what works best for you on any given question.

Strategies for Finding the Main Idea

- Paraphrase each sentence.
- Identify any comparison, contrast, or transition words.
- Predict the main idea.
- Use the process of elimination.

Paraphrasing Each Sentence in the Text

Paraphrasing can help you find a text's main idea because putting information in your own words makes the meaning of each sentence clearer. A nonfiction paragraph's main idea expresses a general statement based on what ALL of its sentences discuss.

Consider the following main idea question:

> Compared with wild strawberries, many of today's cultivated strawberries contain lesser quantities of volatile organic compounds, giving these berries lower aroma intensities and blander flavor. For instance, methyl anthranilate, a molecule found in many wild strawberries that contributes a strong, sweetish aroma, and methyl cinnamate, which contributes a spicy note, are not present in many of the cultivated strawberries available in grocery stores.

Which choice best states the main idea of the text?

Sentence Paraphrasing

S1	Farm-grown strawberries have lower compound levels than wild strawberries.
S2	Molecules improving taste in wild strawberries are absent in farm-grown strawberries.

Identifying Words That Signal a Comparison, Contrast, or Transition

Some nonfiction texts might include words that indicate that a comparison or contrast is being discussed. Nonfiction texts may also include transitions—words that signal what idea follows and that show how information in the paragraph is connected.

Signal	Indicators in a Text	Expresses
Comparison	More, less, words ending in –er (ex. high**er**, great**er**, etc.)	Two or more things are compared
Contrast	But, however	An opposite idea follows the previous one
Transition	For example, for instance	A specific example of a previous idea follows

When text compares or contrasts ideas, the correct answer often includes these elements. Note how a paragraph's information is organized when looking for its main idea.

Compared with wild strawberries, many of today's cultivated strawberries contain less**er** quantities of volatile organic compounds, giving these berries low**er** aroma intensities and bland**er** flavor. For instance, methyl anthranilate, a volatile molecule found in many wild strawberries that contributes a strong, sweetish aroma, and methyl cinnamate, which contributes a spicy note, are not present in many of the cultivated strawberries available in grocery stores.

Which choice best states the main idea of the text?

Signal	Text Word or Phrase
Comparison	compared, lesser, lower, blander
Transition	for instance

The text begins with the word "compared," which indicates that a comparison will be discussed. Words ending with the suffix "-er" such as "lesser," "lower," and "blander" in Sentence 1 also indicate that a comparison is being expressed. The transition phrase "for instance" in Sentence 2 signals a shift to specific examples of strawberry compounds.

Predicting the Main Idea

Based on your understanding of the text, come up with your own idea about what the main idea will be. Compare your prediction with the answer choices to see if one matches.

Given the paraphrasing for this text, the main idea should express both the comparison found in Sentence 1 and the details about compounds provided by Sentence 2.

Prediction: Wild strawberries taste better than cultivated strawberries lacking compounds that improve aroma and flavor.

Using the Process of Elimination

Identify answer choices that contain details or ideas that aren't discussed in the text and eliminate them, narrowing your search for the correct answer.

The correct answer often uses a *general* word to express the same meaning of a *specific* word in the text.

Compared with wild strawberries, many of today's cultivated strawberries contain lesser quantities of volatile organic compounds, giving these berries lower aroma intensities and blander flavor. For instance, methyl anthranilate, a volatile molecule found in many wild strawberries that contributes a strong, sweetish aroma, and methyl cinnamate, which contributes a spicy note, are not present in many of the cultivated strawberries available in grocery stores.

Which choice best states the main idea of the text?

A) Volatile molecules are not often found in strawberries that are cultivated today.

B) Wild strawberries are widely praised for their intense color and attractive appearance.

C) Wild strawberries have more of the compounds that improve taste than cultivated strawberries.

D) Farmers find it more challenging to profit from harvesting wild strawberries than from growing cultivated strawberries.

✗ **Choice A:** The text explains that cultivated strawberries have lower levels of volatile compounds and lack two flavor-enhancing molecules. It doesn't discuss how frequently these compounds and molecules are found in them.

✗ **Choice B:** The text doesn't describe the appearance of wild strawberries or whether they are praised.

✓ **Choice C:** The text explains how lesser quantities of two compounds decrease the flavor and aroma of cultivated strawberries. Because wild strawberries have higher quantities of these volatile molecules, they have better flavor and aroma.

✗ **Choice D:** Although it's possible that more profit is made from cultivated strawberries sold in stores, the **text doesn't discuss** the profit farmers make from any type of strawberries.

Example

To protect themselves against the cold during the Ice Age, Paleolithic people made clothes from animal hides using tools for specific tasks. For example, scrapers were used to clean the inside surface of an animal's hide, stone blades were used to cut it precisely, and bone awls were used to make holes in the hide. Finer bone awls were used as needles to sew hide segments together.

Which choice best states the main idea of the text?

A) Stone blades and bone awls were not commonly used by Paleolithic people to make clothing.

B) Paleolithic people made clothes using various tools designed for specialized purposes.

C) Paleolithic people are widely admired for their innovative tools for making clothes.

D) During the Ice Age, Paleolithic people found it difficult to make clothing from stone tools.

Sentence Summary

S1	Paleolithic people used different tools for separate tasks needed to make clothes.
S2	On hides, scrapers were used to clean, blades to cut, and awls to pierce.
S3	Bone needles were used to sew clothing together.

The phrase "For example" that begins Sentence 2 indicates that specific examples follow the previously stated explanation of Paleolithic tools.

Prediction: The main idea is probably about how Paleolithic people made clothes with different tools that were used for separate purposes: cleaning, cutting, and piercing.

Process of Elimination

✗ **Choice A:** The text mentions that these tools were used by Paleolithic people, but it doesn't discuss whether these tools were commonly or seldomly used.

✓ **Choice B:** The text's three sentences each discuss the separate tools that Paleolithic people used to perform different tasks involved in making clothes.

✗ **Choice C:** The text doesn't explain whether Paleolithic people are admired for their clothes-making tools nor whether those tools are considered innovative.

✗ **Choice D:** The text doesn't describe the difficulty or challenges Paleolithic people experienced when making clothing from stone tools.

Practice

1. Scientists have suggested that humans originally hunted horses as prey and later began to protect and breed horses to ensure a steady supply of meat. This domestication seems to have occurred independently in different areas of the world over the centuries. New uses of horses developed over time as humans used them for milk, hides, and transportation, but these animals may also have been domesticated to help with the hunting of wild horse herds.

Which choice best states the main idea of the text?

A) Though originally used for food, horses were later domesticated for a variety of purposes.

B) Even though horses were domesticated for different reasons, improved transportation was most beneficial to humans.

C) Horses are no longer domesticated by humans to ensure a supply of food.

D) Interaction between different societies now leads to the domestication of horses for similar benefits.

See Appendix for answer

2. Believing that art and artist are more, not less, connected by technology, Eric Standley designs works that are inspired by the intricate geometric forms ornamenting Gothic and Islamic architecture. Taking months to complete, his stained-glass windows are made from laser-cut stacks of paper with thousands of details in each layer that are drawn with a gaming mouse using CAD software. The complex, pattern-based art expresses the universal complexity and vulnerability of people across cultures, creating a unifying effect on viewers as well as connecting the artist to his work.

Which choice best states the main idea of the text?

A) Though creating complex works of art such as those designed by Standley can connect people, it is time-consuming and inefficient.

B) Designing artwork like the stained-glass windows made by Standley is the most effective method of creating a unifying effect on viewers.

C) Standley is an artist who has long argued that artists should use technology to create their art.

D) Though complex, the intricate designs of the stained-glass windows by Standley brings together people, technology, and art.

See Appendix for answer

Things to Remember

- Restate the text's sentences in your own words.
- Note words indicating transition, contrast, or comparison.
- Predict the text's main idea.
- Eliminate answers not supported by the text.

Main Idea: Nonfiction
Check for Understanding

1. Before World War I, many literary critics looked beyond a literary work to research an author's life and the historical and cultural elements of society that likely influenced his writing—an approach called Historical Criticism. For example, an interpretation of the mix of religious and secular elements in the Anglo-Saxon poem *Beowulf* might be based on that society's shift from paganism to Christianity around 600 CE. But poet and theorist John Crowe Ransom asserted that Historical Criticism distracted from a work's meaning and called for New Criticism, an approach that disregards the author and focuses only on the work itself to reveal its meaning more clearly.

   Which choice best states the main idea of the text?

   A) John Crowe Ransom argued that the meaning of a literary work is not fully evident from a critical approach that had previously been used to understand literary works.

   B) John Crowe Ransom theorized that a literary work's meaning is not contained fully in the work itself but is established through the reader's knowledge and response to it.

   C) An approach to *Beowulf* using Historical Criticism may seem to include contradictory influences, but they can be easily understood from the evidence about the author and historical period.

   D) Literary works that were written in previous centuries are more difficult for audiences to comprehend than twenty-first-century literature.

2. Using artistic creation as his subject, video artist Chris Milk designed his interactive installation *Treachery of the Sanctuary* in 2012 to represent the three stages of creativity: inspiration, critical response, and transformation. First, a viewer's on-screen shadow changes to a flock of birds symbolizing inspiration. On the second screen, the birds attack the viewer's shadow, representing critical response. On the third screen, giant wings flap from the shadow's body as the viewer's arms move, demonstrating how a creative idea transforms into something greater than the original thought.

   Which choice best states the main idea of the text?

   A) Though creating an art installation that immerses viewers in the creative process can be lively, it makes understanding the art more difficult.

   B) Symbolic of creativity, *Treachery of the Sanctuary* by Chris Milk engages ordinary viewers in an interactive art experience.

   C) Designing art installations like Chris Milk's *Treachery of the Sanctuary* is the most powerful way to create an immersive art experience for viewers.

   D) As an artist, Chris Milk has supported other artists who create immersive videos that project digital art onto screens.

3. Researchers Kevin Stanek and Deniz Ones have discovered a positive relation between extroverts—energetic people who seek out social interaction and enjoy small talk—and intelligence. This may seem surprising because intellectuals are often thought of as introverts who enjoy quietly studying alone in their rooms, but Stanek and Jones note that the mental and social activities of people with extroverted personalities typically require the more advanced cognitive abilities of memory, visualization, and decision-making.

   Which choice best states the main idea of the text?

   A) Although it may seem odd that extroverted people who enjoy being socially active tend to be smart, that cognitive ability is based on too much energy and enthusiasm to be sustainable over time.

   B) Although introverted people are more likely to be intellectuals, people with extroverted personalities gain advanced cognitive abilities during their social activities.

   C) Although one might think that people with extroverted personalities are less likely to be intellectuals, extroverts use advanced cognitive abilities when interacting with others during social activities.

   D) Although people with introverted personalities tend to be intellectuals, their cognitive abilities may increase significantly from engaging with others.

Evidence

Novel and Short Story

To identify which **quoted lines from a novel or short story best support a question's claim,** students must understand what is being asked and what each answer means.

This section discusses the following strategies for answering an SAT question that requires evidence in the form of lines from a novel or short story:

- Paraphrasing the claim
- Determining the claim's criteria
- Summarizing the answer choice quotations
- Using the process of elimination

These strategies are meant to be helpful suggestions; some may be more effective for you than others, so use whichever ones assist you with locating the right answer to the question.

Paraphrasing the Claim

The text begins by identifying the title of a novel or short story, the year it was written or published, and the name of the author. This information is followed by a sentence stating a claim that ends with a blank. Put that claim in your own words to simplify the idea by using language that makes sense to you.

Example

"Rip Van Winkle" is an 1819 short story by Washington Irving. In the story, Irving characterizes Rip Van Winkle as someone who willingly helps others but avoids his own responsibilities: ______

Which quotation from "Rip Van Winkle" most effectively illustrates the claim?

Background information

"Rip Van Winkle" is an 1819 short story by Washington Irving. In the story,

Claim

Irving characterizes Rip Van Winkle as someone who willingly helps others but avoids his own responsibilities: ______.

Claim Paraphrase: Rip Van Winkle is described as someone who assists others but does not take care of his own business.

Determining the Claim's Criteria

Determine the parts of the claim that must be fulfilled by the correct answer. You can find these criteria by locating the important ideas asked about in the claim.

Claim: In the story, Irving characterizes Rip Van Winkle as someone who willingly helps others but avoids his own responsibilities.

Claim's Criteria: For the above example, the claim has two parts that must be fulfilled by the correct answer. The quotation must show that 1) Rip Van Winkle is helpful to others and 2) Rip Van Winkle does not take care of his responsibilities.

Summarizing the Answer Choice Quotations

Once you know the information you are looking for, it's helpful to restate the main point of each quotation to better understand each answer choice.

Consider these answer choices for the question about "Rip Van Winkle":

A) "Rip was ready to attend to anybody's business but his own; but as to doing family duty, and keeping his farm in order, he found it impossible."

B) "Times grew worse and worse with Rip Van Winkle as years of matrimony rolled on; a tart temper never mellows with age, and a sharp tongue is the only edged tool that grows keener with constant use."

C) "Rip Van Winkle, however, was one of those happy mortals, of foolish, well-oiled dispositions, who take the world easy, eat white bread or brown, whichever can be got with least thought or trouble, and would rather starve on a penny than work for a pound."

D) "Poor Rip was at last reduced almost to despair; and his only alternative, to escape from the labour of the farm and clamour of his wife, was to take gun in hand and stroll away into the woods."

The summary of each one might look something like this:

Choice A: Rip willingly paid attention to everyone else's responsibilities but neglected his own property and family.

Choice B: Rip was in a marriage made difficult by anger and abusive language that got worse as time went by.

Choice C: Rip was content with whatever he had and would rather go hungry than work.

Choice D: Rip went hunting to get away from farm work and his unpleasant wife.

Compare each of these summarized answers with the claim to determine which one shows that Rip helps others but avoids his own responsibilities.

> Usually either paraphrasing the quotations or eliminating wrong answers provides a sufficient strategy for finding the correct answer.

Using the Process of Elimination

Another strategy is to eliminate any of the quotations with information unrelated to the claim. In the "Rip Van Winkle" question, that would mean getting rid of answers that don't contrast Rip helping others with Rip avoiding his own work.

✓ **Choice A:** This answer states that Rip was willing to help others but found it impossible to take care of his farm, which was his responsibility.

✗ **Choice B:** This answer focuses on Rip's marriage and life getting worse over time because of anger and hurtful words. It doesn't mention Rip helping others or his responsibility.

✗ **Choice C:** This answer shows why Rip doesn't want to work, but it doesn't discuss his willingness to help others.

✗ **Choice D:** This answer shows what Rip does instead of working on the farm, but it doesn't contain information about Rip helping others.

Eliminating answers that don't discuss both of Rip's contrasting qualities makes the correct answer easier to find. By getting rid of answers that don't satisfy ALL of the claim's criteria, you can more easily identify the quotation that best supports the claim.

Always read every choice to make sure you haven't overlooked the best answer.

Example

Of Human Bondage is a 1915 novel by W. Somerset Maugham. In the novel, Maugham portrays nine-year-old Philip Carey as being unable to accept his mother's death: ______

Which choice most effectively uses a quotation from *Of Human Bondage* to illustrate the claim?

A) "When they reached the house Mrs. Carey had died in—it was in a dreary, respectable street between Notting Hill Gate and High Street, Kensington—Emma led Philip into the drawing-room."

B) "He had often been in the room when his mother was not in it, but now it seemed different. There was something curious in the look of the chairs."

C) "The strangeness of the room left it, and it seemed to him that his mother had just gone out for a walk. She would be in presently and would come upstairs to have nursery tea with him."

D) "Philip came gradually to know the people he was to live with, and by fragments of conversation, some of it not meant for his ears, learned a good deal about himself and about his dead parents."

Claim Paraphrase: Philip refuses to accept that his mother is dead.

Claim's Criterion: The right answer must show Philip doing or saying something indicating that he does not accept his mother's death.

Process of Elimination: Only one of these sets of lines indicates that Philip is in denial about his mother's death.

✗ **Choice A:** These lines describe the location of the house where his mother died and how Emma takes Philip into the front room. They don't suggest a lack of acceptance of her death.

✗ **Choice B:** These lines discuss how being in his mother's room feels different now, but they do not indicate that Philip believes that she is still alive.

✓ **Choice C:** These lines say that Philip feels like his mother is out walking and will be back soon. This information shows that Philip hasn't accepted his mother's death.

✗ **Choice D:** These lines reveal that Philip discovers information about his new caretakers, himself, and his dead parents. However, there is no mention that Philip is denying that his mother is dead.

Practice

1. "The Other Two" is a 1904 short story by Edith Wharton. In the story, Mr. Waythorn ponders what aspects of her identity Alice has given up in each of her marriages: ______

Which choice most effectively uses a quotation from "The Other Two" to illustrate the claim?

A) "He had fancied that a woman can shed her past like a man. But now he saw that Alice was bound to hers both by the circumstances which forced her into continued relation with it, and by the traces it had left on her nature.'"

B) "Alice Haskett – Alice Varick – Alice Waythorn – she had been each in turn, and had left hanging to each name a little of her privacy, a little of her personality, a little of the inmost self where the unknown god abides."

C) "He could fancy how pretty Alice must have looked, in a dress adroitly constructed from the hints of a New York fashion-paper; how she must have looked down on the other women, chafing at her life, and secretly feeling that she belonged in a bigger place."

D) "Though she had put on her most engaging teagown she had neglected to assume the smile that went with it, and Waythorn thought he had never seen her look so nearly worried."

See Appendix for answer

2. "The Birth-Mark" is an 1843 short story by Nathaniel Hawthorne. In the story, Aylmer is disturbed by his wife Georgiana's appearance: ______

Which quotation from "The Birth-Mark" most effectively illustrates the claim?

A) "Until now he had not been aware of the tyrannizing influence acquired by one idea over his mind, and of the lengths which he might find in his heart to go for the sake of giving himself peace."

B) "He now knelt by his wife's side, watching her earnestly, but without alarm; for he was confident in his science, and felt that he could draw a magic circle round her within which no evil might intrude."

C) "In order to soothe Georgiana, and, as it were, to release her mind from the burden of actual things, Aylmer now put in practice some of the light and playful secrets which science had taught him among its profounder lore."

D) "Aylmer's sombre imagination was not long in rendering the birthmark a frightful object, causing him more trouble and horror than ever Georgiana's beauty, whether of soul or sense, had given him delight."

See Appendix for answer

Things to Remember

- Paraphrase the introductory claim to better understand it.
- Determine the criteria asked for in the claim.
- Summarize the quotation in each answer choice.
- Eliminate answers with information that does not fulfill ALL the question's criteria.

Evidence: Novel and Short Story
Check for Understanding

1. *Daisy Miller* is an 1878 novella by Henry James. In the novella, James portrays Winterbourne as unaccustomed to women like Daisy: ______

   Which choice most effectively uses a quotation from *Daisy Miller* to illustrate the claim?

   A) "Winterbourne was a man of imagination and, as our ancestors used to say, sensibility; as he looked at her dress and, on the great staircase, her little rapid, confiding step, he felt as if there was something romantic going forward."

   B) "He was inclined to think Miss Daisy Miller was a flirt—a pretty American flirt. He had never, as yet, had any relations with young ladies of this category."

   C) "She gave Winterbourne a history of her movements and intentions and those of her mother and brother, in Europe, and enumerated, in particular, the various hotels at which they had stopped."

   D) "Winterbourne listened with interest to these disclosures; they helped him to make up his mind about Miss Daisy. Evidently she was rather wild."

2. "The Sculptor's Funeral" is a 1905 short story by Willa Cather. In the story, the narrator points out his disapproval of another character's behavior: ______

   Which choice most effectively uses a quotation from "The Sculptor's Funeral" to illustrate the claim?

   A) "You pretend to have some sort of respect for me; and yet you'll stand up and throw mud at Harvey Merrick, whose soul you couldn't dirty and whose hands you couldn't tie."

   B) "Harvey Merrick and I went to school together, back East. We were dead in earnest, and we wanted you to all be proud of us some day. We meant to be great men."

   C) "Oh, you needed me hard enough, and you'll go on needing me; and that's why I'm not afraid to plug the truth home to you this once."

   D) "It's not for me to say why, in the inscrutable wisdom of God, a genius should ever have been called from this place of hatred and bitter waters;"

Evidence

Play

To identify which **lines from a play best support an assertion** made in the question, it's important to understand the information given in the text and to identify the claim. The answer choices will contain quotations from the play, but only the correct one will support the claim.

This section discusses the following strategies for questions that ask for evidence from a play:

- Paraphrasing the claim
- Formulating an idea about the answer
- Summarizing the answer choice quotations
- Using the process of elimination

These strategies are just a guide; some may work better than others, so use whichever ones help you the most to answer any given question.

Paraphrasing the Claim

The text will begin by identifying the name of the play, the approximate year it was written or published, and who wrote it. There may be a brief summary of a part of the play before a claim that will be followed by a blank. The question will ask which lines from the play best support the claim.

A claim is an assertion or declaration that a statement is true. To better understand a claim, it's helpful to paraphrase it, or to restate the claim in your own words.

Example

Background information

The *Three Sisters* is a 1901 play by Anton Chekov. In the play, Chebutykin

Brief summary of part of the play

is a doctor whose patient died the previous week. He expresses uncertainty

Claim

over his abilities, as is evident when he ______.

Claim Paraphrase: Chebutykin is no longer certain about his skills.

Predicting the Answer

After paraphrasing the claim, you can come up with your own idea about what a good answer to the question would be based on the information in the text.

In the above example, the claim has to do with a doctor named Chebutykin no longer having faith in his abilities because one of his patients has recently died. Therefore, the best quotation from the play will be the one with information showing the doctor's lack of confidence.

Summarizing the Answer Choice Quotations

To find the answer, it's beneficial to summarize the quotations in each choice.

Example

Which choice most effectively uses a quotation from *The Three Sisters* to illustrate the claim?

A) responds to Irina, "In a year I shall be on the retired list. Then I'll come here again and spend the rest of my life near you."

B) reacts to strangers asking for advice, "I've forgotten all I did know, I remember nothing, absolutely nothing. "

C) says to Andrey, "Perhaps I'll come back in a year. Though goodness knows....It doesn't matter one way or the other."

D) gives advice to Andrey, "Put on your cap, you know, take your stick and walk off... walk off and just go, go without looking back."

The summary of each one might look something like this:

Choice A: Chebutykin tells Irina he will be retired in a year and will live out the rest of his life nearby her.

Choice B: When asked for advice, Chebutykin says he doesn't remember anything that he knows.

Choice C: Chebutykin says to Andrey that he might return in a year but that it doesn't matter whether he does so.

Choice D: Chebutykin tells Andrey to leave and not look back.

Now you can compare the paraphrased answers with the claim to see which one indicates that Chebutykin doubts his abilities.

Using the Process of Elimination

Eliminate any of the quotations with information unrelated to the claim. For the above example, eliminate answers that do not relate to Chebutykin's uncertainty.

✗ **Choice A:** This answer discusses Chebutykin's retirement and how he wants to live near Irina. There is no hint of a lack of confidence.

✓ **Choice B:** When Chebutykin states that he has forgotten everything he knows and that he can't remember anything, he shows his uncertainty about his abilities.

✗ **Choice C:** Although Chebutykin says that it doesn't matter whether he returns, there is no indication that the reason he feels this way is that he has lost confidence in himself.

✗ **Choice D:** Chebutykin's advice to someone about leaving and not looking back doesn't indicate that the reason for this proposed action is that Chebutykin no longer has faith in himself.

Example

A Doll's House is an 1879 play by Henrik Ibsen. In the play, the character Nora realizes that both her husband and her father have controlled her life. She expresses a need for independence, as is evident when she ______

Which choice most effectively uses a quotation from *A Doll's House* to illustrate the claim?

A) says to her husband, "We have been married now eight years. Does it not occur to you that this is the first time we two, you and I, husband and wife, have had a serious conversation?"

B) says about her father, "When I was at home with papa, he told me his opinion about everything, and so I had the same opinions; and if I differed from him I concealed the fact, because he would not have liked it."

C) tells her husband, "I must stand quite alone, if I am to understand myself and everything about me. It is for that reason that I cannot remain with you any longer."

D) says, "I find it impossible to convince myself that the law is right. According to it a woman has no right to spare her old dying father, or to save her husband's life.

Claim Paraphrase: Nora wants to be independent.

Formulated Answer: Nora says something that shows that she wants to be on her own.

Answer Choice Summary

Choice A: Nora points out to her husband that they haven't had a serious conversation in eight years.

Choice B: Nora states that she agreed with her father's views so that he wouldn't be upset with her.

Choice C: Nora says that to understand herself, she must be on her own and can't live with her husband anymore.

Choice D: Nora indicates that she disagrees with any law that doesn't allow a woman to protect her dying father and to save her husband's life.

Process of Elimination

✗ **Choice A:** This quotation discusses a lack of communication but not Nora's need for independence.

✗ **Choice B:** This quotation expresses Nora's desire for approval but says nothing about her wanting to be independent.

✓ **Choice C:** This quotation states Nora's realization she must live on her own so that she can understand who she is. Because it shows her need for independence, this answer illustrates the claim.

✗ **Choice D:** This quotation shows Nora questioning the law; it doesn't say anything about Nora's desire for independence.

Practice

1. *Pygmalion* is a 1912 play by George Bernard Shaw. In the play, Professor Henry Higgins boasts that he can teach working-class Eliza Doolittle how to speak and act like an upper-class lady. Higgins expresses his confidence in his ability to transform Eliza, as is evident when he ______

Which choice most effectively uses a quotation from *Pygmalion* to illustrate the claim?

A) says to himself, “in six months—in three if she has a good ear and a quick tongue—I'll take her anywhere and pass her off as anything."

B) responds to Eliza's request, "If I decide to teach you, I'll be worse than two fathers to you."

C) tells his friend, "I suppose the woman wants to live her own life; and the man wants to live his; and each tries to drag the other on to the wrong track."

D) tells Eliza's father, "Your daughter had the audacity to come to my house and ask me to teach her how to speak properly."

See Appendix for answer

2. *The Importance of Being Earnest* is an 1895 play by Oscar Wilde. In the play, Jack Worthing pretends to be named Ernest when he proposes to Gwendolen; likewise, Algernon pretends to be named Ernest when he proposes to Cecily. Confusion arises when the two women discuss their engagements, as is evident when ______

Which choice most effectively uses a quotation from *The Importance of Being of Being Earnest* to illustrate the claim?

A) Gwendolen comments to Cecily, "Personally I cannot understand how anybody manages to exist in the country, if anybody who is anybody does."

B) Cecily says to Gwendolen, "To save my poor, innocent, trusting boy from the machinations of any other girl, there are no lengths to which I would not go."

C) Gwendolen says to Cecily, "I was growing almost anxious. It would have been terrible if any cloud had come across a friendship like ours, would it not?"

D) Cecily responds to Gwendolen, "I am afraid you must be under some misconception. Ernest proposed to me exactly ten minutes ago."

See Appendix for answer

Things to Remember

- Read the text to locate the claim and then paraphrase it.
- Formulate an idea about the content of the answer.
- Summarize the answers to better understand what they discuss.
- Eliminate answers not supporting the claim.

Evidence: Play
Check for Understanding

1. *Othello* is a circa 1603 play by William Shakespeare. In the play, the character of Othello believes that his wife is cheating on him. He then expresses his torment over this, as is evident when he ______

   Which choice most effectively uses a quotation from *Othello* to illustrate the claim?

   A) describes their love, "She loved me for the dangers I had passed. / And I loved her that she did pity them."

   B) reflects on his actions, "Then you must speak / Of one that loved not wisely but too well."

   C) says to himself, "O, now, for ever / Farewell the tranquil mind; farewell content."

   D) says about his wife, "She wished she had not heard it, yet she wished / That heaven had made her such a man."

2. *Tamburlaine* is a circa 1592 play by William Shakespeare. In the play, the character of Tamburlaine is a shepherd bandit who ultimately becomes Persia's emperor. He believes he is divinely protected, as is evident when he ______

   Which choice most effectively uses a quotation from *Tamburlaine* to illustrate the claim?

   A) asserts, "Our quivering lances, shaking in the air, / And bullets, like Jove's dreadful thunderbolts, Enroll'd in flames and fiery smouldering mists, / Shall threat the gods more than Cyclopian wars;"

   B) states, "Draw forth thy sword, thou mighty man-at-arms, / Intending but to raze my charmed skin, / And Jove himself will stretch his hand from heaven, / to ward the blow, and shield me safe from harm."

   C) says, "What better precedent than mighty Jove? / Nature, that fram'd us of four elements / Warring within our breasts for regiment, / Doth teach us all to have aspiring minds:"

   D) proclaims, "Though Mars himself, the angry god of arms, / And all the earthly potentates conspire / To dispossess me of this diadem, / Yet will I wear it in despite of them,"

Evidence

Poem

Questions asking which **poetry lines provide evidence require you to understand the claim** in the question and the literal meaning of quotations from the poem. Only the correct one will successfully support the claim that ends with a blank.

This section explains steps to successfully answer an SAT question that asks for evidence provided by lines of a poem.

Strategies for Finding Poetry Evidence

- Summarize the claim
- Predict the answer
- Paraphrase the poem's lines
- Use the process of elimination

These strategies are suggestions to help you find the correct answer. Use only the ones that work best for you on each question.

Summarizing the Claim

The text will begin by identifying the name of the poem, the year it was written or published, and who wrote it. This information will be followed by a sentence containing the claim that ends with a blank. A quick summary of the claim can help clarify the idea that must be supported.

Example

Identifying information

"The Bells" is an 1848 poem by Edgar Allan Poe. In the poem, the speaker

Claim

describes the sound of the bells as warning signals of danger: ______

Which quotation from "The Bells" most effectively illustrates the claim?

Claim Summary: In the poem, bells indicate a dangerous situation.

Predicting the Answer

In the "The Bells" question, the claim is that the sound of bells communicates a potentially harmful set of circumstances. Come up with your own idea for information that would best end the sentence.

Prediction: The answer will contain a quotation in which the ringing of the bells relates some kind of danger to the people hearing them.

Paraphrasing the Poem's Lines

Putting the lines from the poem into your own words can help you better understand each answer choice and whether it supports the claim. You don't have to take a lot of time to do this. You just want a general idea about what the quotation says. If the lines are challenging to understand, look for key words that would support the claim.

Suppose these were the answer choices for "The Bells":

A. "Hear the sledges with the bells— / Silver bells! / What a world of merriment their melody foretells! / How they tinkle, tinkle, tinkle, / In the icy air of night!"

B. "How [the ringing] dwells / On the Future! how it tells / Of the rapture that impels / To the swinging and the ringing / Of the bells, bells, bells,"

C. "Hear the loud alarum bells— / Brazen bells! / What a tale of terror, now their turbulency tells! / In the startled ear of night / How they scream out their affright."

D. "And his merry bosom swells / With the paean of the bells! / And he dances, and he yells; / Keeping time, time, time / In a sort of Runic rhyme,"

> The forward slash (/) indicates where one line of poetry ends and the next begins.

The paraphrase of each answer might look something like this:

Choice A: Listen to the silver sleigh bells; their tune declares happy times on a cold night.

Choice B: The swinging and ringing bells predict a future full of joy.

Choice C: Listen to the loud, harsh bells sounding a frightening alarm that tells a scary story of a disturbing night.

Choice D: Someone's heart is happy because of the bells' joyous song, so he dances and keeps time to the magical sound.

> Usually either paraphrasing the quotes or eliminating wrong answers is sufficient to locate the correct choice.

Using the Process of Elimination

Another possible strategy is to eliminate any of the quotations that state something unrelated to the claim. For this example, look for specific words and phrases in each quotation to help you determine what the sound of the bells means and get rid of any answer choices that don't associate the sound of bells with danger.

✗ **Choice A:** The word "merriment" in this quotation relates how the bells declare happy times.

✗ **Choice B:** The word "rapture" describes the sound of the bells as indicating a joyful future.

✓ **Choice C:** Several words and phrases in this answer indicate signals of danger, including "alarum bells," "terror," "turbulency," and "scream out their affright."

✗ **Choice D:** This answer uses the words "merry," "paean" (joyous song), and "dances" to show that the bells are ringing to announce an enjoyable occasion.

Eliminating answers that don't fulfill the claim's requirements can help you quickly identify the correct quotation.

Read ALL the choices to make sure you haven't overlooked the best answer.

Example

"The Dream" is an 1816 poem by Lord Byron. In the poem, Lord Byron suggests that during sleep, dreams have a life of their own: ______

Which quotation from "The Dream" most effectively illustrates the claim?

A) "[Dreams] leave a weight upon our waking thoughts, / They take a weight from off our waking toils,"

B) "A slumbering thought, is capable of years, / And curdles a long life into one hour."

C) "[Dreams] make us what we were not—what they will, / And shake us with the vision that's gone by."

D) "And dreams in their development have breath, / And tears, and tortures, and the touch of joy;"

Claim Summary

Dreams have their own lives just like the people who are doing the dreaming.

Answer Prediction

A description of a dream that makes it seem like it is a living thing.

Quotation Paraphrase

Choice A: Sleep occurs in a world that exists between life and death.

Choice B: The thoughts people have when asleep can make a long life seem like a short time.

Choice C: Dreams create a different reality and allow people to see the past more clearly.

Choice D: Dreams contain elements—like breath, tears, problems, and happiness—that make them seem like living people.

Process of Elimination

✗ **Choice A:** These lines indicates that sleep is a state between life and death; they don't depict sleep as something that is living.

✗ **Choice B:** The focus of these lines is on how the thoughts people have when asleep affect the perception of time, not on how sleep is a living thing.

✗ **Choice C:** These lines assert that dreams make us into different people and change our view of reality; they don't depict dreams as having life.

✓ **Choice D:** These lines give dreams human characteristics. They breathe and have both sadness and happiness, just like people. Therefore, this quotation illustrates the claim that dreams have a life of their own.

Practice

1. "Renascence" is a 1912 poem by Edna St. Vincent Millay. In the poem, the speaker describes feeling empathy for another, writing ______

Which quotation from "Renascence" most effectively illustrates the claim?

A) "Ah! Up then from the ground sprang I / And hailed the earth with such a cry / As is not heard save from a man / Who has been dead, and lives again."

B) "A man was starving in Capri: / He moved his eyes and looked at me; / I felt his gaze, I heard his moan, / And knew his hunger as my own."

C) "But, sure the sky is big, I said; / Miles and miles above my head; / So here upon my back I'll lie / And look my fill into the sky."

D) "I know not how such things can be; / I only know there came to me / A fragrance such as never clings / To aught save happy living things;"

See Appendix for answer

2. "My Mother's Kiss" is an 1896 poem by Frances E. W. Harper. In the poem, the male speaker disagrees with those who minimize the memory of his mother's affection, writing ______

Which quotation from "My Mother's Kiss" most effectively illustrates the claim?

A) "My mother's kiss, my mother's kiss, / I feel its impress now; / As in the bright and happy days / She pressed it on my brow."

B) "The world has scattered round my path / Honor and wealth and fame; / But naught so precious as the thoughts / That gather round [my mother's] name."

C) "You say [my mother's kiss] is a fancied thing / Within my memory fraught; / To me it has a sacred place-- / The treasure house of thought."

D) "My hair is silvered o'er with age, / I'm longing to depart; / To clasp again my mother's hand, / And be a child at heart."

See Appendix for answer

Things to Remember

- Summarize the idea in the claim.
- Predict the answer's idea.
- Paraphrase the poetry lines.
- Eliminate answers not supported by the text.

Evidence: Poetry
Check for Understanding

1. "Workworn" is a 1917 poem by Emily Pauline Johnson. In the poem, the speaker is perplexed by the contradiction between a neighbor's negative circumstances and positive attitude, writing ______

   Which quotation from "Workworn" most effectively illustrates the claim?"

   A) "Across the street, an humble woman lives / To her 'tis little fortune ever gives; / Denied the wines of life, it puzzles me / To know how she can laugh so cheerily."

   B) "This morn I listened to her softly sing, / And, marvelling what this effect could bring / I looked: 'twas but the presence of a child / Who passed her gate, and looking in, had smiled."

   C) "O! weary singer, I have learned the wrong / Of taking gifts, and giving naught of song; / I thought my blessings scant, my mercies few, / Till I contrasted them with yours, and you;"

   D) "If I had watched the woman o'er the way, / Workworn and old, who labours day by day, / Who has no rest, no joy to call her own, / My tasks, my heart, had much the lighter grown."

2. "Thanksgiving Day" is an 1844 poem by Lydia Maria Child. In the poem, the speaker describes experiencing a feeling of impatient anticipation: ______

   Which quotation from "Thanksgiving Day" most effectively illustrates the claim?

   A) "Over the river, and through the wood, / To grandfather's house we go; / The horse knows the way / To carry the sleigh / Through the white and drifted snow."

   B) "Over the river, and through the wood— / Oh, how the wind does blow! / It stings the toes / And bites the nose / As over the ground we go."

   C) "Over the river, and through the wood / Trot fast, my dapple-gray! / Spring over the ground, Like a hunting-hound! / For this is Thanksgiving Day."

   D) "Over the river, and through the wood, / And straight through the barn-yard gate. / We seem to go / Extremely slow,— / It is so hard to wait!"

Evidence

Nonfiction

To identify which **information provides the best evidence that addresses a claim in a nonfiction text,** you must understand the claim and whether the answer requires information that supports or weakens the claim.

This section discusses the following strategies for answering an SAT question about a nonfiction text that requires evidence:

- Analyzing the question
- Locating the claim or hypothesis
- Summarizing the answer choices
- Using the process of elimination

These strategies are meant to be helpful suggestions; some may be more effective than others in locating the correct answer to a question, so just use the ones that assist you.

Analyzing the Question

Analyze the question first to determine if you are looking for information that would support or weaken a claim or hypothesis.

Supporting information includes facts or examples that strengthen the point being made. For instance, if a university claims that that they are graduating more students, then showing that the number of graduates has increased from 9,000 to 10,000 in the last two years would support that point.

Weakening information includes facts or examples that conflict with what is stated. For instance, if the percentage of graduates decreased from 83% to 82% in the last two years, that information would weaken the university's claim that they are graduating more students.

Some common questions that that you will encounter include the following:

Support	**Weaken**
Which finding, if true, would most directly support the hypothesis?	Which finding undermines the hypothesis?
Which quotation most effectively illustrates the claim?	Which finding weakens the claim?
Which response supports the explanation?	
Which statement supports the underlined claim?	

Locating the Claim or Hypothesis

As you read the text, look for information specifically related to what is asked for in the question.

The claim (information asked for in the question that may or may not be true) is often located in the final sentence of the text.

Consider the following sample question:

> Despite the creation of new labor unions, like the ones recently developed by the employees of Starbucks and Trader Joes, the percentage of workers who belong to all labor unions decreased slightly from 10.1% in 2022 to 10.0% in 2023. Researchers speculate there are several reasons for this decline: large-scale organizational challenges, resistance by company owners, and a larger workforce that increased labor union members but decreased the percentage of unionized workers overall. Despite a smaller share of the US workforce, union leaders argue that all workers benefit from organized labor, even nonunion employees.

Which finding, if true, would most directly support the union leaders' argument?

A) After going on strike, both Writers Guild and Actors Guild union members received improved compensation from studios.

B) Healthcare benefits for the majority of corporate employees are similar to benefits of those companies' executives.

C) Most of the increase in union membership has been among younger workers under the age of 45.

D) Members and nonunion members received a raise after the United Auto Workers Union struck a deal with employer General Motors.

The question asks for information that would support the argument made by union leaders The last sentence of the text provides that information: "union leaders argue that all workers benefit from organized labor, even nonunion employees."

Summarizing the Answers

Once you know the evidence that is needed, it's helpful to look for the main points of each answer choice to determine which one supports the claim.

A summary of each answer choice for the above question about labor unions might look something like this:

Choice A:	Union member writers and actors got more money after they refused to work until their demands were met.
Choice B:	Both the employees and executives of companies receive similar healthcare benefits.
Choice C:	The number of people under 45 who joined unions was higher than the number of people over 45 who did so.
Choice D:	Once union autoworkers made a deal with General Motors, autoworkers who weren't a part of a union also got more money.

Compare each of these summarized answers with the claim to determine which one shows that all workers, even nonunion employees, benefit from unions in the workplace.

Usually either summarizing answers or eliminating wrong answer choices provides a sufficient strategy for finding the correct answer.

Using the Process of Elimination

Another strategy is to eliminate any of the answers with information that is only partially correct or that is unrelated to the claim. In the labor union question above, that would mean getting rid of answers that DON'T show non-union employees benefiting from the efforts of labor unions.

✗ **Choice A:** This answer discusses the benefits that union actors and writers received; it doesn't contain any information about nonunion workers.

✗ **Choice B:** This answer indicates a similar benefit received by both workers and management; it doesn't mention union or nonunion employees.

✗ **Choice C:** This answer contrasts the number of workers who joined unions with those who didn't. It doesn't discuss benefits to either group.

✓ **Choice D:** This answer states that nonunion workers received more money for their work after union members struck a deal with General Motors. Therefore, nonunion workers as well as unionized workers benefited.

Eliminating answers that discuss something other than what is asked for in the question or that don't satisfy ALL of the question's criteria can help you more easily identify the statement that best supports the claim.

Read every choice to make sure you haven't overlooked the best answer.

Example

Nigerian singer Sikuru Ayinde Barrister's 1983 album *Nigeria* primarily contains songs focusing on political corruption in an appeal to the country's leaders to have honor and keep their promises to constituents made while campaigning for office. His 1994 album *The Truth* comments on his country's flawed educational and healthcare systems, as well as the inflation prevalent in its economy. Together these albums don't just serve as a musician's artistic expression; <u>they also constitute a type of musical journalism that highlights the many challenges Nigeria has faced</u>.

Which statement about the albums, if true, would most directly support the underlined claim?

A) Between them, *Nigeria* and *The Truth* provide information about social, economic, and political problems facing Barrister's country,

B) *Nigeria* includes songs that address different aspects of the same subject, whereas *The Truth* contains tracks that explore multiple topics.

C) The songs found on *Nigeria* focus on Barrister's political aspirations, whereas *The Truth* primarily includes songs commenting on different social issues.

D) Between them, *Nigeria* and The *Truth* depict the varied history of Nigeria and the experience of its people.

The question asks for support, and the claim is easily located because it's underlined. The claim wants to know how Barrister's songs represent a type of reporting in which he discusses the difficulties the country of Nigeria has experienced.

Answer Choice Summary:

- **Choice A** lists Nigeria's problems that are reported on in two of Barrister's albums.
- **Choice B** contrasts how one album focused on different parts of the same issue whereas the other investigated several different topics.
- **Choice C** mentions how one album explored Barrister's hopes to be a politician, which isn't supported by the text, while another album made statements about problems in society.
- **Choice D** provides inaccurate information because there is nothing in the text that provides details about Nigerian history. Instead, the focus of the two albums is the political and social issues experienced by the Nigerian people.

Process of Elimination:

✓ **Choice A:** Because social, economic, and political issues are also topics covered by journalists, this answer supports the idea that the songs on Barrister's albums function in a similar way to news reporting.

✗ **Choice B:** The number of topics each album explores doesn't provide any information about whether Barrister's songs about "political corruption," or "flawed educational and healthcare systems" created a form of reporting through music.

✗ **Choice C:** Although this answer discusses the content of both albums, it doesn't say how this information is a kind of journalism. Also, the text doesn't indicate whether Barrister wanted to be a politician.

✗ **Choice D:** This answer doesn't show how exploring Nigerian history or its people's experiences via Barrister's music is connected to a method of reporting.

Practice

1. Ironically, political candidates who want to be elected to office claim that government workers are inefficient, lazy, and politically biased. Focusing on the experiences of US federal employees from 2016 to 2020, Jaime Kucinskas and James L. Perry researched the validity of this claim by interviewing and surveying workers in multiple high-level US state departments. Kucinskas and Perry noted the good work ethic displayed by most federal employees, regardless of their preferred political party.

Which finding from Kucinskas and Perry's survey, if true, would most directly weaken the claim made by the political candidates?

A) Government administrators admitted that salary and job security were the primary reasons for taking their current positions.

B) When government employees were temporarily not working due to budgetary shutdowns by Congress, they welcomed their time off as a way to relax.

C) Leaders of several government agencies implemented ways to streamline operations so that they could serve the public in a more efficient manner.

D) Government employees were less likely to follow the directives of a president who belonged to a different political party than their own.

See Appendix for answer

2. Direct social cooperation is a circumstance in which two or more individuals work together—a student group studying together for the next course exam, for instance, or a co-op working together to grow food that is shared by all its members—to accomplish a common goal. In recent research, Yu Kou and her colleagues discovered that cooperation between strangers has increased since the 1950s. The researchers explained that an increase in collaboration likely has occurred due to more people living in cities where they are forced to cooperate with strangers for the well-being of everyone concerned.

Which response from a survey given to city dwellers who use public transit best supports the researchers' explanation?

A) "The first time I rode on a city bus, the driver was so helpful in directing me to the courthouse that I nominated him for the city Employee of the Month award."

B) "When I want to explore a place, to get a sense of its culture, people, and neighborhoods, there is no better way to travel than public transportation."

C) "I am a strong proponent of riding the subway to reduce traffic in the city. I use it several times a week and encourage others to do the same."

D) "While transit in my city is not ideal, I make do because it saves me thousands of dollars a year and makes me a happier, healthier person."

See Appendix for answer

Things to Remember

- Identify whether the evidence should support or weaken the claim.
- Read the text to find its claim or hypothesis.
- Summarize each answer choice to understand its contents better.
- Eliminate answers not supported by the text.

Evidence: Nonfiction
Check for Understanding

1. Hexagonal boron nitride (h-BN), a thin, soft chemical compound shaped like a honeycomb, is often used to give cosmetics a silky texture. Cubic boron nitride (c-BN), a compound with a different chemical formula but a similar molecular arrangement, has a three-dimensional lattice structure resembling a diamond at the molecular level and is used to make cutting tools and drills. Researchers have found that despite the differences between h-BN and c-BN, combining them creates interesting properties that hold even more potential than either compound has on its own, which has led a team to hypothesize that combining these two compounds could create a coating material effective at high temperatures.

   Which finding, if true, would most directly support the researchers' hypothesis?

   A) A material composed of a combination of h-BN and c-BN functioned better in colder climates than it did in warmer ones.

   B) The shape of the composite substance made from combining both h-BN and c-BN retained some of the molecular characteristics of each one.

   C) The combination of h-BN and c-BN created a substance that flashes brightly when a laser beam is pointed at it, a property that could improve radiation therapy.

   D) A composite of h-Bn and c-BN was used to insulate a high-powered electronic device to help regulate its temperature when it became overheated.

2. The Cretaceous period ended 66 million years ago, presumably when an asteroid hit the Earth, causing the extinction of dinosaurs. Paleontologists Kyle Atkins-Weltman and Eric Snively examined three bones of what they thought was a juvenile specimen of a caenagnathid—an already known species of dinosaur from this time period—in order to assess its maturity and found their specimen was an adult dinosaur from a completely different species. Atkins-Weltman and Snively claim that there could be even more dinosaur species that have yet to be discovered—potentially even through re-examination and reclassification of fossils already in museum collections.

   Which finding, if true, would most directly weaken Atkins-Weltman's and Snively's claim?

   A) Additional caenagnathid bones are examined by other paleontologists who state that some of these bones have not been correctly classified.

   B) Paleontologists reexamine a large number of previously catalogued dinosaur bones only to find that all of the species have been identified correctly.

   C) Paleontologists agree that dinosaur species were in decline during the Cretaceous period despite the discovery of Atkins-Weltman and Snively.

   D) Paleontologists determine that another method identifying dinosaur species is more accurate than analyzing fossilized bones.

Inference

Completes Text

An inference is a conclusion that is logical because it is based on evidence; it is not a conclusion reached by random guessing or unsupported speculation. The SAT asks students to understand what isn't directly stated in the text by examining it for clues that help them identify an inference that is based on that information.

Many inference questions have an incomplete statement that is followed by a blank at the end of the text. The same question is asked after the blank: "Which choice most logically completes the text?"

Other inference questions might not have text that ends with a blank—instead, below the complete text they ask what can "most reasonably be inferred." Regardless of the question format, the strategies for inference questions are the same.

This section explains the following strategies to arrive at a logical conclusion that is based on the text.

- Break down the text into its main ideas to improve comprehension.
- Highlight transitions in the text and evaluate what they signal about its information.
- Use the process of elimination.

Breaking Down the Text

Success on SAT inference questions begins with understanding the text. If what is discussed isn't understood, a logical conclusion can't be drawn.

To improve understanding, use the test's annotation tool that allows students to highlight and make notes about the text's main ideas. For example, create a brief list of ideas to clarify what the passage discusses and highlight any transition words in the text. Then examine the answer choices to determine which one seems logical based on the text's ideas.

Because SAT questions such as those about punctuation, parts of speech, and words in context can be answered quickly, readers have more time to spend on questions that require an inference.

Highlighting Transitions and Evaluating What They Signal

Many of the texts in inference questions include transitions that show the connection between the ideas in the sentences.

Pay particular attention to transitions that indicate a contrast or contradiction, such as "but," "however," "although," and "nonetheless." By signaling conflicting ideas, these transitions show how the information after them differs from what was discussed previously. In inference questions, most transitions indicate a contrast.

Using the Process of Elimination

If any part of an answer contradicts the information in the text, that choice should be eliminated—even if it includes other information that is correct.

The correct answer will be a logical conclusion *based on the text*. Look for details in the text that provide evidence of the likelihood that the main idea in an answer choice is true.

Examine the following paragraph to

- note its main ideas
- identify transitions
- eliminate answer choices that aren't supported by the text

The *Mona Lisa* painted by Leonardo da Vinci depicts a noble woman, Lisa Gherardini. Some art experts have claimed that the figure's mysterious smile is an expression of happy contentment, but others suggest that the smile conceals deeper emotions of sorrow and melancholy. The fact that the figure has a puzzling smile, therefore, ______

Which choice most logically completes the text?

A) indicates that the woman was often happy and content.

B) does not conclusively reveal the woman's emotions.

C) eliminates the likelihood that the woman was happy.

D) would make it easy to understand the woman's emotions.

Main ideas:

S1	The *Mona Lisa* portrays a noble woman.
S2	Experts disagree about what her smile expresses.
S3	Because her smile is puzzling...

Transition:

In the text, the word "but" indicates a contrast between what is stated before and after it. In this case, it signals the different views art experts have about Mona Lisa's smile: it might express happiness and it might express sadness. Understanding that contrast makes it easier to identify the correct answer.

Eliminate answers:

- **Choice A:** The woman's smile may indicate that she is happy, but the text doesn't address whether she felt contentment frequently. Therefore, it can't be concluded that she was "often happy."
- **Choice C:** According to some experts, the woman's smile expresses "happy contentment." Therefore, the idea that Mona Lisa was happy can't be eliminated.
- **Choice D:** The text describes the smile as "puzzling," which indicates that it is difficult to know what emotion Mona Lisa's smile expresses. This information in the text contradicts the idea that her emotions were easy to understand.

After breaking down the text, noting transitions, and using the process of elimination, readers can more easily identify the correct answer.

Choice B is correct. Because art experts have conflicting understandings of what the woman's smile means, the emotions behind that smile remain mysterious and cannot be conclusively interpreted.

Example

In argumentative essays that take a stance on an issue, writers generally include information that supports their position. Professional writer Stefani Holloway argues that writers naturally tend to include referenced information that agrees with their opinion, but the strongest and most convincing arguments also include a consideration and rebuttal of opposing views argued by others. Discussing views in a composition that conflict with the writer's opinion could therefore ______

Which choice most logically completes the text?

A) cause the writer's argumentative essay to become less persuasive to readers with opposing views.

B) make writer's opinions more understandable to readers who lack knowledge of the topic.

C) align the writer's opinion with the views that are broadly held by the audience.

D) help the writer improve the arguments made in an argumentative essay.

Text breakdown:

S1	Writers usually include information supporting their argument.
S2	Holloway claims including opposing views creates stronger arguments.
S3	Including opposing views therefore...

Transition:

The word "but" indicates a contrast between what writers generally do and what Holloway argues they should do.

Argumentative essay writers generally include supportive information only, but Holloway argues that writers who discuss views conflicting with their opinions create the "strongest and most convincing arguments." Comparing the information in each answer choice to what the text states helps eliminate incorrect answers and find the one that's correct.

Process of Elimination:

✗ **Choice A** states that including opposing views makes the essay less persuasive, but that contradicts Holloway's claim that including them makes the argument "more convincing."

✗ **Choice B** expresses an idea about the audience's knowledge that isn't discussed in the passage.

✗ **Choice C** states an idea about views of the writer and audience becoming aligned (agreeing), but the views of the audience are not discussed in the text.

✓ **Choice D** is correct. The passage states that arguments are "strongest and most convincing" when they discuss conflicting views. An argument is improved if it becomes stronger and more persuasive.

All parts of a correct answer will be based on information in the passage.

Practice

1. A team of international researchers led by Geoffrey Hill and Miguel Carneiro investigated the factors that enabled scientists to crossbreed yellow canaries with red siskins to create what are now called red factor canaries. These red canaries were given that name because the researchers found the genetic "factor" that moved from red siskins into yellow canaries. Their study showed that the gene CYP2J19 enables a color change in other birds like the African weaver bird and the zebra finch.

It can most reasonably be inferred from the text that the finding about the factor enabling color changes in birds is significant for which reason?

A) The red flesh of salmon and trout is caused by the same genetic factor that enables birds to have red plumage.

B) The ability to have red coloration due to the gene CYP2J19 is unique to red factor canaries.

C) The genetic factor that enables birds to have red feathers and beaks is likely present in many bird species that have the same gene.

D) The genetic factor that creates red pigmentation might be key to developing new medications.

See Appendix for answer

2. The Koa tree is found on two islands that are on opposite sides of the world, with *Acacia koa* (*A. koa*) in Hawaii and its descendant *Acacia heterophylla* (*A. heterphylla*) growing 18,000 kilometers away in Réunion. Plants spread by seeds that are carried by wind, animals, or humans and generally grow in areas much closer to each other. To explain how the Koa tree traveled from Hawaii to Réunion despite the great distance between them, scientists used genetic evidence to estimate the rate of change between tree populations and determined that the dispersal occurred 1.4 million years ago, long before humans arrived in Réunion. Given that Koa seeds soaked in water won't germinate and that wind couldn't carry a seed that far, researchers concluded that ______

Which choice most logically completes the text?

A) the Koa tree growing in Réunion must have predated the Koa tree growing in Hawaii.

B) a seabird likely brought a Koa tree seed from Hawaii to Réunion in its belly or stuck to its feet.

C) a Koa seed from Hawaii likely landed on a floating object and drifted to the island of Réunion.

D) the Koa tree originally came from Australia and traveled from there to Kauai, one of the older Hawaiian islands.

See Appendix for answer

Things to Remember

- Break the information down by making brief notes to better understand the text.
- Locate transition words that signal something about the relationship of ideas in the text.
- Use the process of elimination to determine a logical conclusion based on the text.
- Eliminate an answer if any part of it isn't supported by the text.

Inference: Completes Text
Check for Understanding

1. J. K. Rowling's *Harry Potter* fantasy series remains widely popular among young adults because it addresses familiar, universal themes. For example, *Harry Potter and the Sorcerer's Stone* dramatizes a clash between good versus evil and includes a fast-paced plot with an exciting conflict of love and hate. Despite each book averaging 600 pages, the series has become a hugely successful global media franchise. But following Rowling's adult detective series *Cormoran Strike* requires younger adults to confront books that are over 1,000 pages in length, themes that are less familiar, and stories that have a slower pace. Consequently, __________

   Which choice most logically completes the text?

   A) many younger readers will likely consider Rowling's *Cormoran Strike* series less appealing than her *Harry Potter* series.

   B) some of the books in Rowling's *Harry Potter* series are more relevant to adult audiences than her crime series.

   C) Rowling's *Harry Potter and the Sorcerer's Stone* is the most interesting novel to read in the series.

   D) readers with knowledge about detective work and crime solving generally prefer Rowling's *Cormoran Strike* series over her *Harry Potter* series.

2. Between two closely related species of Mexican tetra fish—the blind cave-dwelling species and the sighted surface-dwelling species— cave tetras seem to have acquired a superior sense of smell by developing larger nose tissues, which, according to scientists, help these fish survive in the darkness. Maryline Blin and her colleagues studied both species' ability to smell food by testing their response to amino acids in different foods. They found that the cave-dwelling tetras reacted to food when surface-dwelling tetras did not, suggesting that ______

   Which choice most logically completes the text?

   A) food detected by cave-dwelling fish can also be detected by surface-dwelling fish despite their inferior sense of smell.

   B) researchers should not assume having a superior sense of smell is necessarily an adaptation for living in an extreme environment.

   C) researchers can assume the greater sense of smell in cave-dwelling fish is an ability that was learned rather than an evolutionary change.

   D) cave-dwelling fish can survive in a dark environment because of an adaptation enabling them to detect food they cannot see.

3. In 2013, researchers discovered evidence of a previously unknown, small-brained species of extinct human (*Homo naledi*) in South Africa's Rising Star cave that may have lived 335,000 to 236,000 years ago. Three studies claim that *H. naledi* deliberately buried their dead and made geometric rock art, practices that are signs of higher cognitive ability. However, according to other archeologists, there is no evidence indicating whether the burial cavities were deliberately excavated by the Naledi or were simply shallow depressions already present in the ground, nor is there proof of when the markings on the walls were made, suggesting that ______

   Which choice most logically completes the text?

   A) South Africa's Rising Star cave discoveries show that the cognitive abilities varied among the *Homo naledi*.

   B) a more cognitively evolved, unknown species, not the smaller-brained *Homo naledi*, made the cave art.

   C) the cognitive abilities of *Homo naledi* aren't demonstrated conclusively by what was discovered in the Rising Star cave.

   D) *Homo naledi* were more cognitively evolved and capable than the claims made in the three studies.

Graphic Displays

Bar Graphs

You must understand how a bar graph's data relate to the text that follows it because you are often asked a question that requires information from both. This section focuses on how to connect what a bar graph shows to what is understood about a text.

These steps can help you strategically find the correct answer to a bar graph question:

- Determine what the question asks.
- Examine the graph's title, labels, and key.
- Look for text information and graph data that connect to the question.
- Use the process of elimination.

Determining What the Question Asks

Note whether the question is asking for **data that support** or **data that weaken** what a statement claims or concludes.

Types of Bar Graph Questions

Filling in a blank	A question may ask for graph data that *support* an incomplete sentence by asking test takers to fill in a blank.
Complete sentence	A question may ask for graph data that *support* a claim or conclusion stated in a complete sentence of the text without a blank.
Text statement	A question may ask for graph data that *weaken* a claim or conclusion stated in text without a blank.

Supporting facts or examples demonstrate the likely truth of a claim or conclusion.

For example, if someone claims that Netflix has been spending less on content than it did previously, data that show the company's content expenses *decreasing* over time will support that claim.

Most bar graph questions ask for support, but a question may ask for information that weakens a claim or conclusion.

Weakening facts or examples conflict with what is stated in a claim or conclusion. Any conflicting evidence showing the claim's likelihood of being false weakens the statement.

For example, if someone claims that Netflix has been spending less on content than it did previously, data that show the company's content expenses *increasing* suggests the opposite. Evidence demonstrating that Netflix has been spending more weakens the claim that it spent less, showing that the claim is inaccurate.

Example

Examine the text and question below that might accompany a bar graph.

> Evaluating population growth information from around the world, the US Census Bureau projected the number of people aged 60 or older living in different regions by 2050. In their report, analysts estimated that, globally, the number of people aged 60 or older would increase, but some regions would experience a greater increase than others; **for instance**, ______
>
> Which choice most effectively uses data from the graph to **complete the example**?

The text's final sentence with a blank begins with "for instance," which indicates that the question requires an answer with information from the graph that **supports** the idea stated just before it.

Notice also that the question includes the phrase "complete the example," another clue that the question requires an answer *supporting* the text.

Bar graph questions sometimes include language clues.

Location	Language clue	Indicates
In text	"for instance" or "for example"	Question focuses on the statement *before* "for instance" or "for example"
In question	"complete the example"	Answer must *support* a statement with data from the graph

Examining the Graph's Title, Labels, and Key

The **title** reveals the graph's topic. In graphs, the horizontal line at the bottom of its bars is the X-axis, and the vertical line on the left is the Y-axis.

The **labels** on the X-axis and Y-axis tell what the bars on a graph represent. Bars extending up from the X-axis represent various amounts that are indicated by the numbers on the Y-axis.

The **key** indicates the category each bar is displaying.

X-axis (horizontal line)	Identifies **what** is being measured
Y-axis (vertical line)	Expresses a **measurement** for each item
Key (below the X-axis label)	Identifies what each bar represents

Once the graph's labels are clearly understood, its bars can be examined to identify what each indicates. The top of each bar shows an amount that is expressed by numbers on the Y-axis.

Example

Examine the bar graph below:

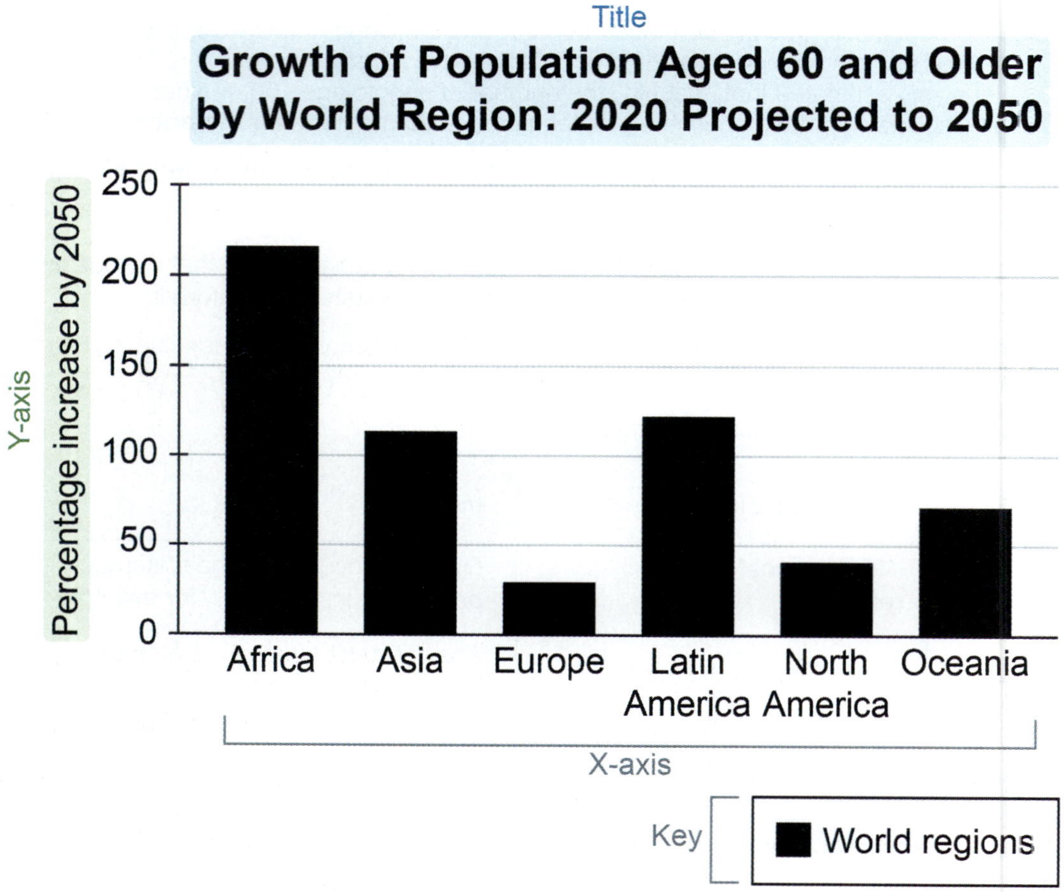

The graph's **title** informs viewers that its bars display the projected growth of people aged 60 or older by regions of the world. The **Y-axis label** on the left shows that the numbers are percentage increases by 2050, and the **X-axis label** below the bars shows that the graph focuses on six regions in the world.

The **key** indicates world regions are represented by each bar.

The heights of the bars indicate that percentage increases of older people by 2050 will differ by region, with Africa having the highest increase and Europe having the lowest.

Looking for Text Information and Graph Data

Examine the text and the graph data to connect the information to the claim.

The task at this point is to evaluate which data fulfill the question's criteria. Look at the illustration below that combines the previously discussed bar graph and text about population growth.

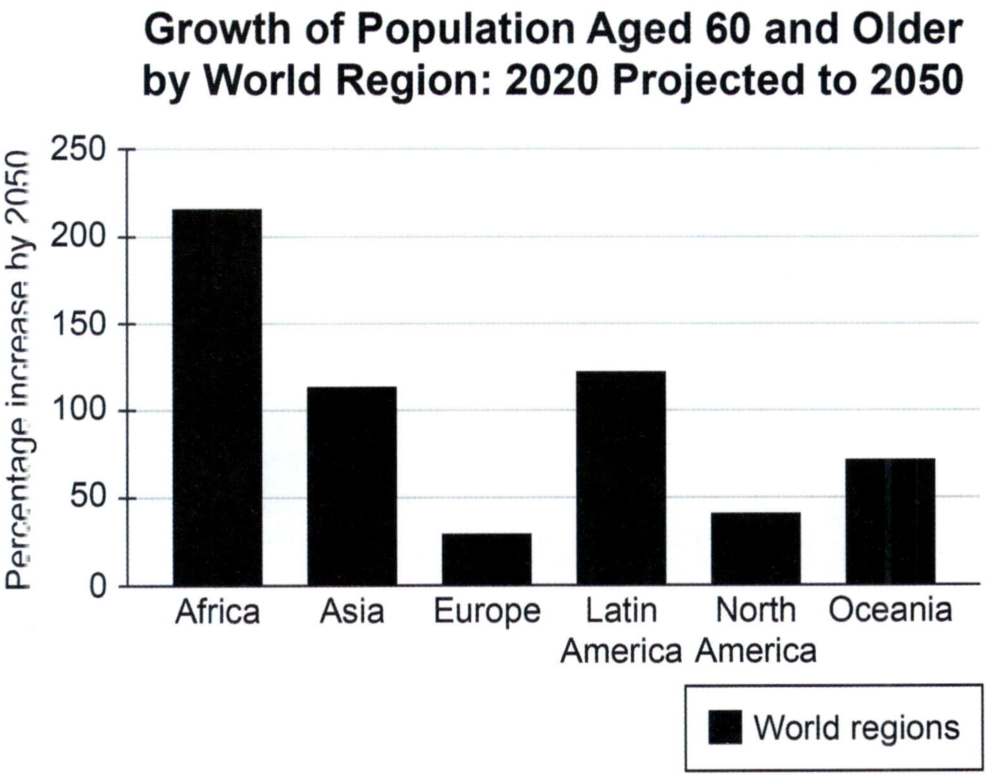

Evaluating population growth information from around the world, the US Census Bureau projected the number of people aged 60 or older living in different regions by 2050. In their report, analysts estimated that, globally, the number of people aged 60 or older would increase, but some regions would experience a greater increase than others; for instance, ______

Which choice most effectively uses data from the graph to complete the example?

The text provides Census Bureau information about the projected increase in the number of older people in different regions by 2050. The final sentence calls for graph data projecting a higher increase in one region compared to the increase in another.

The bars represent six regions. Heights of the bars vary, indicating that projected increases differ by region. Given the data in this bar chart, it's clear to see that the regions with higher bars like Africa and Latin America are projected to have greater increases than regions like Europe and North America.

Using the Process of Elimination

- Eliminate any answer that is unrelated to what the question asks.
- Eliminate any answer that doesn't accurately reflect the graph's data.
- If a question requires *support* for a statement, eliminate any answer choice that lacks the data needed to demonstrate the accuracy of its claim.
- If asked for information that *weakens* a statement, eliminate any answer that provides data that support the text's claim.

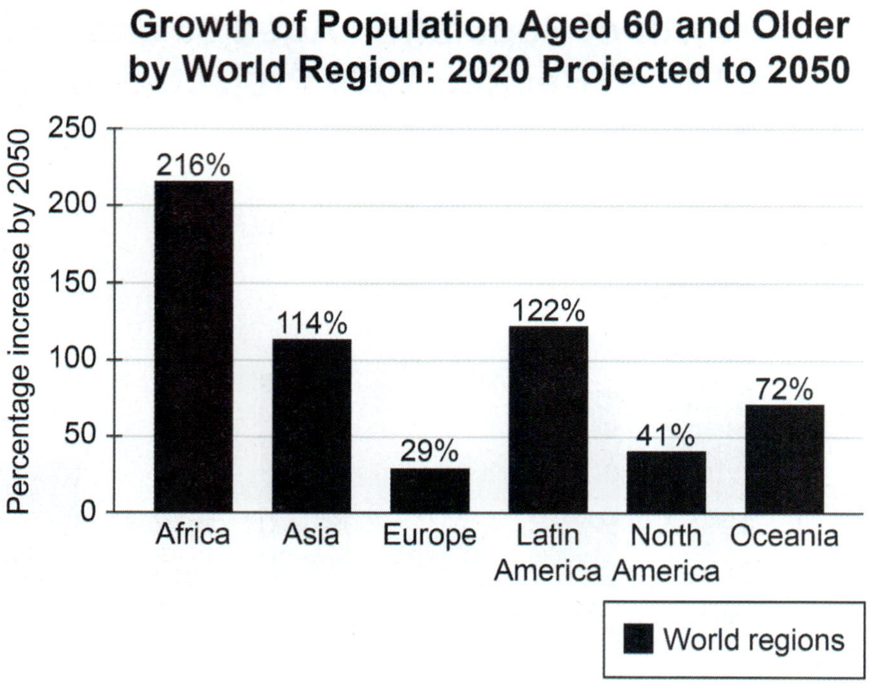

Evaluating population growth information from around the world, the US Census Bureau projected the number of people aged 60 or older living in different regions by 2050. In their report, analysts estimated that, globally, the number of people aged 60 or older would increase, but some regions would experience a greater increase than others; **for instance**, ______

Which choice most effectively uses data from the graph to complete the example?

A) Europe is projected to have a 40% increase and Asia a 200% increase in people aged 60 or older.

B) Africa is projected to have an increase of 200% and 240% in people aged 60 or older but a 20%–40% increase in North America.

C) Oceania is projected to have a less than 50% increase of people aged 60 or older

D) Asia is projected to have a less than 100% increase in people aged 60 or older.

Process of Elimination

X **Choice A:** This answer includes inaccurate data that isn't supported by the graph. The graph indicates that Europe will have a 20–30% increase, not a 40% increase, and Asia will have a 100%–120% increase, not a 200% increase.

✓ **Choice B:** The graph indicates that Africa will have roughly a 210% increase, which falls between 200% and 240%, the range stated in the answer. North America is projected to have an approximately 30% increase, which falls in the range between 20 and 40%.

X **Choice C:** The answer incorrectly reports data from the graph. Oceania is projected to have an increase higher than 50%, so describing it as "less than 50%" doesn't match graph data. Because the answer discusses only one region, it can't demonstrate the percentage increase of different regions required by the question.

X **Choice D:** Asia is projected to have an increase of more than 100%, so "less than 100%" is not supported by the graph. Because the answer discusses only one region, it can't demonstrate the percentage increase of different regions required by the question.

Example

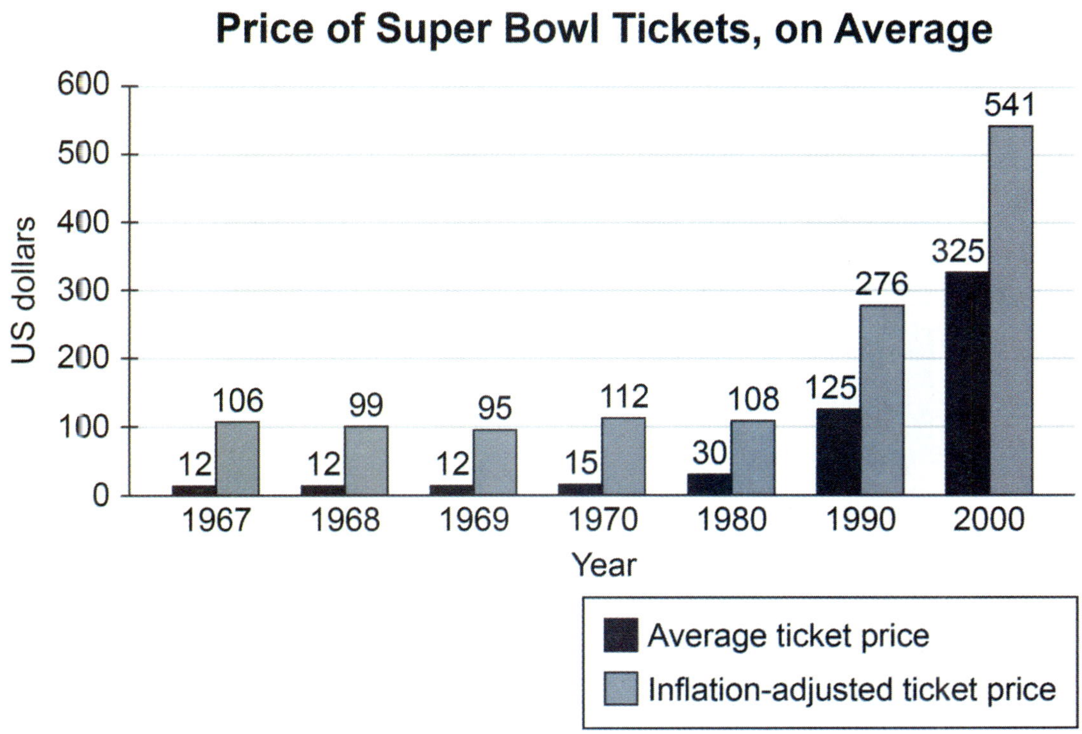

An NFL football fan compared ticket prices for the Super Bowl from its inception in 1967 to 2000. He examined both the average Super Bowl ticket price and its inflation-adjusted price. The fan concluded that the actual price of Super Bowl tickets adjusted for inflation increased each year during that time.

Which choice best describes data from the graph that weaken the fan's conclusion?

A) The average price of Super Bowl tickets was less than the inflation-adjusted price in every year evaluated.

B) The average cost of Super Bowl tickets in 1967 was less than the cost of tickets in 2000.

C) From 1967 to 1980, the average cost of Super Bowl tickets was about the same when adjusted for inflation.

D) From 1980 to 1990, the average cost of Super Bowl tickets more than doubled in price.

✗ **Choice A:** Comparing the average ticket price to its inflation-adjusted price can't demonstrate whether the inflation-adjusted cost of tickets had gone up during the years considered. Unadjusted prices are *unrelated* to a conclusion about inflation-adjusted prices.

✗ **Choice B:** The fan's conclusion is about inflation-adjusted prices. Comparing the price of tickets in the years 1967 and 2000 shows an overall increase in cost, which *supports* the conclusion that prices rose over time. This comparison doesn't demonstrate whether ticket costs rose "each year."

✓ **Choice C:** Showing that inflation-adjusted ticket prices stayed about the same from 1967 to 1970 conflicts with the fan's conclusion and *weakens* it. In 1968 and 1969, the inflation-adjusted price was lower than the prior year's adjusted price.

✗ **Choice D:** The difference in ticket costs between 1980 and 1990 shows a rise in prices during a 10-year period, which *supports* the fan's conclusion.

Practice

1.

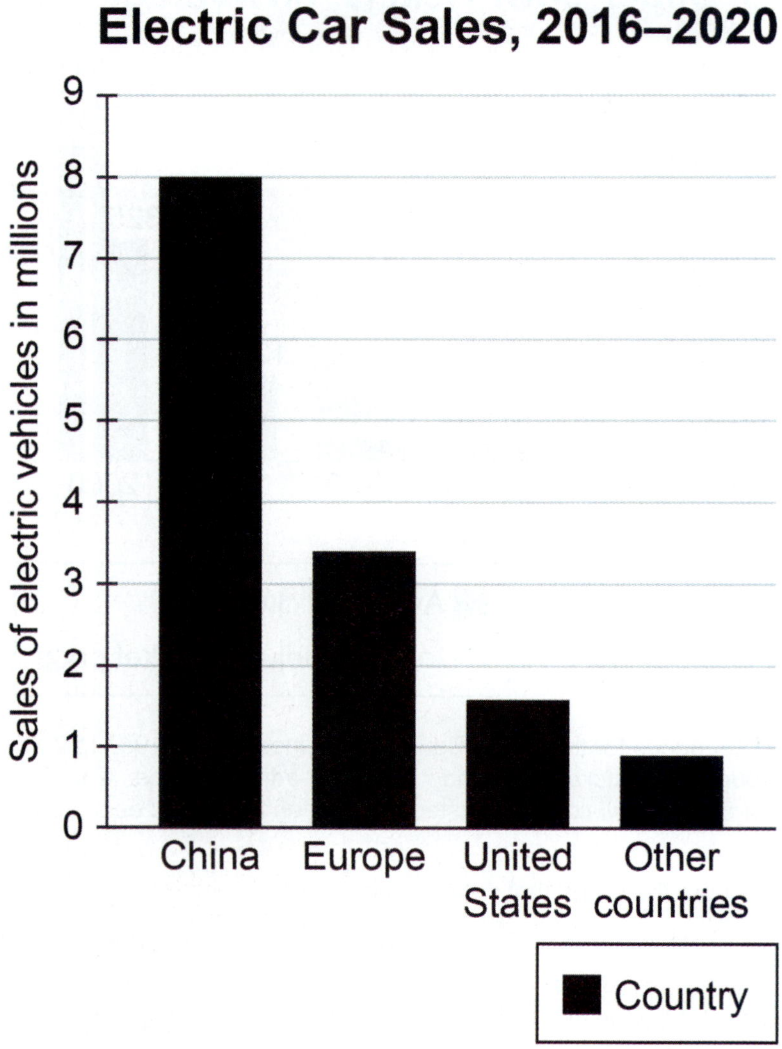

Most electric vehicles (EVs) significantly lower carbon emissions because they are powered by lithium-ion batteries. EVs are estimated to make up only 18% of the new car sales worldwide in 2023, but based on recent trends, electric vehicles are becoming more popular. According to sales data from 2016 to 2023, China accounted for about 8 million EV sales, and ______

Which choice most effectively uses data from the graph to complete the text?

A) the US sold more EVs than European countries sold during that time.

B) countries outside of China, Europe, and the US had more than 1 million in EV sales.

C) the United States had between 1 and 2 million in EV sales.

D) Europe had fewer than 3 million in EV sales.

See Appendix for answer

2.

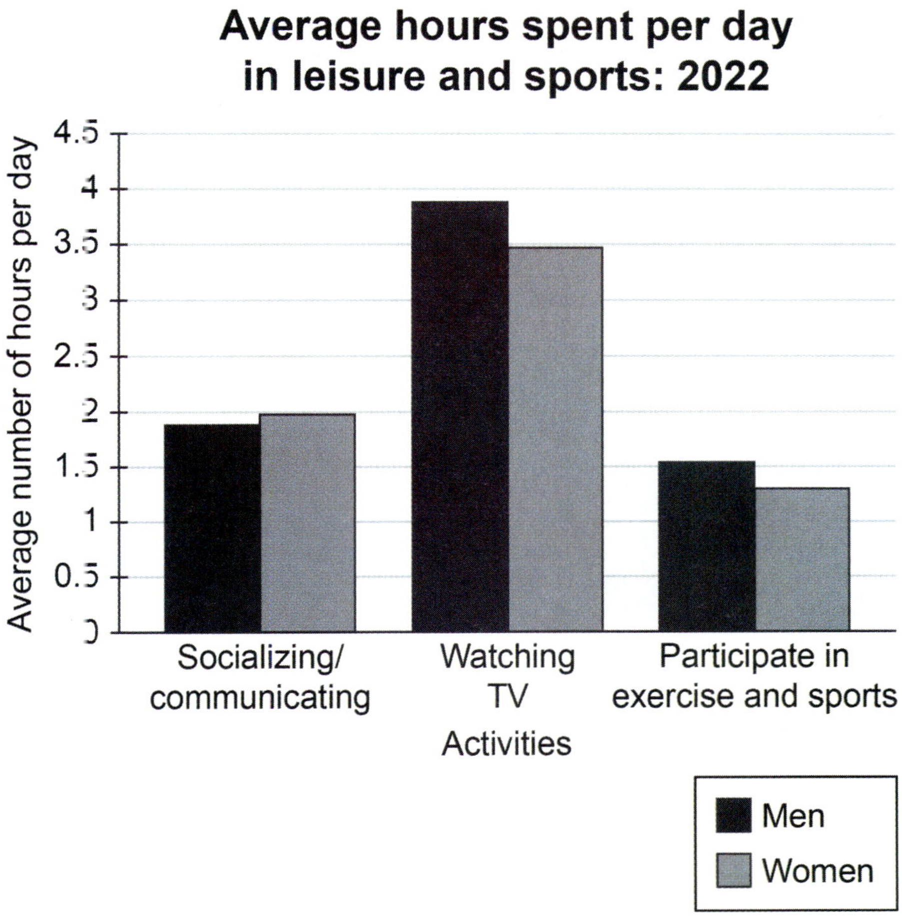

The purpose of the American Time Use Survey is to measure how US adults spend their time. To collect this information, interviewers ask respondents to recall their activities over 24 hours and report every activity they took part in during that time. Using the responses, one analyst concluded that watching television is the preferred pastime of men, while women prefer other activities.

Which choice most effectively uses data from the graph to weaken the analyst's conclusion?

A) Women and men spent the most amount of leisure time watching TV.

B) The time men and women spent socializing and communicating was about the same.

C) Women spent more time than men in socializing and communicating activities.

D) The time spent participating in sports and exercise was greater among men than women.

See Appendix for answer

Things to Remember

- Determine whether the question requires information that supports or weakens a conclusion.
- Carefully examine the graph's title, labels, and key.
- Look for graph data that provide what the question requires.
- Use the process of elimination.

Graphic Displays: Bar Graph
Check for Understanding

1.

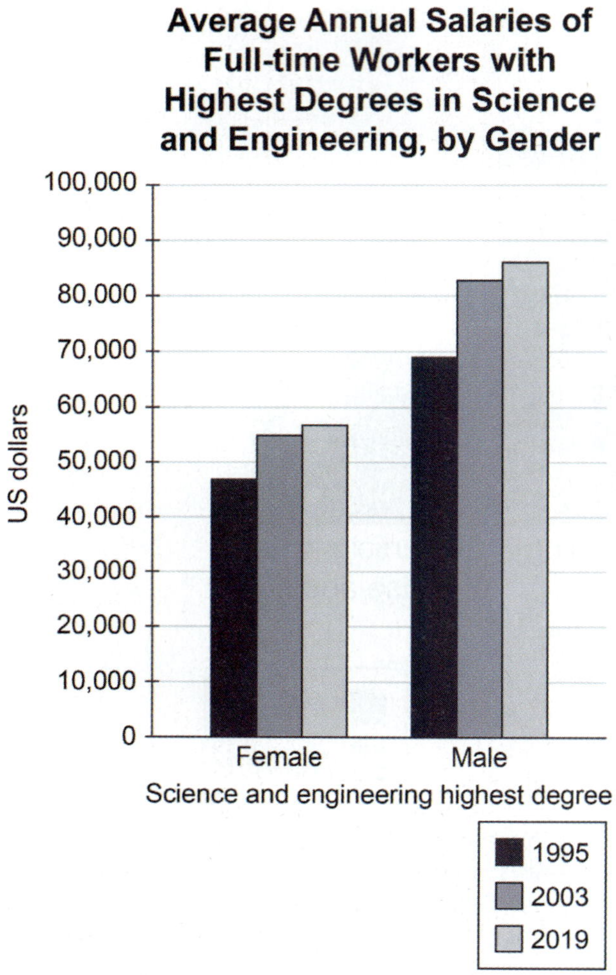

U.S. Census Bureau, American Community Survey (ACS), 2019

The US Census Bureau conducted a survey to learn about the average salaries of male and female workers in science and engineering careers. In science and engineering careers, salary differences between men and women have persisted, with females generally given lower pay than their male counterparts. Even though the average annual salary for females in science and engineering has increased over the years, salaries have also increased for males. As a result, the average salaries for women in science and engineering careers have remained lower than average salaries of men in the same careers. For example, ______

Which choice most effectively uses data from the graph to complete the example?

A) men received a lower average salary increase between 2003 and 2019 than they did between 1995 and 2003.

B) women earned a higher average salary in 2003 than they earned in 2019.

C) men and women earned about the same increase in average salaries between 1995 and 2003.

D) the average salary for men was higher than for women in 2019, just as it was in 1995 and 2003.

2.

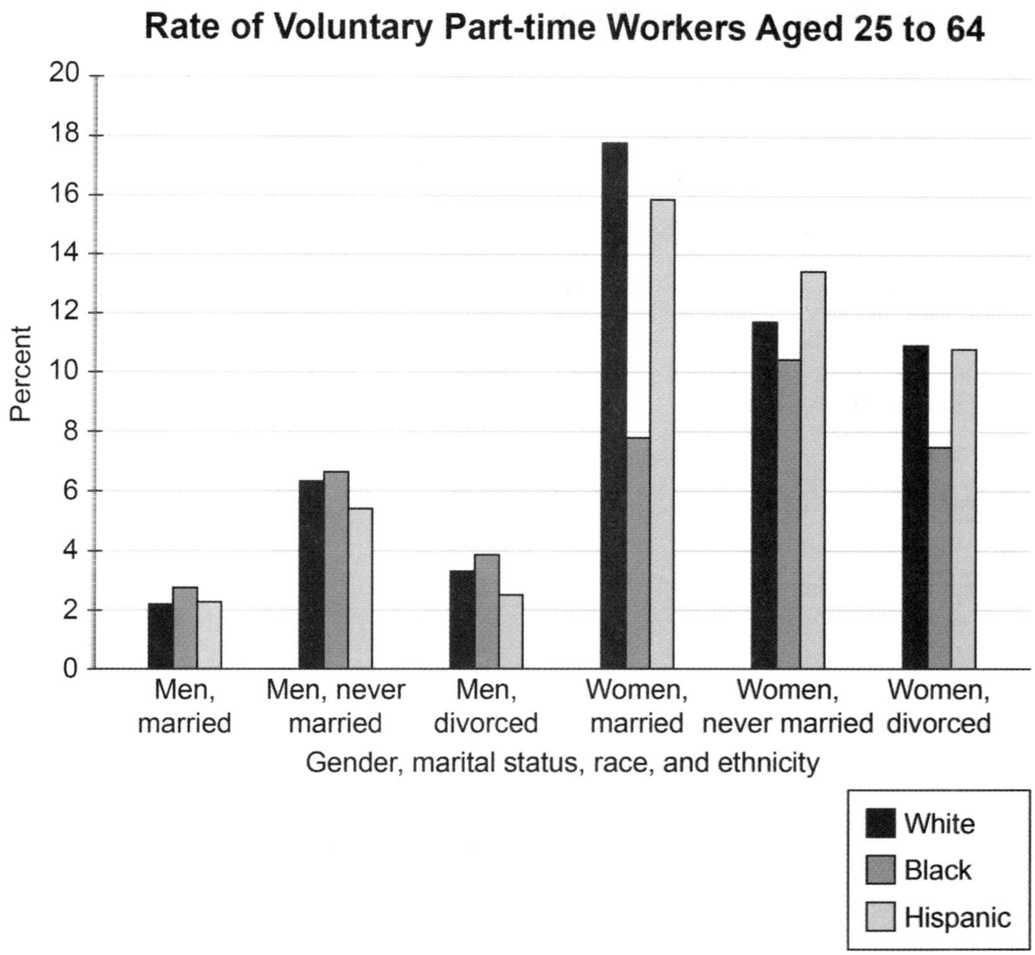

Part-time employees are those who work 1 to 34 hours a week. Researchers sampled 60,000 households in a 2016 Current Population Survey report to see if gender and marital status affected voluntary part-time labor. Percentages of part-time laborers varied somewhat in connection with the race and marital status of workers. However, the percentage of people who worked part time differed the most by gender, with survey data showing that ______.

Which choice most effectively uses data from the graph to illustrate the claim?

A) the percentage of married men of each race surveyed was about the same.

B) the percentage for all women who worked part time was higher than the percentage rates for all men.

C) the percentage of both married men and men who were divorced was lower than among men who never married.

D) the percentage of both Hispanic men and Hispanic women was highest among married women and men who never married.

Graphic Displays

Tables

A table can display a wide range of information about several subjects discussed in a text. Correctly answering questions that include a table and text depends on **understanding how the table's data relate to the text's information**.

A question may ask students to use table data to **complete** an example or sentence. It may ask students to identify table data that **support** a claim, conclusion, or hypothesis. This section will discuss how to approach table questions successfully.

These strategies can help you answer a table question correctly:

- Identify the information that must be supported by table data.
- Examine the table's title and labels.
- Compare the text and table data to find the required information.
- Eliminate wrong answers to find the correct choice.

Strategies for Table Questions

Identify the Information That Must Be Supported by Table Data

A table question includes phrases to indicate whether **supporting** or **weakening** (opposing) data are needed.

> Most table questions ask for information that *supports* a previous statement.

Support a Statement

Support typically includes data from the table that demonstrate how a statement is probably true. For example, suppose someone claims that certain vehicle models manufactured by a particular company average between 35 and 40 miles per gallon. Data showing those vehicles get 37 miles per gallon on average would support the claim.

A question may *directly* ask for data from a table that support a claim, hypothesis, or conclusion. Some of these questions even include the word "support."

However, sometimes a question is an incomplete statement ending with a blank. These questions don't include the word "support" but use other wording such as the following:

- "Complete the idea"
- "Complete the example"
- "This can be seen most clearly"

Table questions that use expressions like those above require supporting data even though they don't include the word "support."

Support an Unexpected Discovery

A question's text may include language describing a student or researcher as "surprised to discover" something. This phrasing indicates that what was expected didn't occur, so the correct answer should complete the text with support based on the table that **conflicts** with that expectation.

Helpful Clues

A word or phrase in a question may provide clues about where in the text the required data can be found.

Examine the text below about teachers who left the profession to determine:

1. *what* statement must be supported by table data, and
2. *where* that information can be found.

> The National Center for Education Statistics (NCES) surveyed teachers to assess how many teachers quit their teaching positions after the 2020–2021 academic year and to understand why they left. The data from the survey showed that a higher percentage of teachers in private schools left the teaching profession than did teachers in public schools. For example, although the percentage of public-school teachers who left the profession was 8%, the percentage of __________
>
> Which choice most effectively uses data from the table to **complete the example**?

The phrase "complete the example" indicates that the correct answer should **support** a statement in the text with an information from the table.

The text's final sentence begins with "for example," a phrase that refers to something *previously* stated and a clue that the answer must support the statement that more teachers in private schools left the teaching profession than did teachers in public schools.

Read the Table's Title and Examine Its Labels for Each Column and Row

The **title** explains the table's contents. The column and row **labels** indicate what the amounts in the table represent. Tables may have numbers that are percentages, averages, or total amounts for various categories of related items. The numbers provide measurement data, but the labels at the top of each column and to the left of each row explain *what* this data means.

Example

Teachers Who Left a Teaching Position in 2021

Teacher decisions	Public-school teachers	Private-school teachers
Stayed at the same school	84%	82%
Went to a different school.	8%	6%
Left the teaching profession	8%	12%

The **title** announces that the table is about teachers who left a teaching position in 2021.

The **column** labels divide the subject into three categories: teacher decisions, private-school teachers, and public-school teachers.

The **row** labels in the first column indicate whether teachers stayed at the same school, left to teach in a different school, or left teaching altogether. Awareness of the table's title and label information gives meaning to the percentages listed.

Compare the Text and Table Data to Find the Required Information

Keeping the table's title and labels in mind makes the meaning of the data clear. Understanding the text helps in seeing how the data connect to the ideas being presented, which guides you to the correct answer.

The challenge is to identify table data in an answer choice that provides what the question requires.

Sometimes a wrong answer choice includes correct table data that is unrelated to the question or that conflicts with the text's statement. Other wrong answers may inaccurately describe the table data.

Teachers Who Left a Teaching Position in 2021

Teacher decisions	Public-school teachers	Private-school teachers
Stayed at the same school	84%	82%
Went to a different school.	8%	6%
Left the teaching profession	8%	12%

The National Center for Education Statistics (NCES) surveyed teachers to assess how many teachers quit their teaching positions after the 2020–2021 academic year. The data from the survey showed that a higher percentage of teachers in private schools left the teaching profession than did teachers in public schools. For example, although the percentage of public-school teachers who left the profession was 8%, the percentage of __________

Which choice most effectively uses data from the table to complete the example?

The text states that, compared to public-school teachers, a "higher percentage" of private-school teachers *left the teaching profession*, so the data must come from the final row about teachers who left the profession. According to that data, 12% of private-school teachers who left the teaching profession is a higher percentage than the 8% of public-school teachers who left the profession.

The connection between ideas in the text and data about percentages guides you to look for an answer that includes the data from the final row.

Use the Process of Elimination to Find the Correct Answer

When a question calls for support, the correct answer choice must show that the claim or conclusion is likely true based on data from the table. Eliminate answers that lack the data needed to support the text's statement.

Examine the answer choices for the table question to eliminate the ones that don't accurately complete the example.

Teachers Who Left a Teaching Position in 2021

Teacher decisions	Public-school teachers	Private-school teachers
Stayed at the same school	84%	82%
Went to a different school.	8%	6%
Left the teaching profession	8%	12%

The National Center for Education Statistics (NCES) surveyed teachers to assess how many teachers quit their teaching positions after the 2020–2021 academic year and to understand why they left. The data from the survey showed that a higher percentage of teachers in private schools left the teaching profession than did teachers in public schools. For example, although the percentage of public-school teachers who left the profession was 8%, the percentage of

____

Which choice most effectively uses data from the table to complete the example?

A) public-school teachers who stayed at the same school was 84%.

B) private-school teachers who left the teaching profession was 12%.

C) private-school teachers who went to a different school was 6%.

D) public-school teachers who went to a different school was also 8%.

✗ **Choice A, C, and D:** These answers include accurate data. However, they don't compare the percentage of teachers in public and private schools who left the teaching profession.

✓ **Choice B:** The phrase "for example" indicates that the information in the blank should complete the text with support for the preceding idea: more private-school teachers left the profession. This answer includes data that support the idea that a higher percentage of private-school teachers left the profession (12%) than did public-school teachers (8%).

Example

Number of US Students Taking the SAT and Their Mean Scores, 2017–2023

Year	Students taking the SAT	Mean scores
2017	1,715,481	1082
2019	2,220,087	1059
2021	1,509,133	1060
2023	1,913,742	1028

A student used a table as part of a research report on college admissions in the last seven years. The student pointed out that, according to the table, from 2017 to 2023 ______

Which choice most effectively uses data from the table to complete the statement?

A) the number of students taking the SAT increased, but mean scores on the test decreased.

B) both the number of students taking the SAT and their total mean scores remained unchanged.

C) the number of students taking the SAT decreased, but mean scores remained unchanged.

D) both the number of students taking the SAT and mean scores increased.

✓ **Choice A:** The number of students who took the SAT increased from 1,715,481 in 2017 to 1,913,742 in 2023, and their mean scores decreased during the overall time period from 1082 to 1028.

✗ **Choice B:** The number of students taking the SAT between 2017 and 2023 changed each year, and their mean scores decreased each year, so neither remained "unchanged."

✗ **Choice C:** The number of students taking the SAT didn't decrease; it *increased* from 1,715,481 in 2017 to 1,913,742 in 2023, and their total mean scores changed, decreasing from 1082 to 1028.

✗ **Choice D:** The number of students taking the SAT did increase in 2023 compared to 2017. However, the total mean scores from those two years show a decrease, not an increase.

Practice

1.

Complainants by Age Group, 2023

Age group	Complaints	Losses
Under 20	18,174	$40.7 million
20–29	62,410	$360.7 million
30–39	88,138	$1.2 billion
40–49	84,052	$1.5 billion
50–59	65,924	$1.7 billion
60 and older	101,068	$3.4 billion

To combat the threat of cybercrimes such as online fraud, identity theft, and hacking, the FBI established the Internet Crime Complaint Center (iC3) in May of 2000. The center provides the public a way to report cybercrime to the FBI, which has received over 8 million complaints from the center's inception through 2023. The data collected from complaints were analyzed for the FBI's 2023 Internet Crime Report, with larger numbers of complaints and losses indicating vulnerability to cybercrime. Compared to other age groups of victims, complainants 60 and older ______

Which choice most effectively uses data from the table to complete the statement?

A) had 101,068 complaints, indicating that vulnerability was lessened by their ability to report complaints to law enforcement.

B) had lower amounts of both complaints and losses than the other groups, indicating they were less vulnerable to cybercrime than might have been expected.

C) had over $3 billion in losses, indicating that not all victims over the age of 60 were financially vulnerable to begin with.

D) had the highest number of complaints and highest amount of losses, indicating they were most vulnerable to cybercrime.

See Appendix for answer

Things to Remember

- Determine what the question requires.
- Pay attention to the table's title and labels.
- Locate the table data that connect to the text.
- Use the process of elimination.

Graphic Displays: Tables
Check for Understanding

1. Bite Force of Dog's Canine Teeth

Study	Year	Estimation method	Approximate bite force (newtons)
Lindner	1995	Transducers	13–1,394
Ellis	2008	Electronic stimulations	147–926
Kiltie	1984	Equation	340–588
Thomason	1991	Equation	351–571
Bourke and Wroe	2008	Finite element analysis	220–560

Veterinarians often consider a dog's bite force to determine teeth restoration materials and develop implants for damaged canine teeth. Bite force measurements also enable veterinarians to assess appropriate foods, chew toys, and dental treats. Measuring the minimum and maximum bite force of a dog can be challenging, however, and researchers have concluded that the estimate of the bite force of dogs' canine teeth may be significantly influenced by the method used to generate that estimate.

Which choice best describes data from the table that support the researchers' conclusion?

A) The study by Lindner used transducers and produced the highest estimated minimum bite force, while the study by Thomason produced the lowest estimated minimum bite force.

B) In their study, Bourke and Wroe used Finite Element Analysis to produce an estimated minimum bite force of 220 newtons and a maximum bite force of 560 newtons.

C) The bite force estimates produced by Thomason and Kiltie were similar to each other, but the estimates produced by Ellis and by Lindner differed substantially from all the other estimates.

D) The highest estimated bite force produced by Thomason was lower than the highest estimated bite force produced by Kiltie, even though both researchers used the same type of method to produce their measurements.

Graphic Displays

Line Graphs

Line graphs are helpful when showing trends or data over time, generally using intervals of hours, days, weeks, month, or years. A question often requires you to compare text to data in the graph, asking you to find data in the graph that support a conclusion or complete a statement in the text. **Examine the graph AND the text** to determine how the graph's data relate to the text's information.

This section focuses on how to connect what a line graph shows to what the text discusses.

These strategies can help you find the correct answer to a line graph question:

- Note what the question asks to determine what data it requires.
- Examine the graph's title, labels, and key.
- Look for data in the graph that connect to the question.
- Use the process of elimination.

Noting What the Question Asks to Determine What Kind of Data Is Required

A line graph question often requires **support** for a claim or conclusion. Sometimes, the claim is underlined and must have data from the graph as support. Other times, the text may end with a blank and ask for data that will "complete the text" or "complete the statement."

Format	Example
Underlined	The student claimed that <u>there were more girls who actively participated in National Honor Society events than boys</u>.
Incomplete statement (blank)	Researchers concluded that *Arabidopsis thaliana* _____

Example

Average home-game attendance to National Football League (NFL) games varies among teams in the NFC East, a division that includes the Dallas Cowboys, New York Giants, Philadelphia Eagles, and the Washington Commanders. The graph displays the average number of fans attending home games over a three-year period. A student notes that among the teams shown in the graph, the team with the highest average attendance to home games in all three years was the ______

Which choice most effectively uses data from the graph to complete the text?

In the sentence with a blank, a student "notes" that one team had the highest average attendance every year. The question calls for data showing which team had the highest attendance in each of the three years examined.

Examine a Graph's Title, Axis Labels, and Key

Understanding the information that a graph presents is an important step to answering correctly.

The **title** reveals the graph's topic.

The **labels** on the X-axis and the Y-axis tell what the lines on a graph represent. The horizontal line at the bottom is the X-axis, and the vertical line on the left is the Y-axis.

The **key** indicates what each line is displaying.

X-axis (horizontal line)	Often identifies **intervals of time**
Y-axis (vertical line)	Expresses a **measurement** for each item
Key	Identifies what each line represents

The labels on a line graph's X-axis often refer to months, years, or other indicators of time.

The data points on the line signify amounts that are indicated by numbers on the Y-axis.

Example

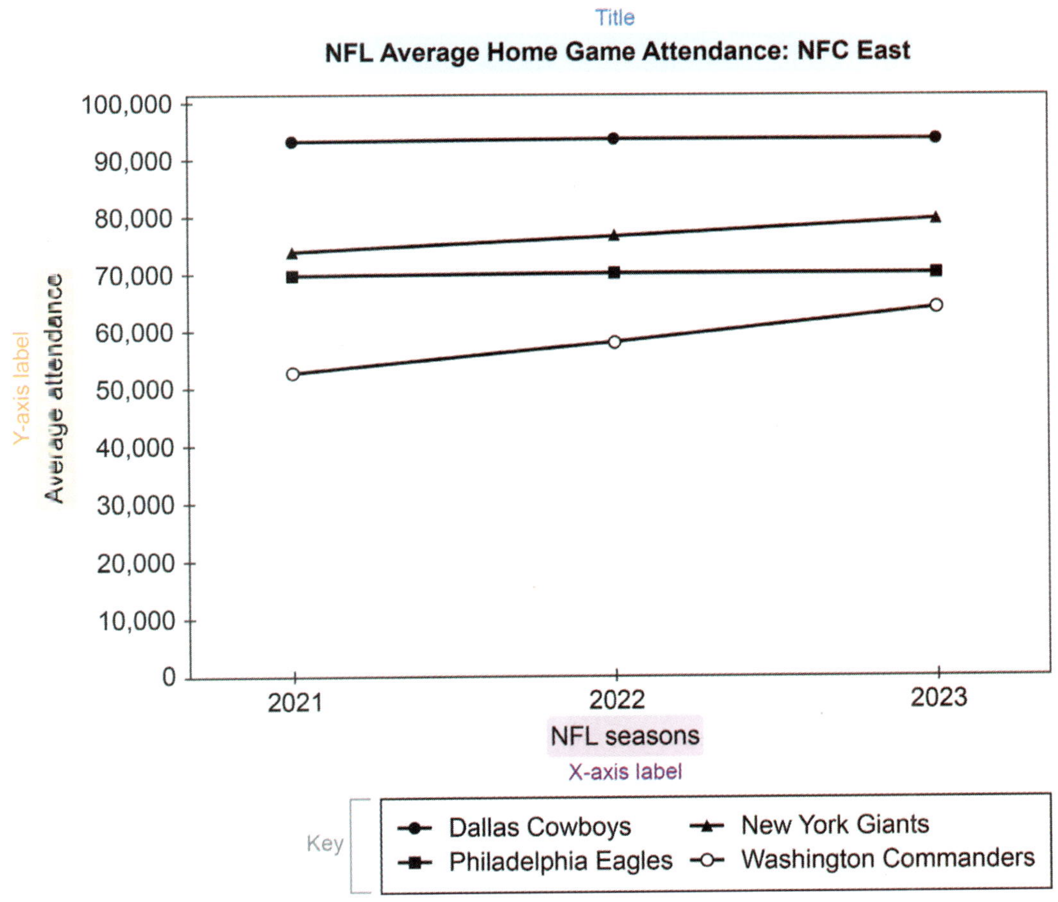

The graph's **title** informs viewers that its lines display the average National Football League (NFL) home game attendance for teams in the NFC East.

The **X-axis label** below the lines shows that the graph focuses on three NFL seasons: 2021, 2022, and 2023. The **Y-axis label** on the left shows that the numbers represent the average number of attendees.

The **key** reveals that each line represents an NFL team.

Noting this information enables you to see that Washington has the lowest attendance and the Cowboys have the highest attendance.

Look for Data in the Graph That Connects to the Question

The next task is to predict which data fulfill the question's criteria. Some data are irrelevant based on what the question asks. Only the correct answer will provide the graph information called for by the question.

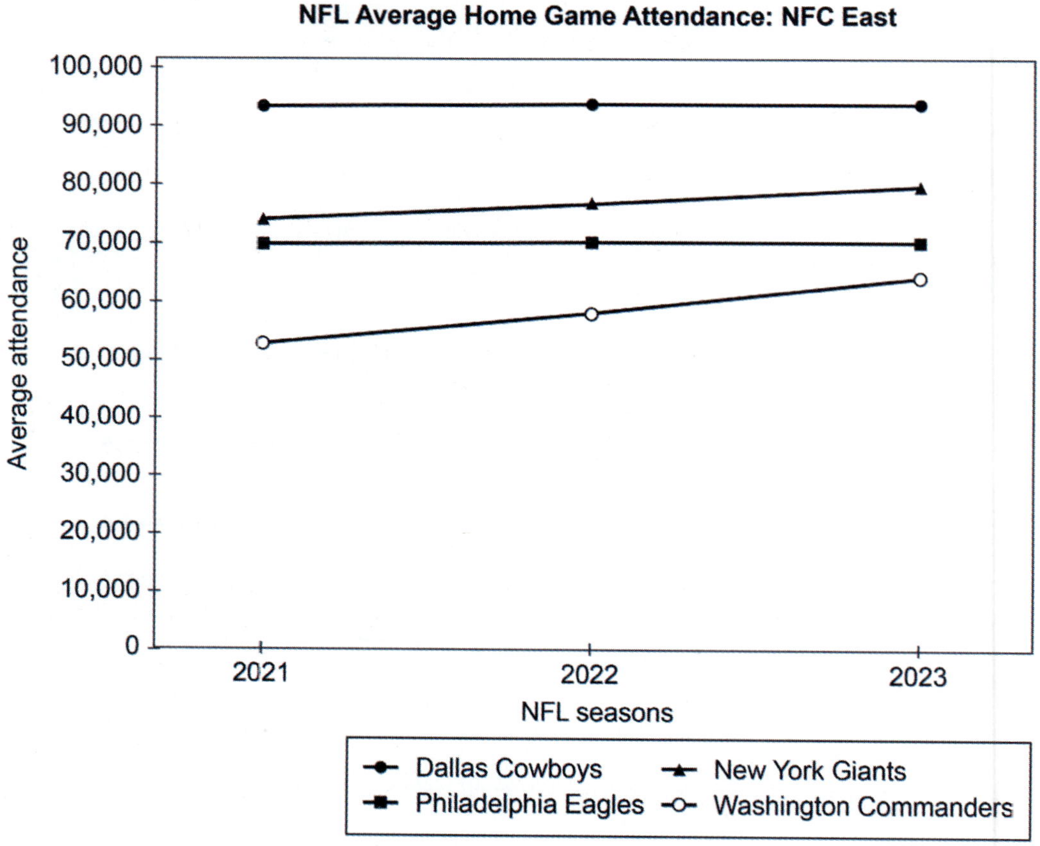

Average home-game attendance to National Football League (NFL) games varies among teams in the NFC East, a division that includes the Dallas Cowboys, New York Giants, Philadelphia Eagles, and the Washington Commanders. The graph displays the average number of fans attending home games over a three-year period. A student notes that among the teams shown in the graph, the team with the highest average attendance at home games in all three years was the ______ Conclusion

Because the incomplete sentence begins with a claim about the team with the highest average attendance over three seasons, look for graph information that accurately identifies which team averaged the highest number of fans.

Use the Process of Elimination to Remove Incorrect Answers

Eliminate any answers that make inaccurate statements about data in the graph. If a question requires support for a statement, eliminate any answers that provide information unrelated to what the question asks.

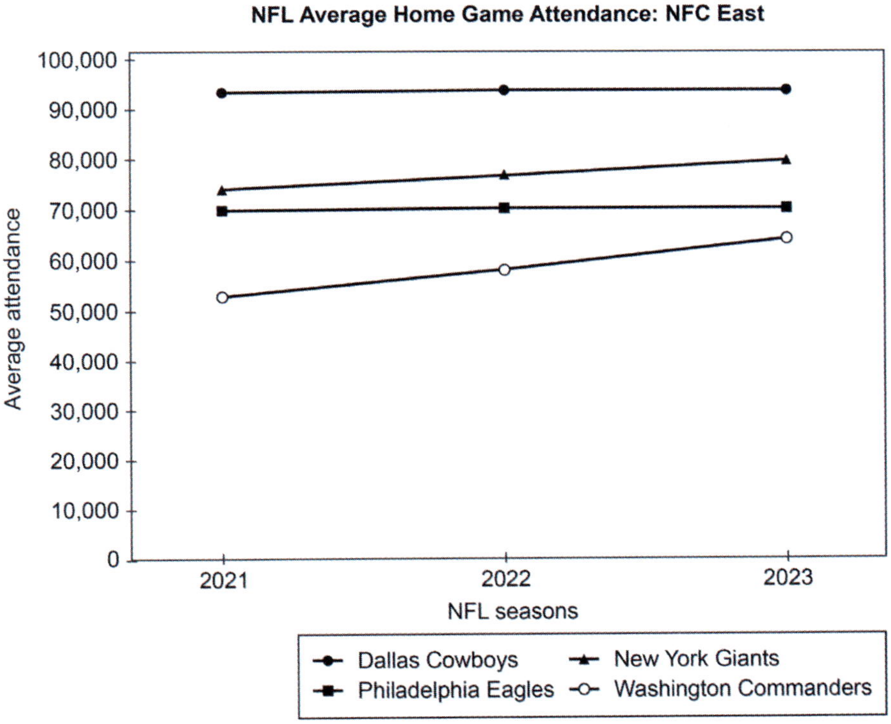

Average home-game attendance to National Football League (NFL) games varies among teams in the NFC East, a division that includes the Dallas Cowboys, New York Giants, Philadelphia Eagles, and the Washington Commanders. The graph displays the average number of fans attending home games over a three-year period. A student notes that among the teams shown in the graph, the team with the highest average attendance to home games in all three years was the ______

Which choice most effectively uses data from the graph to complete the text?

A) Philadelphia Eagles

B) New York Giants

C) Dallas Cowboys

D) Washington Commanders

X **Choices A, B and D:** The lines for Philadelphia. New York, and Washington are beneath the line for Dallas, indicating that their attendance at home games was *lower* than attendance at Dallas home games in each season.

✓ **Choice C:** The line for Dallas is higher than the other lines for all three seasons, indicating that its home-game attendance was higher than the home-game attendance for the other teams.

Practice

1.

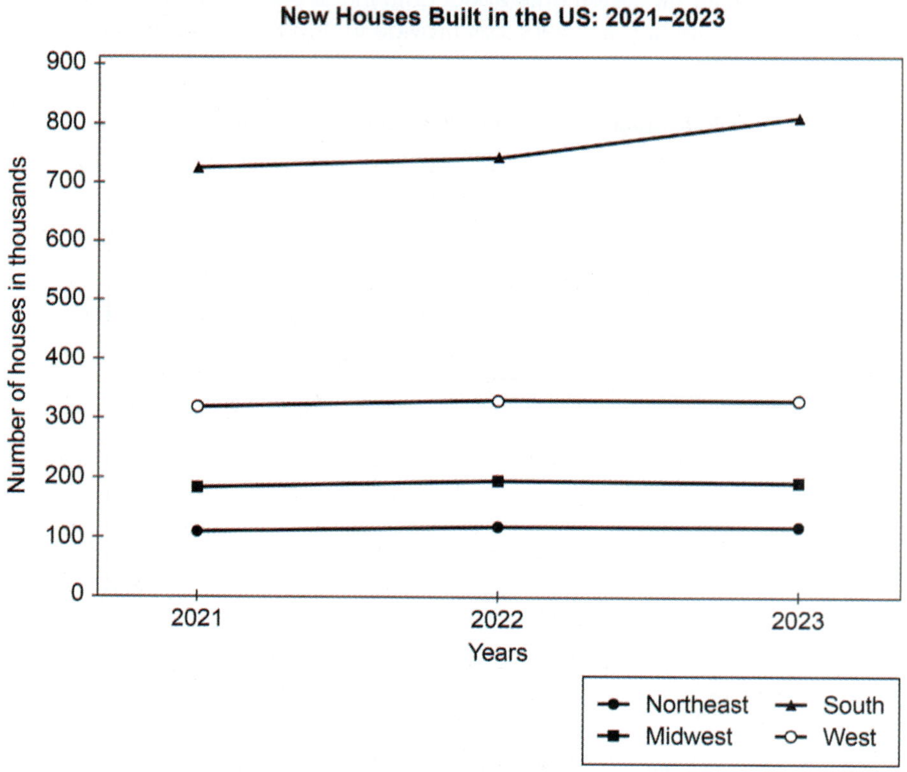

The US Census Bureau calculated the number of new single-family homes built in four US regions: the Northeast, Midwest, South, and West. The graph shows the number of new houses built in each of these regions during a 3-year period. A student notes that among the different areas shown in the graph, the region with the lowest number of new homes built from 2021 to 2023 was the ______

Which choice most effectively uses data from the graph to complete the text?

A) Northeast

B) Midwest

C) West

D) South

See Appendix for answer

2.

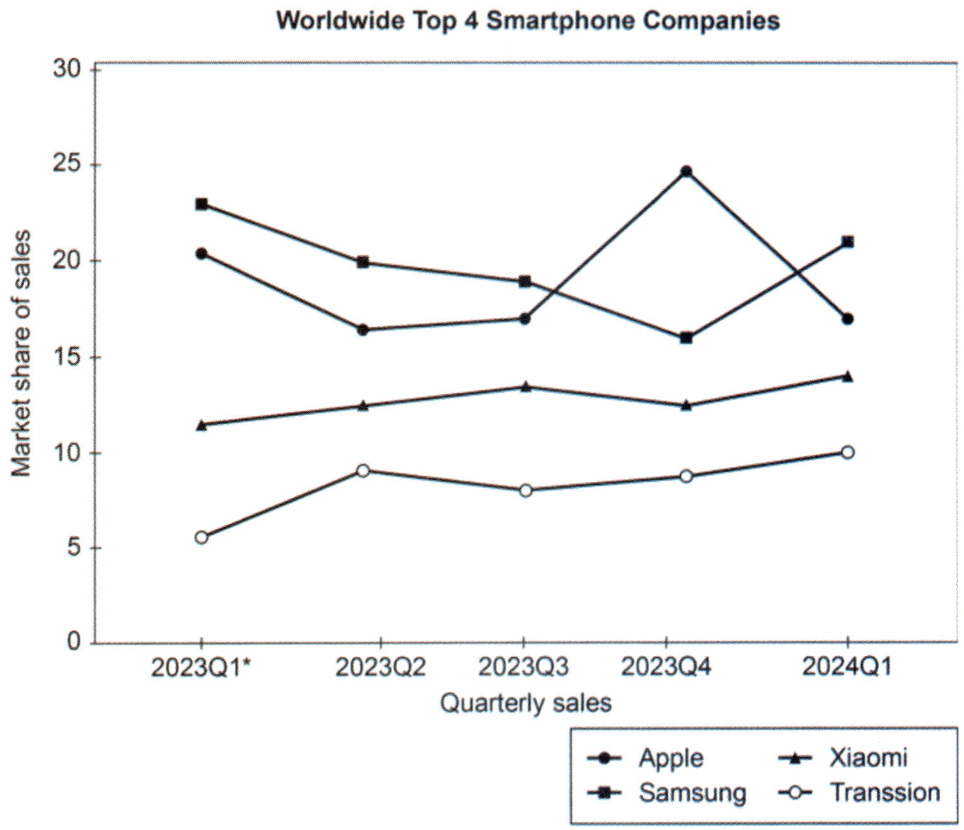

*Q = Quarter of the year

Retail analysts have observed worldwide sales trends based on phone manufacturers. The graph shows the number of phones made by US and Chinese manufacturers that were sold in each quarter of the last year. Based on the data in the graph, analysts claim that in the most recent quarter, <u>there were more sales of Samsung-made phones than sales of phones made by other companies.</u>

Which choice most effectively uses data from the graph to support the underlined claim?

A) The lowest percentage of the worldwide smartphone market was held by Transsion in the first quarter of 2023.

B) The highest percentage of the worldwide smartphone market was held by Samsung with about 21% of sales in the first quarter of 2024.

C) In the first quarter of 2023, Xiaomi gained a higher percentage of the worldwide smartphone than Apple did.

D) In the first quarter of 2024, Samsung and Apple had about the same percentage of the worldwide smartphone market.

See Appendix for answer

Things to Remember

- Identify what a question asks to determine the data it requires.
- Pay attention to a graph's title, labels, and key.
- Look for the text's claim and the graph's data that support it.
- Use the process of elimination.

Graphic Displays: Line Graphs
Check for Understanding

1.

Texas Teachers Receiving New State Certifications

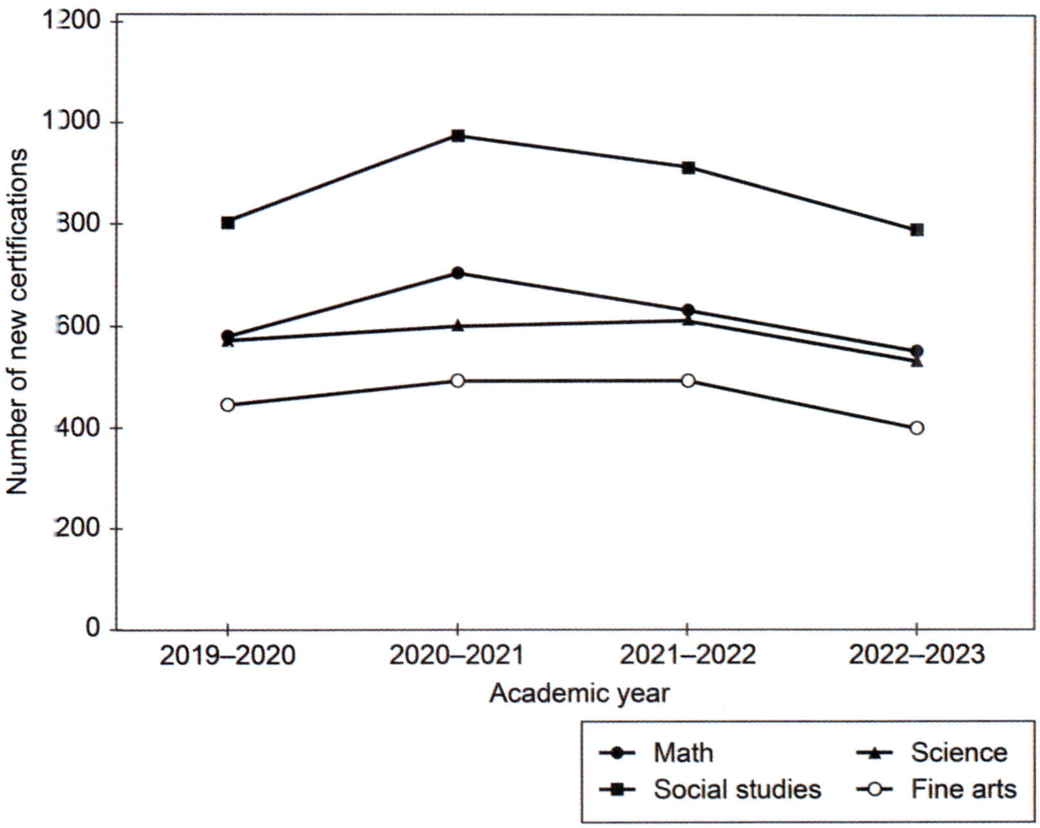

Between 2019 and 2023, Texas teacher certification in four subjects decreased. The graph shows the number of teachers by subject who received state certification each school year. A researcher notes that among the subjects shown in the graph, the subject with the highest number of certified teachers in all four academic years was ______

Which choice most effectively uses data from the graph to support the underlined claim?

A) fine arts.

B) science.

C) math.

D) social studies.

2.

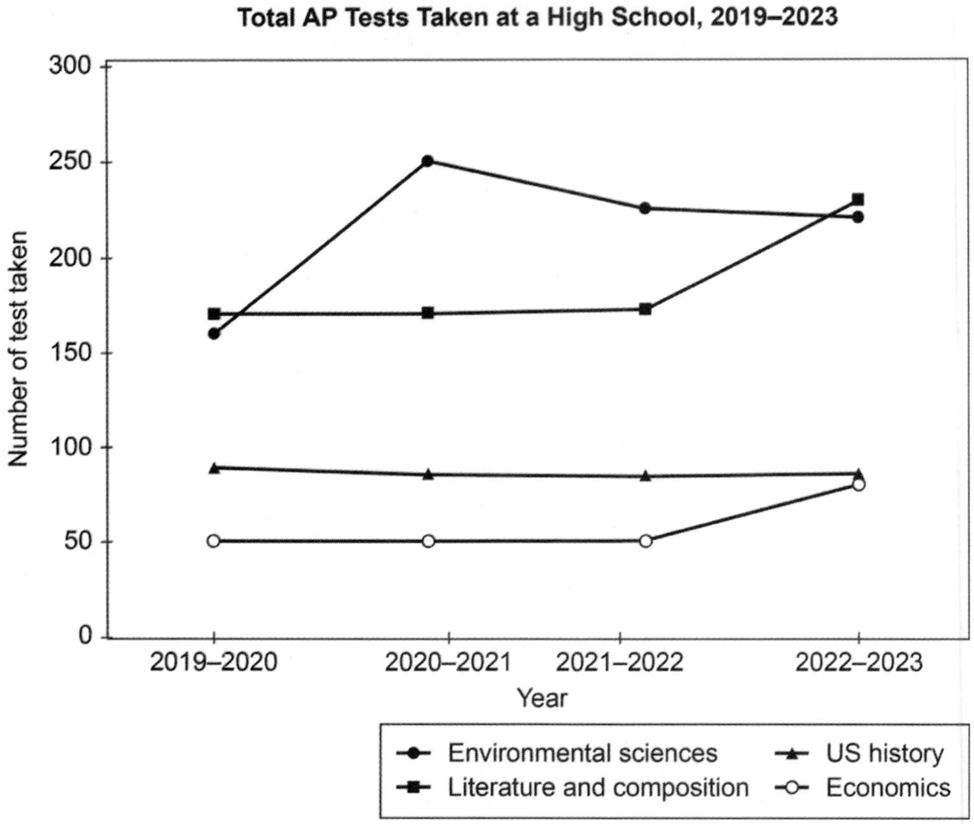

A student is researching trends in the number of Advanced Placement (AP) tests taken by students at his high school. The graph shows the number of AP tests taken each year in Environmental Science, US History, Literature and Composition, and Economics. Based on the data in the graph, the student claims that <u>there were more US History AP tests taken by students in 2023 than in any other year</u>.

Which choice most effectively uses data from the graph to support the underlined claim?

A) The lowest number of AP Economics tests taken in a year was approximately 50 in 2020.

B) The highest number of AP US History tests taken during the period shown is approximately 230 in 2023.

C) In 2020, the number of AP Environmental Science tests was the same as the number of AP US History tests.

D) In 2023, there were more AP Literature and Composition tests taken than there were AP US History tests.

Unit 3: Expression of Ideas

3.1	Transitions: Conjunctive Adverbs	196
3.2	Synthesis: Notes	205

Transitions

Conjunctive Adverbs

Readers can become confused when writing jumps abruptly from one topic to another. To prevent confusion, writers use a transition to show the connection between the ideas before and after it.

Transitions are like road signs that indicate what is coming next.

Knowledge about two aspects is helpful:

- Types of transition
- Strategies for transition questions

This section will discuss how to answer transition questions successfully.

Types of Transition

A transition expresses the **connection between different ideas**. Knowing the relationships indicated by different transitions can help identify the missing one in an SAT question.

Some transitions have multiple meanings and can indicate more than one type of connection.

Types of Transitions	
Additive	Adds more information about previously mentioned ideas
Contrast	Presents opposing information to previous ideas
Cause and Effect	Indicates the result of a previously discussed cause
Time and Order	Reveals a step in a sequence or an order of events

Additive Transitions

Additive Transition	**What it Signals**
Accordingly	Summary
Additionally	More detail
Besides	Additional information
For example	An example
For instance	An example
Furthermore	New, supportive information
In addition	More detail
In comparison	A comparison
Increasingly	An addition related to size, extent, or quantity
Indeed	Emphasis or supportive proof
In fact	An example, support, or emphasis
In other words	A restatement that clarifies
Likewise	A similarity
Moreover	Additional information
Similarly	A comparison
Specifically	More detail to clarify
To conclude	Conclusion or summary

Additive transitions indicate that a previous idea will be **expanded on** with a comparison, example, details, restatement, support, or conclusion.

Oedipus punished himself by giving up his royal position as king of Thebes. Furthermore, he voluntarily blinded himself and went into exile.

The transition "furthermore" indicates that more *detail* will be *added* about what Oedipus "gave up" in addition to his throne—his sight and his community.

Contrast Transitions

Contrast Transition	What It Signals
Actually	Contrasting fact or something unexpected
Alternatively	A different option or idea
Besides	An exception
By contrast	Contrasting idea
However	Conflicting information
In contrast	Contrasting details
Indeed	Emphasis or proof
In fact	Introduce an opposite idea
Instead	Different idea
Nevertheless	Contrasting idea despite previous idea, an exception
Nonetheless	Contrasting idea despite previous idea
Regardless	Dismissal of previous idea
Still	Conflicting information
Though	Conflicting information

Contrast transitions indicate that the previous idea will be followed by a **different** or **opposing** idea.

Esmeralda enjoys eating vegetarian food. However, her sister prefers meat.

"However" tells readers that what follows will contrast with Esmeralda's enjoyment of vegetables. In this case, the difference is her sister's preference for meat.

Cause-and-Effect Transitions

Cause-and-Effect Transition	What It signals
Accordingly	As a consequence, so
As a result	An effect resulting from something
Consequently	A consequence of something
For this reason	An effect will be explained
Therefore	The reason an effect occurs
Thus	An effect will be explained

A cause-and-effect transition indicates that an **effect** follows its previously mentioned **cause**.

After a late night, Amanda overslept. Consequently, she arrived at the office late.

The information after "consequently" explains the effect of Amanda oversleeping: not getting to her job on time.

Time and Order Transitions

Time and Order Transition	What It Signals
Afterward	Occurring at a later time
Currently	Occurring in the present
Finally	Introducing a last item in a series, such as a step or time period
In turn	Happening afterward
Meanwhile	Occurring at the same time
Second	Introducing something that follows a first item or step
Subsequently	Occurring afterward

A time and order transition indicates **when** the information that follows a previous statement occurs in time or **where** something occurs within a sequence.

> Jameson graduated from Baylor College of Medicine. Subsequently, he was matched at Emory School of Medicine for his residency, specializing in ophthalmology.

The transition "subsequently" indicates that Jameson started his residency at Emory *after* he completed medical school at Baylor.

Strategies for Transition Questions

Four strategies for success will be discussed in this section:

- Read all the text.
- Paraphrase sentences to identify the text's ideas.
- Evaluate how the two ideas relate to each other.
- Eliminate answers to select the one that signals how the two ideas are connected.

Read ALL the text to understand the context for the transition

The text will include two or three sentences, each expressing a separate idea. A blank for a missing transition will be in one of two places in the text: at the beginning of a sentence or in the middle of a sentence.

Identifying the correct transition requires understanding the ideas expressed in the sentences *before* and *after* the blank regardless of where the blank is located in a sentence. When the blank appears in the middle of a sentence, it might seem like you only have to read that sentence to find the answer, but this mistaken idea can lead to choosing an incorrect answer.

Paraphrase the idea expressed by each sentence to determine what the missing transition should join.

Evaluate what each sentence expresses. Mentally paraphrase the text to identify how the ideas before and after the blank are related to determine the correct transition.

> Shreya is a high school student. Her friend Sai, however, dropped out.

Idea 1	Shreya is in high school.
Idea 2	Sai is not in school.

Knowing what each idea expresses is essential to determining how they are related. In this case, understanding Shreya is in school but Sai dropped out allows you to see that those ideas are opposite. The transition "however" appropriately indicates that an opposing idea follows it.

Evaluate the relationship between the ideas before and after the transition

The relationship between ideas will vary. Identifying their relationship will help you decide which transition expresses their connection.

> Hoping for an early start, Boris packed the family's camping gear and clothes in the car the night before. <u>In addition</u>, he got up early the next morning to load the ice chest.

Idea 1	Boris loaded stuff.
Idea 2	Boris loaded more stuff.
Relationship	Idea 2 expresses **additional** things that Boris loaded.

The second idea adds a *similar* action to what is described by the first idea: Boris loaded things in the car. Because "in addition" signals that more detail follows about the previous statement, it is a logical transition between the two ideas.

Knowing the main idea in each sentence shows an additional loading of an ice chest. Thus, "in addition" is the appropriate transition.

Eliminate choices that don't indicate the relationship between the text's ideas. What will be left is the transition that does show their connection.

Plug each answer into the blank and eliminate the ones that don't indicate the relationship between the text's ideas.

> Colter goes to remote forests to enjoy natural beauty and peace. Penny, ______, stays in the city to enjoy its culture and convenience.
>
> Which choice completes the text with the most logical transition?
>
> A) finally
>
> B) in other words
>
> C) though
>
> D) consequently

✗ "Finally" indicates the last step of a sequence, but the sentences don't describe an order in which Colter and Penny go to the forest or stay in the city.

✗ "In other words" indicates that a restatement or summary of a previous idea follows, but describing Penny's preference for the city doesn't restate Colter's desire to be in remote forests.

✓ "Though" indicates a contrast with a previous idea. This transition logically signals the difference between Penny's city pleasure and Colter's enjoyment of forests.

✗ "Consequently" indicates an effect that results from a cause, but Colter's enjoyment of the forest doesn't cause Penny's enjoyment of city life.

By eliminating answers that don't express the relationship between the two ideas, the correct answer becomes easier to identify.

Example

Charles Ives is often considered the leading creator of twentieth-century art music. A modernist interested in experimental music, Ives used innovative techniques. For his *Concord Sonata*, he instructed the pianist to use a piece of wood to create a large chord. ______ he combined trumpet, flutes, and a string quartet in an unusual mix of instruments for his piece *The Unanswered Question*.

Which choice completes the text with the most logical transition?

A) Nonetheless,

B) In addition,

C) Still,

D) Therefore,

S1: Background	Ives was an art music composer.
S2: Claim	Ives used innovative musical techniques.
S3: Example 1	In his *Concord Sonata*, Ives created large piano chords with a wood piece.
S4: Example 2	In his *The Unanswered Question*, Ives blended an unusual mix of instruments.

In this case, the sentence before the blank gives an example of Ives's techniques and the sentence after the blank **adds** a second example.

✗ "Nonetheless" indicates a *contrast* to what was previously stated. However, adding a second example after the first example in the previous sentence includes something *similar*.

✓ "In addition" indicates something is *added* to what was previously stated. Because the information after the blank *adds* a second example, this answer creates a logical transition.

✗ "Still" indicates that a *contrast* follows. (Ex. I don't like chicken. Still, I'll eat wings with pleasure.) However, the information following the blank adds a *similar* example of Ives's musical innovation.

✗ "Therefore" indicates that an *effect* was caused by something discussed previously. Adding a second example of Ives's musical innovation is *not* caused by the first example before the blank.

Example

Moths are winged insects primarily active at night, rest with their wings spread out to their sides, and spin a cocoon for the pupal stage before metamorphosis. Butterflies, ______ are primarily active during the day, rest with their wings folded above their backs, and form a chrysalis for the pupal stage before metamorphosis.

Which choice completes the text with the most logical transition?

A) for example,

B) nevertheless,

C) in contrast,

D) in other words,

✗ "For example" indicates that an example of moths follows, but Sentence 2 discusses butterflies, not moths.

✗ "Nevertheless" indicates that *despite* previous information, something different follows. However, butterflies don't differ from moths *despite* their traits.

✓ "In contrast" indicates that a contrast follows. Sentence 2 contrasts butterflies with the previous description of moths: when they are active (night versus day), how they rest their wings (spread out versus folded), and what their means of metamorphosis is (cocoon versus chrysalis).

✗ "In other words" indicates that a restatement follows. However, the information about butterflies isn't restating the preceding information about moths.

Example

Plants have adapted to survive in adverse environments. The leaves of aloes, ______ have developed water-storing tissues called parenchyma that enable them to endure drought.

Which choice completes the text with the most logical transition?

A) thus,

B) though,

C) for example,

D) meanwhile,

Claim	Plants evolved adaptations to survive.
Example supporting claim	Aloes developed tissues that help them survive drought.

Sentence 1 makes a general claim, and Sentence 2 provides an example. Understanding those ideas helps reveal the relationship between them that the missing transition should express.

✗ "Thus" indicates an *effect* that follows a previously discussed cause. However, an example of plant adaptation provides *support* for a prior claim, not an effect caused by something.

✗ "Though" indicates a *contrast* follows. (Ex. I love English courses. Math classes, though, I can barely tolerate.) However, an example *supporting* the claim follows the blank, not a contrast.

✓ "For example" indicates that an example follows for something previously stated. The aloes example follows the discussion about plant adaptation in the preceding sentence.

✗ "Meanwhile" indicates that what follows occurred at the same time as something previously discussed. However, time isn't mentioned in the text.

Practice

1. The US Department of Education reports that, while students have traditionally taken AP courses in high school to gain college credit, evidence indicates that more students are choosing a different option. ______ students are enrolling in dual credit courses to gain both high school and college credit—a trend shown by a significant rise in dual credit enrollment from 2002 to 2024.

Which choice completes the text with the most logical conclusion?

A) Additionally,

B) Increasingly,

C) Likewise,

D) Thus,

See Appendix for answer

2. Most insect species in the Arthropoda phylum of animals are oviparous. That is, they lay eggs that hatch outside of their bodies. However, not all species of Arthropoda are oviparous. Scorpions, ______ produce eggs that hatch within the mother's body.

Which choice completes the text with the most logical conclusion?

A) for example,

B) nonetheless,

C) meanwhile,

D) furthermore,

See Appendix for answer

3. In his 1916 poetry collection *Mountain Interval*, Robert Frost creates meditative poems inspired by a person, object, or event. His poem "The Road Not Taken" centers on a fork in a woodland path that sparks reflection about life's journey. ______Frost's poem "Birches" describes trees bent over by ice that leads to contemplation of escaping from and returning to life, despite its troubles.

Which choice completes the text with the most logical conclusion?

A) Therefore,

A) In contrast,

B) Similarly,

C) Specifically,

See Appendix for answer

Things to Remember

- Transitions can indicate an addition, contrast, cause and effect, or sequence in order or time.
- Read all sentences in the text.
- Identify the ideas expressed before and after the blank.
- Evaluate how the two ideas relate to each other.
- Eliminate answers to select the transition indicating the ideas' connection.

Transitions: Conjunctive Adverbs
Check for Understanding

1. Searching for kivas (buried religious structures) in New Mexico can be difficult and time-consuming. In years past, archeologists uncovered ancient Pueblo kivas by searching the red desert sands on foot. ______ researchers are helped by drones and thermal imaging that detect subtle temperature differences caused by a structure heating and cooling.

   Which choice completes the text with the most logical transition?

   A) Currently,

   B) Similarly,

   C) Specifically,

   D) Though,

2. Spatula-shaped adhesive toe pads called setae are found on the feet of most gecko species. Electrostatic interaction between their setae and a surface creates adhesion. ______ geckos can climb almost any surface and even travel upside down across ceilings.

   Which choice completes the text with the most logical transition?

   A) For example,

   B) Alternatively,

   C) Similarly,

   D) Consequently,

3. Archeologists believe evidence in an ancient shrine indicates that the Blemmyes people worshipped Egyptian gods but practiced their own unique rituals. First, a column inside the shrine depicts the Egyptian god Harpocrates and an unidentified figure believed to be the Egyptian god Khonsu. ______ researchers found the remains of fifteen headless falcons sacrificed within the shrine, a ritual that wasn't practiced elsewhere in Egypt.

   Which choice completes the text with the most logical transition?

   A) However,

   B) Nonetheless,

   C) Specifically,

   D) Second,

4. When sanitation and sewer services are limited by economic or geographic obstacles, waste can be disposed of by installing a septic tank to hold it. ______ waste can be placed in a compost pit where it is stored and converted into biosolids: a form of manure that provides nutrients and organic material for plants to absorb, helping farmers successfully fertilize their crops.

   Which choice completes the text with the most logical transition?

   A) Consequently,

   B) For instance,

   C) Alternatively,

   D) Accordingly,

5. Plays and poetry are two different forms of literature, but some writers have created works that combine aspects of both. William Shakespeare's *Hamlet*, ______ is a verse drama, a five-act play with plot and characters written in iambic pentameter, ten-syllable lines that use a poetic rhythm.

   Which choice completes the text with the most logical transition?

   A) as a result,

   B) for instance,

   C) however,

   D) subsequently,

Synthesis

Notes

Synthesis questions begin with a bulleted list of notes about a given topic. This list is followed by a specific writing goal that a hypothetical student wants to achieve. Your task is to find the answer that satisfies that goal using relevant information from the notes. Usually, all the answer choices contain accurate information from the notes, so focusing on satisfying the GOAL is the key to these questions.

This section will discuss strategies for approaching synthesis questions on the SAT.

Strategies

- Identify key words in the goal
- Eliminate answers based on the goal
- Read the notes, if necessary

Identify Key Words in the Goal

The most important information for answering synthesis questions is contained in the text AFTER the notes, so read this first. The text will look something like this:

> The student wants to **compare** the lifespans of the two rodents. Which choice most effectively uses relevant information from the notes to accomplish this goal?

The highlighted text indicates the student's **goal**. Understanding this goal is critical for answering the question because **the correct answer must completely fulfill that goal.** If an answer contains accurate information based on the notes but does NOT fulfill that writing goal, it is incorrect. Identifying key words in the goal statement will give you a clear idea of what to look for in the answer choices.

In this case, the key words are the action verb "compare" and the object of the verb, "lifespans of the two rodents." Every goal will be made up of those parts: an action and something receiving that action.

Types of Goals

The goal typically falls into one of the following categories, which can be recognized by common key words. The goal will not necessarily contain these exact words or phrases, but it will likely have something similar.

Goal Category	Common Key Words
Comparing	emphasize a **similarity** explain an **advantage** **compare** [something] emphasize a **difference** emphasize [something] **relative to** [something else]
Presenting information	**describe** [something] provide an **explanation** provide an **example** **introduce** [something] **present** [something]

Emphasizing specific detail	**emphasize** [something specific] **specify why** [something occurred] **explain how** [something happened]
Analyzing study	emphasize the **aim of the study** make a **generalization** about the **kind of study** present the **study and its methodology**

There are some additional words to be aware of that could show up in any of the categories:

Additional Key Words	Meaning
and	There are **two parts** to the goal and the answer must satisfy BOTH parts.
audience **unfamiliar** with [a person/thing]	The answer must include basic background information about the person or thing. The person or thing will usually be named directly, but may not be.
audience **familiar** with [a person/thing]	The answer should name the person or thing WITHOUT offering detailed background info.

Identifying these key words in the goal will allow you to analyze and eliminate answer choices without even needing to read the bulleted notes.

Example

While researching a topic, a student has taken the following notes:

- The guinea pig is a rodent native to the South American Andes region.
- Adult guinea pigs typically weigh between 1.5 and 2.6 lbs.
- The average lifespan of a pet guinea pig is 4–5 years.
- The chinchilla is a rodent native to the South American Andes mountains.
- Adult chinchillas typically weigh between 1 and 2 pounds.
- The average lifespan of a pet chinchilla is 10–15 years.

The student wants to **compare** the lifespans of the two rodents. Which choice most effectively uses relevant information from the notes to accomplish this goal?

✗ Some rodents, like South American chinchillas, can live as long as 15 years.

✓ A chinchilla typically lives 10–15 years, while the guinea pig has a shorter lifespan of about 4–5 years.

In this example, the student must compare two things: the lifespans of two rodents. Reading that goal, without reference to the notes, already tells you what to look for in the answer; it must mention the two rodents and show something similar or different about their lifespans.

The incorrect answer accurately discusses the lifespan of the chinchilla, but it does not mention another rodent to compare it to. The correct answer mentions the lifespans of two different rodents, the chinchilla and the guinea pig, and uses the words "while" and "shorter" to highlight their difference. Thus, this answer satisfies all parts of the goal.

Read the question and the answer choices first. Reading the notes is often unnecessary.

Eliminate Answers Based on the Goal

Generally, the answer choices contain accurate information based on the notes, so checking the answer choices for accuracy is not an effective way to eliminate them. Instead, remember that the correct answer must COMPLETELY satisfy the goal, so eliminate any answer choices that do not do so.

Below is a chart that shows what might lead you to eliminate an answer as well as what you might find in the correct answer.

Category	✗ What to Eliminate	✓ What to Look For
Comparing	Mention of only one thing Mention of both things but doesn't show similarity or difference Details too vague	Mention of both things Specific details illustrating similarity or difference Comparison words
Presenting information	Irrelevant details Incomplete details	Details focused on the specific topic
Emphasizing specific detail	Irrelevant details Incomplete details	Information on the specific detail stated in the goal
Analyzing study: aim/purpose	Results of study Methodology	Purpose phrases Ex. "set out to determine," "wanted to know"
Analyzing study: generalization	Details about the specific study Names	NO details General method and aim
Analyzing study: methodology	Results of study Aim/purpose without method	Method phrases Ex. "used . . . to study," "examined," "collected data," "analyzed"

Example

While researching a topic, a student has taken the following notes:

- Yellowstone National Park was established in 1872 as the first national park in the United States.
- It is known for its many impressive geysers.
- It is located mostly in Wyoming, with small parts in Idaho and Montana.
- It covers an area of 3,468 square miles.

The student wants to **emphasize the size** of Yellowstone National Park. Which choice most effectively uses relevant information from the notes to accomplish this goal?

✗ A) Known for its impressive geysers, Yellowstone National Park was established in 1872.

✗ B) Yellowstone National Park, which is located mostly in Wyoming, was established in 1872.

✗ C) The first national park in the United States, Yellowstone National Park is known for its geysers.

✓ D) Yellowstone National Park is situated on 3,468 square miles, mostly in Wyoming.

The goal is to emphasize a specific detail—in this case, the size of the park. Without even checking the notes, you can eliminate choices A, B, and C because none of them mentions the size of the park. Only choice D mentions the size, 3,468 square miles, so this is the correct answer. If you do check the notes, you will see that choices A, B, and C all contain accurate information, but because they do not satisfy the goal, they are not correct.

Don't let the accuracy of the information distract you from the question's goal.

Read the Notes, If Necessary

Usually, the process of elimination will allow you to narrow down to just one answer choice that fulfills the goal. When that is the case, go ahead and pick that answer. If it is the only one fulfilling the goal, it must be correct.

However, if you are left with more than one choice or are unsure what some of the answer choices mean, refer to the notes to get a better understanding of the context. Look for information that is relevant to the goal, and then look for that information in the answer choices.

Example

While researching a topic, a student has taken the following notes:

- A number of women made important contributions to the Apollo 11 mission that landed men on the moon in 1969.
- Judy Sullivan, a biomedical engineer, began working for NASA in 1966 in Spacecraft Operations.
- Computer scientist Margaret Hamilton worked on software used by the military in anti-aircraft defense before joining the MIT Instrumentation Laboratory on the Apollo project.
- Sullivan helped Neil Armstrong in the suit lab before the launch of Apollo 11 and was in the control room monitoring the biomedical systems during the launch.
- Hamilton was responsible for the development of critical on-board flight software that was used in the Apollo 11 spacecraft.

The student wants to **compare** the two women's roles in the Apollo 11 mission. Which choice most effectively uses relevant information from the notes to accomplish this goal?

A) Women made many contributions to the Apollo 11 moon landing; Hamilton and Sullivan are just two examples.

B) As a biomedical engineer, Sullivan monitored biomedical systems for NASA, while Hamilton had experience developing software for the military.

C) Sullivan and Hamilton both played important but different roles in the Apollo 11 mission; for example, Sullivan helped Neil Armstrong in the suit lab.

D) Hamilton developed critical software for Apollo 11, but Sullivan was in the control room monitoring biomedical systems during the launch.

The goal is to compare the roles of the two women in the Apollo 11 mission. Therefore, the answer must discuss both women and show something about their contributions to Apollo 11 specifically.

✗ **Choice A** indicates that Hamilton and Sullivan contributed to Apollo 11, but it does not compare their specific roles, so it can be eliminated.

✗ **Choice B** is tempting. It compares the two women's work, including Sullivan's work monitoring biomedical systems, which is part of what she did for the Apollo 11 mission. However, the answer does not discuss Hamilton's work for Apollo 11, instead focusing on her prior work. In this case, you might choose to look at the notes to confirm that the information does not specifically address the goal, and, therefore, is incorrect.

✗ **Choice C** mentions Apollo 11 specifically and says the women played different roles. However, it only specifies Sullivan's role and does not show Hamilton's, so this answer can also be eliminated.

✓ **Choice D** states a role that each woman played in Apollo 11 and uses the word "but" to show there is a difference between them, thus making a comparison that fulfills all parts of the goal.

Before finalizing your answer, double check the goal to make sure your answer is fulfilling every part of it.

Practice

1. While researching a topic, a student has taken the following notes:

- Sam Gilliam was an American abstract artist known for his *Drape* paintings.
- His *Drape* paintings were made on unstretched canvases or polypropylene fabric and often suspended from the ceiling or walls.
- He created one of these works, *Autumn Surf,* in 1973 for a group exhibition at the San Francisco Museum of Modern Art.
- *Autumn Surf* was hung from several points in the ceiling and spread around the room, creating an area that viewers could enter.

The student wants to describe *Autumn Surf* to an audience unfamiliar with Sam Gilliam. Which choice most effectively uses relevant information from the notes to accomplish this goal?

A) *Autumn Surf*, featured at the San Francisco Museum of Modern Art in 1973, is an example of Gilliam's *Drape* paintings.

B) *Autumn Surf* was created by American abstract artist Sam Gilliam, who was known for his *Drape* paintings.

C) Created in 1973, *Autumn Surf*, one of American abstract artist Sam Gilliam's *Drape* paintings, was hung in such a way that it created an area that viewers could enter.

D) Sam Gilliam's *Drape* paintings, such as *Autumn Surf*, were made on unstretched canvases or polypropylene fabric.

See Appendix for answer

Things to Remember

- Read the goal first and identify key words.
- Eliminate answers that don't satisfy the goal.
- Double check that your answer fulfills all parts of the goal.
- Read the notes only if you find them helpful.

Synthesis: Notes
Check for Understanding

1. While researching a topic, a student has taken the following notes:

   - West Nile virus has become a health threat in an expanded area of Europe.
   - Researchers from the University of Brussels, including Diana Erazo and Simon Dellicour, explored how much of the expansion of West Nile virus is a result of climate change.
   - Erazo and Dellicour used artificial intelligence to project the risk of West Nile virus based on environmental conditions in an area and compared the projections with simulations that removed the effects of climate change.
   - The threat of West Nile virus is related to local climate.
   - The study demonstrated that climate change likely contributed to the expanded area affected by West Nile virus.

   The student wants to emphasize the aim of the research study. Which choice most effectively uses relevant information from the notes to accomplish this goal?

   A) Diana Erazo and Simon Dellicour of the University of Brussels used artificial intelligence to analyze the risk of West Nile Virus in different areas.

   B) Researchers from the University of Brussels have discovered that climate change plays a role in the spread of West Nile virus.

   C) Based on research completed by Diana Erazo and Simon Dellicour, we now know that climate change is responsible for the expanded area threatened by West Nile virus.

   D) Diana Erazo and Simon Dellicour conducted a study because they wanted to know if the expansion of West Nile virus is the result of climate change.

2. While researching a topic, a student has taken the following notes:

   - Traditional electric stoves—the most common type of stove in U.S. homes by 2022—work by heating a burner which in turn heats the pot or pan.
   - Because the electric burner remains hot after it is turned off, there is a risk of burns from the stovetop.
   - Induction stoves, an alternative to traditional electric stoves, use electromagnetic energy to heat the pot or pan directly, without an intermediate heating element.
   - Since the pan is heated directly on an induction stovetop, there is no heating element that remains hot when the stove is shut off, thus reducing the risk of burns.

   The student wants to explain an advantage of induction stoves. Which choice most effectively uses relevant information from the notes to accomplish this goal?

   A) Induction stoves, which rely on electromagnetic energy, use a different heating process than traditional electric stoves do.

   B) If more people used induction stoves, they could avoid a problem inherent in using traditional electric stoves.

C) Because there is no intermediate heating element, induction stoves have a smaller risk of burns compared to traditional electric stoves.

D) Induction stoves are an alternative to traditional electric stoves, which were the most common type of stove in the U.S. in 2022.

3. While researching a topic, a student has taken the following notes:

- In 2009, Afruz Amighi won the Jameel Prize, an award for contemporary art inspired by Islamic tradition.
- Born in Tehran, Iran, Amighi now lives in New York.
- Amighi was awarded the prize for her artwork *1001 Pages*, which was created in 2008 and features intricate patterns inspired by designs from Iran's past and present.
- The detailed designs of *1001 Pages* were hand cut from a sheet of thin plastic, which is suspended to create a shadow on the wall behind it.

The student wants to introduce *1001 Pages* to an audience unfamiliar with the artwork and the artist. Which choice most effectively uses relevant information from the notes to accomplish this goal?

A) Created by Iranian-born American artist Afruz Amighi, the award-winning *1001 Pages* (2008) features intricate, hand-cut designs inspired by Iran's Islamic past and present.

B) The Islamic traditions of Iran, where Afruz Amighi was born, are reflected in the detailed designs of *1001 Pages*.

C) Born in Iran and now living in New York, Afruz Amighi created *1001 Pages* and won the 2009 Jameel Prize, which is awarded for art inspired by Islamic tradition.

D) In 2009, Afruz Amighi's *1001 Pages*, which consists of an intricately cut sheet of plastic hung to create a shadow on the wall behind it, won the Jameel Prize.

Unit 4: Craft and Structure

4.1	Vocabulary: Logical and Precise	214
4.2	Vocabulary: Most Nearly Means	225
4.3	Purpose: Main	229
4.4	Purpose: Portion	239
4.5	Purpose: Sentence	244
4.6	Purpose: Structure	250
4.7	Connections: Between Texts	257

Vocabulary

Logical and Precise

Vocabulary questions consist of one or two sentences with a missing word or phrase. Your task is to use the context—the words around the missing word—to determine the best way to fill in the blank. The key to answering Vocabulary questions is recognizing the context clues that relate to the missing word. Sometimes there are signals in the text that point to a relevant clue.

In this section, you will learn

- what context clues are
- how to find context clues using signals in the text
- strategies to approach vocabulary questions in a step-by-step manner

Context Clues

Context clues are details that help you interpret the rest of the text.

Verb — Adjective

The teacher **praised** the student for her **excellent** essay.

Verb — Adjective

The teacher **criticized** the student for her **terrible** essay.

In the first sentence, the verb "praised" expresses a positive action that makes sense with the positive description "excellent." As seen in the second sentence, however, if either the verb or the adjective is changed, the other also must change for the sentence to make sense.

Because the two parts of the sentence are tied to each other in this way, if you know the meaning of one of the words, it helps you know what to expect for the other one. Recognizing this connection on Vocabulary questions will help you fill in the blank.

Types of Context Clues

Verbs, Adjectives, and Adverbs

Usually, the most helpful details are **actions and descriptions**, so verbs, adjectives, and adverbs are strong clues.

Adjective / Adjective
This is an **important** decision: it will have a **major** effect on the rest of your life.

Adverb / Adjective
He **finally** finished the project after **many** hours of work.

Verb / Adjective
My teacher **explained** the concept in detail, **illustrating** the main points with concrete examples.

Nouns

Although nouns are not usually strong clues, nouns that name an action or idea often are.

Noun / Adjective
After **rejection** from his top choice school, Bob was **upset**.

The noun "rejection" indicates a negative experience, which fits with the negative adjective "upset." Since "rejection" is a noun that refers to an action, it is a strong context clue. The other nouns in the sentence, "school" and "Bob," are not very helpful context clues. They could be changed without affecting the rest of the sentence.

Adverb / Verb
The school **severely restricts** the use of phones. Students think these
Adjective / Noun
harsh restrictions are unnecessary.

Noun
The **dangers** of social media are well established: multiple studies have
Adjective
shown its **harmful** effects on teenagers.

Contrast

Usually, context clues have a similar idea to another part of the sentence, but sometimes there are context clues with contrasting ideas.

Contrast word

Though there are **many** places I'd like to visit, there are a **few** at the top of my list.

In this sentence, the word "though" at the beginning signals that the two clauses should have opposite ideas. The first clause talks about "many" places, and the second clause shows the opposite, "few."

Contrast word

I thought the test was **easy**, but my friend said she found it **difficult**.

Contrast word

The doctor said not to **worry**, so I felt **relieved**.

You can use the SAT testing app highlighting tool to highlight context clues as you read the text.

Finding Context Clues

Vocabulary questions often repeat the same idea in different parts of the text. Certain signals indicate this repetition, which can make it easier to find the relevant context clues. Although not every question will have these signals, it is useful to recognize them when they are there.

Demonstratives

The words **"this," "these," and "such"** indicate that the following word or phrase repeats an idea mentioned earlier in the text.

Demonstrative

My grades **increased** by the end of the year. **This improvement** was the result of many hours of studying.

In the second sentence, the word "this" signals that the "improvement" was already mentioned. The preceding sentence says the grades "increased," so "this improvement" points back to "increased." The first sentence must have an idea relating to "improvement" for the text to make sense.

Demonstrative

When I mentioned my **headache and sore throat**, the doctor said **such symptoms** were mild enough to be treated at home.

The word "such" before the word "symptoms" indicates that some kind of symptoms were mentioned earlier. The previous clause mentions "headache and sore throat," which are symptoms of illness, so "such symptoms" is pointing to "headache and sore throat."

Pay attention to the words "this," "these," and "such." They will point to a matching context clue in the previous sentence or clause.

Example

I have always been **scared** of flying on an airplane. This ______ makes it hard for me to travel.

Which choice completes the text with the most logical and precise word or phrase?

✗ injury
✓ fear

In the text above, the word "this" helps you find the relevant context clue by pointing back to the preceding sentence. The missing word—the thing that "makes it hard for me to travel"—must have been mentioned in that first sentence, which talks about being scared. Thus, the missing word is a similar idea: "fear."

In the incorrect example, "injury" does not match anything in the preceding sentence. Even though the second sentence would make sense on its own—an injury could make it hard to travel—it doesn't fit with the previous sentence because no injury was mentioned. The word "this" indicates there MUST be a matching context clue in the previous clause or sentence.

Punctuation

Both colons (:) and dashes (—) typically introduce an explanation or illustration of the previous statement, so these also indicate a repeated idea.

I finally realized why my skin was so **itchy:** I had wandered through a patch of **poison ivy**.

Colon

The colon in this sentence indicates that the following information will explain the itchiness mentioned before the colon. Since poison ivy can cause skin irritation, this explanation fits.

The weather yesterday was **perfect—**the sun was **shining**, a **slight breeze** rustled in the trees, and the temperature was **ideal**.

Dash

The dash in this sentence indicates that the second clause explains or illustrates the first clause. The first clause claims that the weather was perfect, and each detail in the second clause supports that by giving a specific example of "perfect" weather.

When you see a colon or dash, look for a context clue after the punctuation. This context clue will be similar to the idea of the missing word.

Example

Carlos has always _______ playing sports: he **enjoys** basketball, soccer, and tennis.

✗ hated
✓ loved

The colon indicates that the following information illustrates the previous statement and contains a context clue that matches the word in the blank. "Enjoys" goes with the idea of loving sports, so "loved" is the correct word.

Strategies

Recognizing context clues is the most important part of answering Vocabulary questions, but a step-by-step approach can help as well. Use the following strategies as a guide. You may find that some parts work better for you than others, or that it is easier to work in a different order on some questions. Use what works best for you on any given question.

- Restate the text in simpler terms
- Fill in the blank with your own word
- Eliminate answers and plug in remaining choices

Restate the Text in Simpler Terms

The sentences in Vocabulary questions are often long and complicated. To make them easier to understand, **restate the main points** in simpler words. Use the context clues you identify to make sure the restatement keeps the same main idea as the original text. Focus on actions and descriptions rather than names.

> Researchers, including Robin Franklin, a neuroscientist at Altos Labs-Cambridge Institute of Science, have discovered that an ancient virus may have played an essential role in evolution: a retrovirus likely triggered the production of myelin, a fatty tissue necessary for the development of our complex brains.

Based on the key ideas in this sentence, you might reword it like this:

> Researchers discovered that an ancient virus was essential in evolution. It triggered the production of something necessary for the development of our brains.

Restating the text in simpler terms makes it easier to understand the main idea, which allows you to get a sense of what word could fill in the blank.

> Don't get intimidated by scientific terms or by the names of artists, scientists, etc., in a passage. Try substituting a simple name or word when you restate the text.

Fill in the Blank with Your Own Word

Once you have a good idea of what the sentence is saying, try to fill in the blank with your own word. Don't worry about coming up with a high-level "SAT word." Instead, focus on completing the logic of the sentence. The goal is to predict the *idea* that fits in the blank, which will then make it easier to recognize the correct answer when looking at the answer choices. Do not try to predict the exact answer.

Since the sentences often repeat ideas, you can sometimes fill in the blank with a word that appears somewhere else in the sentence.

Context clue

This is a ______ decision: it will have a **major** effect on the rest of your life.

Colon

In this sentence, the colon indicates a repeated idea, so locate the context clue after it: "major." Use this to fill in the blank.

Context clue

This is a _major_ decision: it will have a **major** effect on the rest of your life.

Colon

Even though this is repetitive, it establishes the correct idea. You would then look for an answer that has the same meaning as major. The final sentence might look like this:

Context clue

This is a **significant** decision: it will have a **major** effect on the rest of your life.

Colon

In other cases, there may not be a direct synonym for the missing word, but there will be words with related meanings.

Context clue

On Saturday, the plumber _fixed_ the **broken** faucet that had been bothering me for weeks.

Something that is "broken" needs to be fixed, so "fixed" makes sense in the blank. Although you might think of other things a plumber could do, such as install a faucet, the word you put must fit with the clue "broken."

If you can't think of a specific word to fill in the blank, try to explain the general idea you are looking for, like "something positive" or "something that describes this action."

Eliminate Answers and Plug in Remaining Choices

Read each answer and eliminate any that don't match the predicted idea or that are unrelated to the context. If you don't know what a particular answer choice means, don't eliminate it yet.

In the SAT testing app, you can cross out answers that you decide to eliminate.

After eliminating answers, plug each remaining choice into the sentence to see what fits most precisely. There are a few possibilities at this point:

- If only one word that you are familiar with fits in the blank, choose that answer. Don't be afraid to pick an answer that seems simple or obvious.
- If more than one word seems to fit in the blank, look again at the context clues to determine which one is the *most precise* fit.
- If none of the words you know fit in the blank, make an educated guess from the remaining words. When considering an answer choice, look for any parts of the word that might be similar to a word that you do know. This could give you an idea of the meaning or connotations of the unfamiliar word.
- If you eliminated ALL the answer choices, then reevaluate the text and the context clues. Plug in each choice to see if it makes sense.

> Make sure to select an answer for every question, even if you don't know the meanings of the words. If you guess, you at least have a chance of getting it correct!

Applying the Strategies

Example

Drawing on her deep connection to her homeland, Alhalkere, Emily Kame Kngwarreye, a twentieth-century Aboriginal Australian artist, created beautiful abstract works that gained her ______ recognition: In 1993, she was one of three artists chosen to represent Australia at the Venice Biennale, an international art exhibition.

Which choice completes the text with the most logical and precise word or phrase?

A) local

B) approximate

C) obfuscated

D) global

Restate the Text in Simpler Terms

✗ Emily Kame Kngwarreye, from Alhalkere, was a twentieth-century Australian aboriginal artist that gained _______ recognition: In 1993, she was at the Venice Biennale.

✓ Deeply connected to her homeland, Emily created works that gained her _______ recognition: She was chosen for an international art exhibition.

The first restatement above gives accurate information based on the text, but it focuses on proper nouns and dates instead of actions and descriptions, so it loses the main idea. Although the artist's name and details would be important for an art history class, they do not affect the connections within the text, so they are not important for Vocabulary questions.

The second restatement simplifies the names to focus on the actions and descriptions. This version makes the main ideas and connections within the text clearer, which should help you figure out the missing word.

Fill in the Blank with Your Own Word

Drawing on her deep connection to her homeland, Alhalkere, Emily Kame Kngwarreye, a twentieth-century Aboriginal Australian artist, created beautiful abstract works that gained her _______ recognition: In 1993, she was one of three artists chosen to represent Australia at the Venice Biennale, an international art exhibition.

✗ local

✓ international

The colon after "recognition" indicates there is a context clue following it that should have a similar idea to the missing word. The sentence says that Emily was chosen for an "international" art exhibition, so it makes sense that her recognition is also "international." Use that word to fill in the blank since that is the *idea* you are looking for.

Eliminate Answers and Plug in Remaining Choices

Drawing on her deep connection to her homeland, Alhalkere, Emily Kame Kngwarreye, a twentieth-century Aboriginal Australian artist, created beautiful abstract works that gained her *international* recognition: In 1993, she was one of three artists chosen to represent Australia at the Venice Biennale, an international art exhibition.

Which choice completes the text with the most logical and precise word or phrase?

✗ A) local

✗ B) approximate

? C) obfuscated

✓ D) global

Eliminate "local" since that is the opposite of the predicted word, "international." "Approximate" is unrelated to "international," so it can also be eliminated. If "obfuscated" is not a familiar word, then you should not eliminate it yet. "Global" is similar to "international," so it looks like a good answer choice.

Since "global" is the only familiar word left after the process of elimination, that should be your answer. You can plug it into the sentence to double check that it makes sense:

✓ Drawing on her deep connection to her homeland, Alhalkere, Emily Kame Kngwarreye, a twentieth-century Aboriginal Australian artist, created beautiful abstract works that gained her *global* recognition: In 1993, she was one of three artists chosen to represent Australia at the Venice Biennale, an international art exhibition.

"Global" fits in the sentence and is the correct answer.

"Obfuscated" means "made harder to see or understand," which does not fit in this context. However, you do not need to know that to answer this question correctly, as long as you see that "global" DOES fit the context.

Practice

1. In a project known as ScanPyramids, which began in 2015, Cairo University and the French HIP Institute (Heritage Innovation Preservation) are using muon tomography, among other technologies, to _______ previously hidden spaces inside the Great Pyramids.

Which choice completes the text with the most logical and precise word or phrase?

A) conceal

B) construct

C) attack

D) uncover

See Appendix for answer

2. In 2023, the US Census Bureau _______ that, although the rate of growth is decreasing, the global population will reach 10.2 billion by the year 2060. This projection is slightly higher than the 10.1 billion estimate made by the United Nations Population Division.

Which choice completes the text with the most logical and precise word or phrase?

A) requested

B) discounted

C) predicted

D) interjected

See Appendix for answer

3. Many people enjoy the flavor of the herb cilantro, but others find it _______ due to a genetic variation that makes them sensitive to a soapy-flavored chemical compound in the herb.

Which choice completes the text with the most logical and precise word or phrase?

A) exciting

B) unappealing

C) delectable

D) unknown

See Appendix for answer

4. Leon Botstein, president of Bard College, believes that by treating adolescents as children, the typical American high school provides an _______ environment for teens: he argues that keeping teens separate from the adult world has damaging effects on students and on society.

Which choice completes the text with the most logical and precise word or phrase?

A) encouraging

B) unhealthy

C) irreverent

D) inviting

See Appendix for answer

Things to Remember

- The most helpful context clues are usually actions and descriptions.
- Many questions rely on repeating similar ideas in different parts of the sentence.
- "This," "These," "Such," colons, and dashes indicate a repeated, similar idea.
- Restate the text to focus on actions and descriptions, not names.
- You can often predict a word by reusing a word in the sentence.
- When eliminating answer choices, keep any words that you are unsure of the meaning.
- Plug in answer choices to find the most precise fit.

Vocabulary: Logical and Precise
Check for Understanding

1. Researchers hoping to use graphene for electronics have long been stumped by a fundamental obstacle: graphene's lack of what is known as a "band gap." Walter de Heer and his team of researchers have made a major breakthrough to address this _______ by using a special process to chemically bond graphene to silicon carbide.

   Which choice completes the text with the most logical and precise word or phrase?

   A) selection

   B) problem

   C) interest

   D) question

2. According to author William Berger, celebrated soprano Maria Callas _______ the essence of a character through her emotional performances, showing the ugly as well as the beautiful.

   Which choice completes the text with the most logical and precise word or phrase?

   A) loved

   B) envisioned

   C) disputed

   D) revealed

3. Professors Sebyung Kang and Sung Ho Park of Ulsan National Institute of Science and Technology are developing an _______ cancer treatment: their creative technique uses nanodrones to activate innate lymphoid cells, which are then able to eliminate target cancer cells.

   Which choice completes the text with the most logical and precise word or phrase?

   A) innovative

   B) ample

   C) inexplicable

   D) obscure

4. Nineteenth-century economist Henry George believed that a tax on the intrinsic value of land should be the _______ source of government revenue. Many modern economists support land value taxation, but they do not rely on it alone, believing instead that it should be combined with a tax on the buildings and improvements on the land.

   Which choice completes the text with the most logical and precise word or phrase?

   A) final

   B) complementary

   C) sole

   D) infrequent

Vocabulary

Most Nearly Means

Some vocabulary questions ask for **the meaning of a particular word or phrase in the text**. The word will often be one that has different meanings in different situations, so it is important to **read the surrounding text to understand how the word is being used**.

This section will discuss strategies for answering questions about the meaning of a word or phrase in the text.

Strategies

- Predict the meaning in your own words.
- Plug in answers to eliminate incorrect choices.

Predicting the Meaning in Your Own Words

To determine the meaning of a word, it is necessary to understand the context around it. Start by carefully reading the whole text. If the text is complex, you can restate it in simpler terms to make it easier to understand. Once you understand the text, **replace the underlined word with your own word or phrase**. Since the underlined word may have multiple definitions, remember to focus on the surrounding ideas to interpret its meaning.

You can treat the underlined word as a blank and use the surrounding context to come up with your own idea to fill in the blank.

Example

The following text is from Louis Bromfield's 1924 novel *Possession.* Lily is Ellen's cousin and Mrs. Tolliver is Ellen's mother.

> It was Lily who still dominated [Ellen's] thoughts when she descended at last to find her mother setting the table for the family supper. This was <u>an operation</u> into which Mrs. Tolliver threw all the great energy and force of her character.

As used in the text, what does the phrase "an operation" most nearly mean?

Prediction

The first sentence mentions Ellen coming downstairs to find her mother getting the table ready for dinner. The second sentence says that this "operation" is something Mrs. Tolliver puts a lot of effort into doing. The word "operation" seems to refer to the act of "setting the table" mentioned in the previous sentence. With that in mind, you could replace "an operation" with something like "a job" or "a chore."

Annotated Text

> It was Lily who still dominated [Ellen's] thoughts when she descended at last to find her mother setting the table for the family supper. This was *<u>a job</u>* into which Mrs. Tolliver threw all the great energy and force of her character.

Plugging in Answers to Eliminate Incorrect Choices

Once you have predicted an idea, look at the answer choices for a word or phrase with a similar meaning. If more than one answer is similar to your predicted word, plug each one into the text to see which fits the best.

If you had trouble predicting an idea or if none of the answers matches your idea, then reread the whole text with each answer choice substituted for the underlined word. Eliminate any answers that don't make sense based on the context.

If you have more than one answer left after plugging in and eliminating, try to locate specific context clues in the text that point to one of the remaining answers.

Example

The following text is from Louis Bromfield's 1924 novel *Possession.* Lily is Ellen's cousin and Mrs. Tolliver is Ellen's mother.

> It was Lily who still dominated [Ellen's] thoughts when she descended at last to find her mother setting the table for the family supper. This was <u>an operation</u> into which Mrs. Tolliver threw all the great energy and force of her character.

As used in the text, what does the phrase "an operation" most nearly mean?

A) A transaction

B) A surgery

C) An organization

D) A task

✗ **A:** "It was Lily who still dominated [Ellen's] thoughts when she descended at last to find her mother setting the table for the family supper. This was **<u>a transaction</u>** into which Mrs. Tolliver threw all the great energy and force of her character."

✗ **B:** "It was Lily who still dominated [Ellen's] thoughts when she descended at last to find her mother setting the table for the family supper. This was **<u>a surgery</u>** into which Mrs. Tolliver threw all the great energy and force of her character."

✗ **C:** "It was Lily who still dominated [Ellen's] thoughts when she descended at last to find her mother setting the table for the family supper. This was **<u>an organization</u>** into which Mrs. Tolliver threw all the great energy and force of her character."

✓ **D:** "It was Lily who still dominated [Ellen's] thoughts when she descended at last to find her mother setting the table for the family supper. This was **<u>a task</u>** into which Mrs. Tolliver threw all the great energy and force of her character."

Choice A: The word "transaction" relates to buying, selling, or exchanging something. There is nothing in the text that suggests any kind of sale or exchange.

Choice B: A "surgery" is a medical operation, but the context does not relate to medical procedures, so this meaning does not fit here.

Choice C: "Organization" is the manner in which something is arranged. The text discusses Mrs. Tolliver performing the action of setting the table, but it does not describe the particular way the table is arranged. Thus, the word "operation" refers to the action rather than an arrangement, so "organization" can be eliminated.

Choice D: A "task" is a piece of work that must be done, like a chore, which is similar to the predicted word "job" and makes sense to refer to "setting the table."

Practice

1. The following text is from Edith Wharton's 1920 novel *The Age of Innocence.* A man is standing outside a quiet, rundown house.

   For a long time he stood there, content to take in the scene, and gradually falling under its drowsy spell; but at length he roused himself to the sense of the passing time. Should he look his fill and then drive away?

As used in the text, what does the phrase "falling under" most nearly mean?

A) Struggling with

B) Disputing over

C) Becoming influenced by

D) Being classified as

See Appendix for answer

2. The following text is from F. Scott Fitzgerald's 1920 novel *This Side of Paradise.* Amory is talking with D'Invilliers, a fellow college student, at lunch and is concerned about what the group sitting nearby will think of him.

   [The others] didn't seem to be noticing, so [Amory] let himself go, discussed books by the dozens—books he had read, read about, books he had never heard of, rattling off lists of titles with the facility of a Brentano's clerk. D'Invilliers was partially taken in and wholly delighted.

As used in the text, what does the word "facility" most nearly mean?

A) Structure

B) Ease

C) Establishment

D) Convenience

See Appendix for answer

Things to Remember

- Use the context to determine a substitute for the underlined word.
- Plug in each choice and eliminate the ones that are unrelated to the context.

Vocabulary: Most Nearly Means
Check for Understanding

1. The following text is from Margaret Lynn's 1913 short story "The Legacy of Richard Hughes." A woman is reflecting on the room in which she has placed her husband's coffin after his death.

    For the library was, above everything else in the world, hers. It was such a room as shows it has been taking on character through succeeding decades, cumulative of its type, slowly drawing to itself an atmosphere of fineness and greatness.

    As used in the text, what does the phrase "drawing to" most nearly mean?

    A) Closing on

    B) Extracting from

    C) Attracting to

    D) Sketching for

2. The following text is from Herman Melville's 1853 short story "Bartleby, the Scrivener: A Story of Wall Street." Bartleby has just refused to do a task that his employer, the narrator, has asked of him.

    I looked at [Bartleby] steadfastly. His face was leanly composed; his gray eye dimly calm. Not a wrinkle of agitation rippled him. Had there been the least uneasiness, anger, impatience or impertinence in his manner; in other words, had there been any thing ordinarily human about him, doubtless I should have violently dismissed him from the premises.

    As used in the text, what does the word "manner" most nearly mean?

    A) Behavior

    B) Arrangement

    C) Class

    D) Type

Purpose

Main

The main purpose of a text is the **goal** the author has for writing it. For example, a writer's goal might be to describe something, to discuss an idea, or to encourage someone. On the SAT, you will be given a short text—it could be nonfiction, fiction, or poetry—and will be asked to identify which answer best states the main purpose.

This section will discuss strategies for approaching questions about a text's purpose and illustrate those strategies in different kinds of texts.

Strategies

- Analyze the text for clues to the author's purpose.
- Paraphrase or note key words and ideas.
- State the purpose in your own words.
- Use the process of elimination.

Analyzing the Text for Clues to the Author's Purpose

As you read the text, look for clues to the author's purpose. These are often the same types of clues that indicate the main idea of a text. Although main idea and purpose are not identical, they are closely related. The author's purpose is WHY the author is conveying the main idea. For example, if the main idea of a text is "smoking is unhealthy," the purpose might be "**to explain** the health risks of smoking" or "**to persuade** people to quit smoking."

Introductory Information

Poems and fiction texts are preceded by brief introductory information. Make sure to read this information because it often includes important context. For example, the title of a poem can be an excellent clue to the author's purpose. In fiction, background information about the plot or setting can make it much easier to understand what is going on in the excerpt.

Topic Sentences

Many texts, especially nonfiction texts, have a topic sentence that states the main idea, providing a strong clue to the author's purpose. It is often near the beginning of the paragraph, but it could be located anywhere. To find the topic sentence, look for a statement that is supported or illustrated with details throughout the rest of the text.

Example

It is widely recognized that long summer breaks from school lead to summer learning loss—by the time students return at the end of the summer, many have forgotten one month's worth of learning. Year-round education is one potential solution to this problem. Year-round school calendars usually consist of the same number of school days as a traditional school year, but the days are distributed such that there are more frequent, shorter breaks. In theory, this gives students the rest they need without the negative effects of extended time away from school.

The paragraph begins by identifying a problem and then discusses a potential solution to that problem. Since the details all relate to year-round education as a solution to summer learning loss, the topic sentence (highlighted in the text above) is the one that states this solution. Thus, the purpose of the paragraph might be **to discuss a potential solution to the problem of summer learning loss**.

Transitions

Each part of a text contributes to its overall purpose, so it is important to understand how the parts fit together. Transition words and conjunctions help establish the flow of ideas and show relationships within the text.

Contrast words, like "but," "yet," and "however," are particularly important to notice because they indicate a shift from one idea to an opposing idea. In most cases, the purpose statement will relate to both ideas in some way.

Example

Year-round education is often suggested as a solution to summer learning loss. Supporters argue that when students are given shorter breaks, they are less likely to lose knowledge and skills. But others point to drawbacks of this approach. Long breaks allow students to immerse themselves in extracurricular activities, such as summer jobs, internships, or specialized camps. With a year-round school schedule, students may miss these valuable opportunities.

The first two sentences discuss support for year-round education, and then the contrast word "But" marks a shift to the opposite point of view, with the remaining sentences presenting an argument against a year-round school schedule. The purpose might be something like this: **to introduce conflicting points of view on year-round education as a solution to summer learning loss.**

Paraphrasing or Noting Key Words and Ideas

Paraphrase

Restating the main parts of the text in your own words can improve your understanding. Take one or two sentences at a time and rephrase what they are saying. This can help you keep track of the ideas in a text.

Note Key Words or Ideas

If you find that you don't understand the text well enough to rephrase it, then you can make note of key words or themes that you notice instead. This can be especially helpful for poetry.

Stating the Purpose in Your Own Words

After reading and analyzing the text, try to express the main purpose in your own words before looking at the answer choices. This gives you an idea of what to look for ahead of time, which can make it easier to avoid distracting answer choices. Try to state the purpose with a phrase that begins with "To [do something]." For example, if a text is about a character trying to make a difficult decision, the purpose might be something like this: **to convey a character's struggle to choose between two options**.

Using the Process of Elimination

Read each answer choice and compare it to the text. If you have notes or if you stated the purpose in your own words first, use those to help eliminate answers. Look for anything in an answer choice that doesn't fit with the text. If even one part of the answer doesn't fit, then it is incorrect.

Applying the Strategies

Nonfiction Example

While studying the skulls of large carnivores, evolutionary biologist Blaire Van Valkenburgh of UCLA noticed that many had broken teeth. In a 2019 study that focused on the skulls of gray wolves from several different areas, she reported that the frequency of broken teeth was linked to the availability of food. Van Valkenburgh identified a higher incidence of broken teeth in places where the ratio of prey to wolves was low. She theorizes that with less food available, wolves are forced to chew all the way down to the bones of their prey, thereby increasing the damage to their teeth.

Which choice best states the main purpose of the text?

A) To indicate how broken teeth affect wolves and other large carnivores

B) To express concern over the lack of food available to gray wolves

C) To introduce Van Valkenburgh as a respected researcher in the field of evolutionary biology

D) To describe Van Valkenburgh's research on large carnivores' broken teeth

Analyze the Text for Clues to the Author's Purpose

In this example, Sentence 2 ("In a 2019 study…") is the topic sentence. It introduces a specific study and its findings, and the following sentences give details about it. This suggests the purpose of the text is related to that specific study.

Paraphrase

S1	Many carnivore skulls have broken teeth.
S2	A study on gray wolves shows broken teeth are tied to availability of food.
S3	More broken teeth = less prey available
S4	Less food means chewing food to the bone, which leads to tooth damage.

State the Purpose in Your Own Words

All the sentences relate to the broken teeth and the study that investigated the reason for the broken teeth. Thus, the purpose might be **to discuss a study about the reason for wolves' broken teeth**.

Use the Process of Elimination

While studying the skulls of large carnivores, evolutionary biologist Blaire Van Valkenburgh of UCLA noticed that many had broken teeth. In a 2019 study that focused on the skulls of gray wolves from several different areas, she reported that the frequency of broken teeth was linked to the availability of food. Van Valkenburgh identified a higher incidence of broken teeth in places where the ratio of prey to wolves was low. She theorizes that with less food available, wolves are forced to chew all the way down to the bones of their prey, thereby increasing the damage to their teeth.

Which choice best states the main purpose of the text?

A) To indicate how broken teeth affect wolves and other large carnivores

B) To express concern over the lack of food available to grey wolves

C) To introduce Van Valkenburgh as a respected researcher in the field of evolutionary biology

D) To describe Van Valkenburgh's research on large carnivores' broken teeth

✗ **Choice A:** The text discusses what might cause the broken teeth, but it does not discuss how that affects the animals.

✗ **Choice B:** The text shows that scarcity of food affects the wolves, but it does not express concern about this. The text is relaying facts, not showing the writer's opinion about those facts.

✗ **Choice C:** The text introduces Van Valkenburgh as an evolutionary biologist, but nothing indicates whether she is viewed with respect by other members of her field.

✓ **Choice D:** The text introduces and provides details about Van Valkenburgh's study on carnivores' broken teeth.

Fiction Example

The following text is adapted from Lucy Maud Montgomery's 1915 novel *Anne of the Island.* Anne's friends Phil and Diana are each celebrating a joyful life event.

> Phil Gordon was married the next week and Anne went over to Bolingbroke to be her bridesmaid. [...] Anne was always glad in the happiness of her friends; but it is sometimes a little lonely to be surrounded everywhere by a happiness that is not your own. And it was just the same when she went back to Avonlea. This time it was Diana who was bathed in the wonderful glory that comes to a woman when her first-born is laid beside her.

Which choice best states the main purpose of the text?

A) To convey that Anne's friends are preoccupied with their own lives and inconsiderate of her feelings

B) To suggest that Anne is bitter because she does not have the happiness that her friends have

C) To reveal Anne's conflicted feelings of happiness and loneliness as she witnesses her friends' joy

D) To illustrate that Anne is tired of celebrating her friends and wants to pursue her own happiness

Analyze the Text for Clues to the Author's Purpose

In this example, the contrast word "but" marks a transition in the text. The preceding clause discusses happiness, and the following clause brings up loneliness. Keep this contrast in mind as you continue to analyze the text.

Paraphrase

S1	Anne is a bridesmaid in her friend's wedding.
S2	Anne is glad to see her friends happy BUT also feels lonely.
S3	She feels the same in Avonlea.
S4	Diana is happy because she just had her first child.

State the Purpose in Your Own Words

Noting the contrast word, you might say the purpose is **to show that Anne feels both glad and lonely as she celebrates her friends' happiness**.

Use the Process of Elimination

The following text is adapted from Lucy Maud Montgomery's 1915 novel *Anne of the Island.* Anne's friends Phil and Diana are each celebrating a joyful life event.

> Phil Gordon was married the next week and Anne went over to Bolingbroke to be her bridesmaid. [...] Anne was always glad in the happiness of her friends; but it is sometimes a little lonely to be surrounded everywhere by a happiness that is not your own. And it was just the same when she went back to Avonlea. This time it was Diana who was bathed in the wonderful glory that comes to a woman when her first-born is laid beside her.

Which choice best states the main purpose of the text?

A) To convey that Anne's friends are preoccupied with their own lives and inconsiderate of her feelings

B) To suggest that Anne is bitter because she does not have the happiness that her friends have

C) To reveal Anne's conflicted feelings of happiness and loneliness as she witnesses her friends' joy

D) To illustrate that Anne is tired of celebrating her friends and wants to pursue her own happiness

✗ **Choice A:** The text mentions her friends' life events, but it does not show anything about their attitudes or how they treat Anne.

✗ **Choice B:** Although Anne feels lonely as she sees her friends' happiness, nothing in the text suggests she is bitter about it. In fact, the text mentions that she is glad for her friends.

✓ **Choice C:** This choice expresses the conflicted nature of Anne's feelings, which is indicated with the word "but." She feels happy but also a bit lonely.

✗ **Choice D:** The text indicates that Anne is a little lonely because she is surrounded by other people's happiness, but it does not suggest she is tired of her friends or that she plans to focus on her own happiness.

Poetry Example

The following text is from Muriel Stuart's 1922 poem "The Seed Shop."

Here in a quiet and dusty room they lie,
Faded as crumbled stone or shifting sand,
Forlorn as ashes, shrivelled, scentless, dry—
Meadows and gardens running through my hand.

Dead that shall quicken at the voice of spring,
Sleepers to wake beneath June's tempest kiss;
Though birds pass over, unremembering,
And no bee find here roses that were his.

Which choice best states the main purpose of the text?

A) To illustrate the process of growth from seeds to fully developed plants

B) To express sorrow over the dry remains of the season's vegetation

C) To highlight a contrast between the outward appearance and the inward potential of seeds

D) To show how seeds are interconnected with the rest of the natural world

Analyze the Text for Clues to the Author's Purpose

Although poems don't have topic sentences, they may have a statement that establishes a clear theme. They can also have transitions to mark a shift in ideas. In this example, however, nothing like that stands out. Instead, look at the title: "The Seed Shop." In the context of the poem, it seems that the speaker is looking at seeds in a shop. "Here in a quiet and dusty room **they** lie" refers to seeds.

Note Key Words and Ideas

Stanza 1	faded, forlorn, shrivelled — meadows and gardens
Stanza 2	Dead — quicken, spring; sleepers — wake; birds unremembering, no bee, roses

Each stanza appears to have contrasting ideas—some words suggest decay or lifelessness, and some suggest growth and life.

State the Purpose in Your Own Words

Based on the above notes, the purpose will likely be related to the contrasting ideas of the seeds' lifelessness and their potential for vibrant life. The purpose statement might be **to show how even though seeds appear lifeless, they contain the potential for vibrant life**.

Use the Process of Elimination

The following text is from Muriel Stuart's 1922 poem "The Seed Shop."

Here in a quiet and dusty room they lie,
Faded as crumbled stone or shifting sand,
Forlorn as ashes, shrivelled, scentless, dry—
Meadows and gardens running through my hand.

Dead that shall quicken at the voice of spring,

Sleepers to wake beneath June's tempest kiss;
Though birds pass over, unremembering,
And no bee find here roses that were his.

Which choice best states the main purpose of the text?

A) To illustrate the process of growth from seeds to fully developed plants

B) To express sorrow over the dry remains of the season's vegetation

C) To highlight a contrast between the outward appearance and the inward potential of seeds

D) To show how seeds are interconnected with the rest of the natural world

✗ **Choice A:** The text implies that plants come from seeds, but it does not discuss the process by which this happens.

✗ **Choice B:** A few phrases suggest something dried up, such as "Forlorn as ashes, shrivelled, scentless, dry," but the speaker is referring to seeds, not the remains of old vegetation, and doesn't express sorrow about their condition.

✓ **Choice C:** The poem describes seemingly dead seeds as "shrivelled" and "dry," yet within them lies the possible life of "Meadows and gardens" that will come alive "at the voice of spring." This portrays a contrast between their outward appearance and their inward potential.

✗ **Choice D:** The poem focuses on seeds and what comes from the seeds. It does mention birds and bees, but rather than showing interconnectedness, it says they "pass over" the seeds and do not find any "roses."

Practice

1. The following text is adapted from Christina Krysto's 1911 short story "Babanchik." The narrator is recalling childhood memories of a family friend.

> It was in those two summers that we came to know Babanchik best and to adore him accordingly. It was he who led our marvelous expeditions to the neighboring peaks, his clothes steaming with the effort of that leadership—he who showed us where to look for mushrooms, and later fried those mushrooms for us. His mind settled, wisely and fairly, all our momentous quarrels, and invented countless new and fascinating games when we had tired of the everlasting croquet.

Which choice best states the main purpose of the text?

A) To identify some of the ways in which Babanchik endeared himself to the others

B) To reveal that the narrator blames Babanchik for problems arising from past actions

C) To convey the love and enthusiasm Babanchik had for the outdoors

D) To describe the types of adventures the narrator experienced as a child

See Appendix for answer

Things to Remember

- Analyze the text and the introductory information for clues.
- Paraphrase or note key ideas as you read.
- State the purpose in your own words.
- Eliminate answers that are not fully supported by the text.

Purpose: Main
Check for Understanding

1. The following text is from the 1903 poem "The Debt" by Paul Laurence Dunbar, a Black American author.

    This is the debt I pay
    Just for one riotous day,
    Years of regret and grief,
    Sorrow without relief.

    Pay it I will to the end--
    Until the grave, my friend,
    Gives me a true release--
    Gives me the clasp of peace.

    Slight was the thing I bought,
    Small was the debt I thought,
    Poor was the loan at best—
    God! but the interest!

    Which choice best states the main purpose of the text?

    A) To express anguish over a seemingly small action that has had long-lasting consequences

    B) To demonstrate that taking out loans with interest is painful but necessary

    C) To show hope for a future that will be free from unhappy memories

    D) To consider whether it is better to enjoy life one day at a time or plan for the future

2. Many scientists believe that handedness—our tendency to use one hand over the other—developed sometime after the evolution of humans and primates diverged and that it may have been tied to the development of language in humans. However, cognitive neuroscientist William Hopkins conducted a study on chimpanzees that he believes suggests otherwise. He found that captive chimpanzees showed a right-handed preference for specific tasks that required precision and manual dexterity. Although his research is not widely accepted, Hopkins hypothesizes that handedness developed earlier than previously thought and is tied to the need for motor coordination rather than language.

    Which choice best states the main purpose of the text?

    A) To explain how the evolution of language and handedness are related

    B) To introduce research that conflicts with commonly held ideas about handedness

    C) To assert that chimpanzees are more closely related to humans than previously thought

    D) To call attention to an issue that was resolved by Hopkins's research

3. The following text is adapted from Theodore Dreiser's 1900 novel *Sister Carrie*. Carrie has just arrived in Chicago to live with her sister.

    In the interval which marked the preparation of the meal, Carrie found time to study the flat. She had some slight gift of observation and that sixth sense, so rich in every woman, of intuition.

    She felt the drag of a lean and narrow life. The walls of the rooms were discordantly papered. The floors were covered with matting and the hall laid with a thin rag carpet. One could see that the furniture was of that poor, hurriedly patched-together quality sold by the installment houses.

Which choice best states the main purpose of the text?

A) To illustrate Carrie's use of intuition to improve her circumstances

B) To convey Carrie's impression of her new surroundings

C) To reveal the generosity of Carrie's sister despite her financial difficulties

D) To emphasize the sharp change in Carrie's living conditions

Purpose

Portion

Some questions ask about the purpose, or **function**, of a particular underlined **portion** of a sentence. These questions require you to **consider the role the underlined portion plays in relation to the rest of the text.**

Sometimes an answer choice will directly state the sentence's relationship to other parts of the text. For example, an answer might look like this: "It introduces an idea that is supported **later** in the text," or "It elaborates on a statement made **earlier** in the text."

In other cases, an answer will include specific details from the text, but the relationship to the other sentences will be implied, like in these examples: "It identifies a problem faced by the researchers," and "It suggests Lara is confused by her neighbor's behavior." Even though statements like these don't directly refer to another part of the text, they refer to details from somewhere else in the text.

This section will discuss strategies to approach questions about the function of a particular portion of a text. To answer these questions, make sure to **read all the sentences in the text** to understand how their ideas fit together.

Strategies

- Paraphrase the text to find the main claim.
- Predict the answer in your own words.
- Use the process of elimination.

Paraphrasing the Text to Find the Main Claim

It is important to understand the main idea of the whole text to see how the underlined portion fits in. Paraphrasing a text can make it easier to understand. Take one or two sentences at a time and rephrase what they are saying. Then you can analyze the ideas in your paraphrased text to determine the main idea and the underlined portion's relationship to it.

Nonfiction texts will usually have a main claim that is supported throughout the text. There may also be counterclaims or contrasting ideas presented. Try to identify the main claim first, then determine whether the underlined portion agrees with the claim or contrasts with it.

If the underlined portion agrees with the main claim, its function might be to elaborate on or to provide details or evidence to support the claim. If the underlined portion disagrees with the main claim, then the function might be to concede an opposing point or to present an objection.

Example

Many people imagine nineteenth-century American "Wild West" towns as filled with guns and lawlessness, but according to Adam Winkler, a professor of American constitutional law, this image is mostly false. Winkler says that, in reality, guns were more strictly regulated in many Western towns at that time than they are today. <u>Although most people did own guns</u>, local laws prohibited weapons of any kind from being carried in public. Visitors would leave their guns with law officers as long as they remained in town.

Which choice best describes the function of the underlined portion in the text as a whole?

Paraphrase

S1	The common idea of guns and lawlessness in "Wild West" towns is inaccurate.
S2	There were strict gun regulations in many Western towns.
S3	Most people did own guns, but the guns couldn't be carried in public.
S4	Visitors in town left their guns with law officers.

The sentences all relate to gun use and rules in the Wild West. The main claim is established in the first sentence: **The popular image of widespread gun use in "Wild West" towns is false.** The underlined portion, however, states that most people did own guns, which seems to **contrast** with the main claim. The text presents this statement as a fact and does not present evidence to disprove it, so the text appears to be **conceding**, or admitting the truth of, this point.

Words like "although" and "while" often introduce a point the author is conceding.

Predicting the Answer in Your Own Words

After reading the text, try to predict the function of the underlined portion before looking at the answer choices. Doing so gives you an idea of what to look for in the correct answer, which can make it easier to avoid distracting answers.

Example

Many people imagine nineteenth-century American "Wild West" towns as filled with guns and lawlessness, but according to Adam Winkler, a professor of American constitutional law, this image is mostly false. Winkler says that, in reality, guns were more strictly regulated in many Western towns at that time than they are today. Although most people did own guns, local laws prohibited weapons of any kind from being carried in public. Visitors would leave their guns with law officers as long as they remained in town.

Which choice best describes the function of the underlined portion in the text as a whole?

Predicted Answer

The underlined portion states that most people at the time owned guns. However, the rest of the text discusses restrictions on guns. Since the underlined portion seems to support an idea opposite of the text's main claim, the function of the underlined portion might be stated like this: **It concedes that gun ownership was widespread even though there were restrictions.**

Using the Process of Elimination

Read each answer choice and compare it to the ideas in the text. If you paraphrased the text and predicted the function of the underlined portion, use that information to help eliminate incorrect answers.

Keep in mind that the entire answer must be accurate for it to be correct. In some cases, the description of the portion itself might be correct, but the explanation of how it relates to the rest of the text is incorrect. If even one part of the answer is inaccurate, you should eliminate it.

Example

Many people imagine nineteenth-century American "Wild West" towns as filled with guns and lawlessness, but according to Adam Winkler, a professor of American constitutional law, this image is mostly false. Winkler says that, in reality, guns were more strictly regulated in many Western towns at that time than they are today. Although most people did own guns, local laws prohibited weapons of any kind from being carried in public. Visitors would leave their guns with law officers as long as they remained in town.

Which choice best describes the function of the underlined portion in the text as a whole?

A) It establishes why Winkler thinks laws of the nineteenth-century American West are relevant in today's society.

B) It identifies a flaw in a widely held belief about the American West.

C) It claims that gun ownership was common mostly among town-dwellers.

D) It acknowledges that weapon restrictions did not prevent people from owning guns.

✗ **Choice A:** The underlined portion focuses on the fact that people owned guns. It does not indicate anything about the laws at the time or their relevance today.

✗ **Choice B:** Even though the text as a whole indicates that a widely held belief about the American West is flawed, the underlined portion does not. Rather, it states a fact that supports that belief.

✗ **Choice C:** The underlined portion talks about gun ownership but does not say anything about whether people in town were more likely to own guns than other people were.

✓ **Choice D:** The majority of the text discusses restrictions on guns, but the underlined portion concedes that most people did own guns, showing that the restrictions were on the use and not the ownership of guns.

Practice

1. The following text is adapted from Gwendolyn B. Bennett's 1927 short story "Tokens." Jenks is a former singer who is now in the hospital dying of tuberculosis.

   Few of the patients there had escaped the lash of [Jenks's] tongue. Sour at life and the raw deal it had dealt him, he now turned his attention to venting his spume on those about him. Nurses, doctors, orderlies, fellow-patients, persistent friends ... all shared alike the blasphemy of his words. Even Bill Jackson, <u>the one friend who continued to brave the sting of his vile tongue</u>, was not spared.

Which choice best describes the function of the underlined portion in the text as a whole?

A) It illustrates why Bill Jackson was unable to understand Jenks's predicament even though they had a close relationship.

B) It indicates why, unlike other acquaintances, Bill Jackson is not afraid to visit Jenks.

C) It suggests that Bill Jackson believes Jenks's attitude reflects a positive character trait that others don't recognize.

D) It implies that Bill Jackson would not have been the only visitor if it weren't for Jenks's behavior.

See Appendix for answer

2. During World War II, the people of North Platte, Nebraska, provided a significant boost to the morale of American troops. As a major rail hub, North Platte saw thousands of soldiers pass through on their way to active duty. With up to twenty-four trains full of troops stopping briefly in their town each day, residents took the opportunity to make the men feel welcome: <u>they provided baskets of food, birthday cakes for anyone celebrating that day, and of course, smiles and encouragement</u>. From 1941 to 1946, the people of North Platte welcomed approximately six million soldiers.

Which choice best describes the function of the underlined portion in the text as a whole?

A) It introduces an alternate explanation for the improved morale described earlier in the text.

B) It provides details about a feature of World War II train travel discussed earlier in the text.

C) It illustrates a claim made earlier in the text about the wartime contributions of a particular town.

D) It gives a physical description of the residents mentioned earlier in the text.

See Appendix for answer

Things to Remember

- Look for the main claim and relate the underlined portion of the text to it.
- State the function of the underlined portion in your own words.
- Use the process of elimination to find the best answer.

Purpose: Portion
Check for Understanding

1. Groundwater levels are decreasing in aquifers around the world, but there is some evidence that this trend can be reversed with appropriate measures. Debra Perrone and Scott Jasechko have found that efforts such as those in Tucson, Arizona, where water is taken regularly from the Colorado River to replenish the nearby aquifer, can successfully restore the groundwater levels. This affects the flow of the Colorado River itself, unfortunately, but evidence shows that without efforts like this, groundwater levels will continue to decline at an accelerated rate.

   Which choice best describes the function of the underlined portion in the text as a whole?

   A) It provides an exception to Perrone and Jasechko's claim that groundwater levels can be replenished.

   B) It calls attention to the importance of taking intentional steps if groundwater depletion is to be reversed.

   C) It illustrates the claim that groundwater levels in Tucson, Arizona, are being restored.

   D) It offers evidence that aquifer replenishment in Tucson, Arizona, is affecting the environment by changing the flow of the Colorado River.

2. Since the 1940s, Gross Domestic Product (GDP)—the measure of the total value of goods and services produced in a country in a given period of time—has been regarded by many as the key measure of a nation's development, leading to policy decisions that prioritize economic growth. According to economists Amit Kapoor and Bibek Debroy, however, we can create policies that better promote societal progress if we focus more on other indicators of well-being, such as economic equality and environmental impact.

   Which choice best describes the function of the underlined portion in the text as a whole?

   A) It explains a widespread perspective on GDP that, according to the text, some economists believe fails to recognize the diverse factors that contribute to a society's welfare.

   B) It presents a popular view of GDP's significance that the text claims has fallen out of favor due to Kapoor and Debroy's research.

   C) It illustrates a common use of GDP that the text indicates has resulted from politicians focusing on their own financial gain.

   D) It describes the traditional interpretation of GDP, which the text implies economists are using to measure the environmental impact of economic growth.

Purpose

Sentence

Some questions ask about the purpose, or **function**, of a particular sentence within a text. These questions require you to **determine the role the sentence plays in relation to the sentences around it**.

Sometimes an answer choice will directly state the sentence's relationship to other parts of the text. For example, an answer might look like this: "It states a claim that is supported **later** in the text," or "It elaborates on a statement made **earlier** in the text."

In other cases, an answer will include specific details from the text but the relationship to the other sentences will be implied, like in these examples: "It identifies a problem faced by the researchers," and "It suggests Lara is confused by her neighbor's behavior." Even though statements like these don't directly refer to another part of the text, they refer to details from somewhere else in the text.

This section discusses strategies for approaching questions about the function of a particular sentence. To answer these questions, it is important to **read all the sentences in the text** to understand how their ideas fit together.

Strategies

- Summarize each sentence and state its function.
- Predict the answer in your own words.
- Use the process of elimination.

Summarizing Each Sentence and Stating Its Function

Summarize the main point of each sentence, and then try to state what the sentence is doing in general terms. For example, it might be stating a claim, giving an example, or describing a setting.

Example

A team at Drexel University is investigating whether house mice that live in cities have begun to develop genetic differences from those that live in rural areas. <u>The researchers collected mice from Philadelphia, New York City, and Richmond and are comparing the DNA of these city mice to that of rural mice</u>. They are particularly interested in whether certain versions of genes related to metabolism are found more frequently in mice from one environment than from the other.

Which choice best describes the function of the underlined sentence in the text as a whole?

	Summary	Function
S1	Scientists are investigating genetic differences of mice in the country versus the city.	Introduces a specific study and its general aim
S2	The researchers are comparing the mice's DNA.	Explains a method
S3	The scientists are interested in the metabolism genes of the mice.	Identifies a specific goal

Predicting the Answer in Your Own Words

After reading and analyzing the text, try to predict the answer before looking at the answer choices. This gives you an idea of what to look for ahead of time, which can make it easier to avoid distracting answers.

Example

A team at Drexel University is investigating whether house mice that live in cities have begun to develop genetic differences from those that live in rural areas. <u>The researchers collected mice from Philadelphia, New York City, and Richmond and are comparing the DNA of these city mice to that of rural mice</u>. They are particularly interested in whether certain versions of genes related to metabolism are found more frequently in mice from one environment than from the other.

Which choice best describes the function of the underlined sentence in the text as a whole?

The chart from the previous strategy showed the functions of the sentences individually, but the question asks for the function of the sentence **in the text as a whole**. Thus, to predict the answer, you must take the individual function and relate it to the rest of the text.

	Summary	Function
S1	Scientists are investigating genetic differences of mice in the country versus the city.	Introduces a specific study and its general aim
S2	**The researchers are comparing the mice's DNA.**	**Explains a method**
S3	The scientists are interested in the metabolism genes of the mice.	Identifies a specific goal

The underlined sentence explains a method used in a study. That study was introduced in the previous sentence, and the following sentence expands on a particular goal of the same study, so the answer will probably be something like this: **It explains a method used in a study introduced in the previous sentence.**

Using the Process of Elimination

Read each answer choice and compare it to the text. If you summarized the sentences or stated the function in your own words first, use those ideas to help eliminate incorrect answers. Look for anything in an answer choice that doesn't agree with the text. If even one part of the answer doesn't fit, then it is incorrect.

Example

A team at Drexel University is investigating whether house mice that live in cities have begun to develop genetic differences from those that live in rural areas. <u>The researchers collected mice from Philadelphia, New York City, and Richmond and are comparing the DNA of these city mice to that of rural mice</u>. They are particularly interested in whether certain versions of genes related to metabolism are found more frequently in mice from one environment than from the other.

Which choice best describes the function of the underlined sentence in the text as a whole?

A) It discusses how the study relates to previous research on the topic.

B) It explains the findings from the research introduced in the previous sentence.

C) It identifies a method the researchers are using in the study.

D) It highlights issues with the study that are resolved later in the text.

✗ **Choice A:** The sentence discusses details of the current study. It does not address any previous research.

✗ **Choice B:** The underlined sentence does not show any results of the research.

✓ **Choice C:** The sentence discusses the method the researchers are using to look for differences in the house mice: they are "comparing the DNA" of the mice from different places.

✗ **Choice D:** The sentence does not indicate any issues with the study and there is nothing resolved later.

Applying the Strategies

Example

The following text is from Upton Sinclair's 1906 novel *The Jungle.*

> Marija took her usual detour, and, to her horror and dismay, saw a crowd of people in front of the bank, filling the avenue solid for half a block. <u>All the blood went out of her face for terror.</u> She broke into a run, shouting to the people to ask what was the matter, but not stopping to hear what they answered, till she had come to where the throng was so dense that she could no longer advance.

Which choice best describes the function of the underlined sentence in the text as a whole?

A) It introduces an idea that is contrasted in the following sentence.

B) It offers a detailed account of a character's thoughts.

C) It suggests that a character is suffering from an unknown illness.

D) It describes a physical reaction to an event depicted in the previous sentence.

Strategy: Summarize Each Sentence and State Its Function

	Summary	Function
S1	Marija sees a crowd in front of the bank and is horrified.	Introduces a scene and a character's emotions
S2	The blood leaves Marija's face, showing her fear.	Describes a physical sign of the character's emotions
S3	She runs toward the bank, asking what is going on but not listening, until the crowd blocks her progress.	Describes the character's actions in response to the situation.

Strategy: Predict the Answer in Your Own Words

The first sentence introduces an event, and the following sentences illustrate different aspects of the character's reaction to the event. The underlined sentence in particular shows a physical indication of the character's emotional reaction. Its function could be stated like this: **It describes a physical sign of a character's reaction to an event mentioned earlier,** or **it describes a physical sign of Marija's distress.**

Strategy: Use the Process of Elimination

The following text is from Upton Sinclair's 1906 novel *The Jungle*.

> Marija took her usual detour, and, to her horror and dismay, saw a crowd of people in front of the bank, filling the avenue solid for half a block. <u>All the blood went out of her face for terror.</u> She broke into a run, shouting to the people to ask what was the matter, but not stopping to hear what they answered, till she had come to where the throng was so dense that she could no longer advance.

Which choice best describes the function of the underlined sentence in the text as a whole?

A) It introduces an idea that is contrasted in the following sentence.

B) It offers a detailed account of a character's thoughts.

C) It suggests that a character is suffering from an unknown illness.

D) It describes a physical reaction to an event depicted in the previous sentence.

✗ **Choice A:** The underlined sentence illustrates that Marija is in "terror." The following sentences continue to show her panicked reaction to the situation, so there is no contrast between the sentences.

✗ **Choice B:** The sentence shows that Marija is terrified, but it does not go into detail about what she is thinking.

✗ **Choice C:** The blood draining from Marija's face is due to her "terror." Nothing in the text implies she is sick.

✓ **Choice D:** The "blood" draining "out of her face" is a physical reaction caused by her "horror and dismay" at the situation described in the previous sentence.

Practice

1. Plants rely on their root systems and on photosynthesis for nutrients, but some plants acquire additional nutrients by catching and eating insects or even small reptiles or mammals. The round-leaved sundew attracts and captures its prey with sugary droplets on its leaves that appear to be nectar or dew. Insects trying to feed on these droplets become trapped in the sticky substance. The sundew plant then uses enzymes to digest the insects and obtain the nutrients it needs.

Which choice best describes the function of the underlined sentence in the text as a whole?

A) It describes the sundew's root system mentioned earlier in the text.

B) It provides information about how the sundew performs the actions referred to in the text.

C) It discusses the different nutrient needs of plants discussed in the text.

D) It identifies the natural habitat of sundew plants described later in the text.

See Appendix for answer

2. The following text is adapted from Dorothy Canfield's 1919 novel *The Brimming Cup*. Marise is playing the piano for some visitors.

> Those well-remembered opening chords, they were by this time not merely musical sounds. They had become something within [Marise], of her own being, rich with a thousand clustered nameless associations, something that thrilled and sang and lived a full harmonious life of its own. That first down-dropping arabesque of treble notes, not only her fingers played those, but every fiber in her, answering like the vibrating wood of a violin, its very cells rearranged in the pattern which the notes had so many times called into existence . . . by the time she had finished she had almost forgotten that she had listeners.

Which choice best describes the function of the underlined sentence in the text as a whole?

A) It reveals that Marise is more interested in music than her listeners are.

B) It hints that Marise would prefer to be playing piano without an audience.

C) It emphasizes the deep connection Marise feels with the piece of music.

D) It provides a detailed description of the musical style Marise has chosen.

See Appendix for answer

Things to Remember

- Summarize each sentence and state its function.
- Look for connections between the sentences to predict the answer.
- Eliminate any answers that are not supported by the text.

Purpose: Sentence
Check for Understanding

1. The following text is from Katharine Butler's 1915 short story "In No Strange Land."

   As the train moved out he sank comfortably back into his seat, and with his chin on his hand he took up his accustomed nightly gaze on the outer landscape. <u>His thoughts ran back to the morning.</u> He saw the room where he had gone to wake his children. It was a large, square room, with colored nursery pictures on the walls and a collection of battered toys in the corner. The place was fresh and cool with the sparkling air of early May, and through the open windows he had seen the lawn thick spread with cobwebs.

   Which choice best states the function of the underlined sentence in the text as a whole?

   A) It illustrates a physical characteristic that was introduced in the previous sentence.

   B) It presents an analysis of the character that is expanded on in the following sentences.

   C) It introduces the description provided in the sentences that follow.

   D) It suggests a change in the setting established in the previous sentence.

2. According to a study at Cambridge Judge Business School, high levels of air pollution can have a detrimental impact on a team's ability to collaborate on complex tasks. <u>Looking at data from escape room games in London from 2018 to 2022, the researchers compared the time it took teams to complete the tasks on days with high levels of air pollution to the time on days with lower pollution levels</u>. The data indicated that it took teams up to 5% longer to finish the sequence of tasks on days when air pollution levels were highest.

   Which choice best states the function of the underlined sentence in the overall structure of the text?

   A) To present a method the researchers used in the study

   B) To show the significance of the study's findings

   C) To state the researcher's aim in conducting the study

   D) To indicate a difficulty encountered by the researchers

Purpose

Structure

Some questions ask you to describe the overall structure of a text. This usually involves **breaking the text down into distinct parts, each with its own function that contributes to the overall purpose.** The answer will reflect each of those parts individually. For example, the structure of a text might be described like this: "It introduces a hypothesis, explains how the hypothesis was tested, and then presents the researcher's conclusion." Identifying these distinct parts is critical for answering structure questions.

Occasionally, the whole text will maintain one function and there won't be separate pieces. In this case, the answer will only reflect that one function rather than multiple parts.

This section will discuss strategies for approaching questions about the overall structure of a text.

Strategies

- Paraphrase the text.
- Look for shifts in the text.
- Explain the structure in your own words.
- Use the process of elimination.

Paraphrasing the Text

Structure questions require you to understand how the individual parts of the text fit together. Take one or two sentences at a time and rephrase what they are saying. This can make it easier to understand the meaning and therefore recognize distinct parts of the text.

Looking for Shifts in the Text

A shift in the text occurs when a new sentence serves a different function from the previous sentence in relation to the overall purpose. For example, there could be a shift from a general statement to specific evidence or examples, or from introducing a problem to explaining a solution. In poetry, there might be a shift from a description of something to a reflection about it.

Shifts are sometimes marked by a conjunction or transition word, but not always. To identify shifts, carefully consider the function of each sentence and how it relates to the sentences around it.

In some cases, especially in poetry, you may not identify any clear shifts. When that occurs, try to define the way in which the text is conveying the author's ideas. For example, the author might use a particular image throughout the text to depict something.

Explaining the Structure in Your Own Words

After reading and analyzing the text, try to describe the structure in your own words before looking at the answer choices. This gives you an idea of what to look for ahead of time, which makes it easier to avoid distracting answer choices.

If you've identified distinct parts of the text, use those to construct your statement. Make sure to keep the parts in the order that they appear. For example, if the author introduces an idea and then gives examples, the structure of the text could be stated like this: **It makes a statement about a topic, then provides examples illustrating that statement**.

Check the answer choices to make sure you've identified the right number of parts in the text. If ALL the answers have two parts (For example, "It presents an idea, then illustrates it), then your structure statement should also have two parts. If the number of parts in the answer choices varies, then this does not apply.

Using the Process of Elimination

Read each answer choice and compare it to the text. If you have notes or if you explained the structure in your own words first, use that to help eliminate answers.

Since the answer choices often have multiple parts, be careful about wrong answers that are *partially* correct. Sometimes the first part of the answer will match the first part of the text, but another part will be incorrect. Remember that if even one part of the answer doesn't fit, it cannot be the right answer.

Applying the Strategies

Nonfiction Example

A study led by Dr. Alice Bridges and Professor Lars Chittka demonstrated that bumblebees can learn through social interaction. In the study, the bees were given a two-step puzzle to solve with a reward at the end. Although individual bees were unable to learn the steps on their own, they were able to solve the puzzle after they watched a trained bee complete it. This type of social learning, which was thought to be unique to humans, suggests bees may have what is known as cumulative culture—the accumulation of increasingly sophisticated skills over generations.

Which choice best describes the overall structure of the text?

A) It presents the findings of a study, gives a specific example to illustrate the findings, and then discusses a conflicting interpretation.

B) It introduces research on a specific topic, addresses an issue encountered in the research process, and then discusses unexpected results stemming from the research.

C) It describes the aim of a study, details several methods used to reach that aim, and then makes a generalization about the study's findings.

D) It states the conclusion of a study, offers details of how researchers came to that conclusion, and then presents an implication of the study.

Paraphrase the Text

S1	A study demonstrated that bumblebees learn from social interactions.
S2	The bees had to solve a two-step puzzle to get a reward.
S3	The bees couldn't solve it until they watched another bee solve it.
S4	Because bees are capable of social learning, they may be able to accumulate skills over generations.

Look for Shifts in the Text

A study led by Dr. Alice Bridges and Professor Lars Chittka **demonstrated** that bumblebees can learn through social interaction. **In the study**, the bees were given a two-step puzzle to solve with a reward at the end. Although individual bees were unable to learn the steps on their own, they were able to solve the puzzle after they watched a trained bee complete it. **This type of social learning**, which was thought to be unique to humans, **suggests** bees may have what is known as cumulative culture—the accumulation of increasingly sophisticated skills over generations.

The first sentence **introduces** a study and what it **demonstrated**.

"In the study" indicates a shift to specific **details** in the next two sentences.

The final sentence shifts again to an idea **suggested** by the results of the study.

Explain the Structure in Your Own Words

Based on the shifts identified previously, the text has three parts. The first part (Sentence 1) introduces the study by stating what it found or "demonstrated." The next part (Sentences 2–3) gives details about what happened in the study. The final part (Sentence 4) discusses something suggested by the results of the study. Thus, the structure statement could look like this: **It introduces the findings of a study, describes details of the study, and then discusses an idea suggested by the study**.

Use the Process of Elimination

A study led by Dr. Alice Bridges and Professor Lars Chittka **demonstrated** that bumblebees can learn through social interaction. **In the study**, the bees were given a two-step puzzle to solve with a reward at the end. Although individual bees were unable to learn the steps on their own, they were able to solve the puzzle after they watched a trained bee complete it. **This type of social learning**, which was thought to be unique to humans, **suggests** bees may have what is known as cumulative culture—the accumulation of increasingly sophisticated skills over generations.

Which choice best describes the overall structure of the text?

A) It presents the findings of a study, gives a specific example to illustrate the findings, and then discusses a conflicting interpretation.

B) It introduces research on a specific topic, addresses an issue encountered in the research process, and then discusses unexpected results stemming from the research.

C) It describes the aim of a study, details several methods used to reach that aim, and then makes a generalization about the study's findings.

D) It states the conclusion of a study, offers details of how researchers came to that conclusion, and then presents an implication of the study.

When using the process of elimination, remember that **if any part of the answer is wrong, the whole answer is incorrect**. Consider each part of the structure statement individually. If you find a part that doesn't make sense, eliminate the whole answer.

✗ **Choice A:** Although the text does present a study's findings, there is no discussion of a conflicting interpretation. The idea that bees might have "cumulative culture" comes from the finding about their social interaction, rather than conflicting with it.

✗ **Choice B:** The text does not address any issues the researchers had, so the middle portion of the answer choice is incorrect.

✗ **Choice C:** The text begins with the study's findings, not its aim. It also only describes one method, and it does not make a generalization.

✓ **Choice D:** The text starts by stating the conclusion of the study, namely that bees can "learn through social interaction." It then gives details of how the study was performed and how the bees acted. Finally, it shows something suggested by the study's findings: bees may have "cumulative culture."

Poetry Example

The following text is from the 1903 poem "A Roadway" by Paul Laurence Dunbar.

Let those who will stride on their barren roads
And prick themselves to haste with self-made goads,
Unheeding, as they struggle day by day,
If flowers be sweet or skies be blue or gray:
For me, the lone, cool way by purling brooks,
The solemn quiet of the woodland nooks,
A song-bird somewhere trilling sadly gay,
A pause to pick a flower beside the way.

Which choice best describes the overall structure of the text?

A) The speaker illustrates the heedlessness of others, then reflects on his own mistakes.

B) The speaker expresses sorrow over the misfortune of others, then admits his own loneliness.

C) The speaker acknowledges the value of a goal-oriented life, then considers how he might make a change in his priorities.

D) The speaker indicates how some choose to live, then details a different lifestyle that he has chosen.

Paraphrase the Text

Lines 1-2	Let people push themselves to hurry if they want to
Lines 3-4	Paying no attention to flowers or blue sky as they struggle through life
Lines 5-6	I will go alone by brooks and quiet woods
Lines 7-8	A bird singing, I stop to pick a flower

Look for Shifts in the Text

Let those who will stride on their barren roads And prick **themselves** to haste with self-made goads, Unheeding, as **they** struggle day by day, If flowers be sweet or skies be blue or gray:	The speaker refers to **other** people and how they live.
For me, the lone, cool way by purling brooks, The solemn quiet of the woodland nooks, A song-bird somewhere trilling sadly gay, A pause to pick a flower beside the way.	The speaker shifts to talk about **himself** and his lifestyle.

Explain the Structure in Your Own Words

The poem's two main parts should be included in the structure statement. The first part describes others as hurrying, struggling, and paying no attention to the natural world, the "flowers" and "skies." The second part describes the speaker going alone in quiet woods and mentions various elements of nature. Since there seems to be a contrast between the speaker's actions and the others' actions, the structure of the text might be stated like this: **It explains how other people act and then contrasts that with how the speaker acts**.

Use the Process of Elimination

The following text is from the 1903 poem "A Roadway" by Paul Laurence Dunbar.

> **Let those** who will stride on their barren roads
> And prick **themselves** to haste with self-made goads,
> Unheeding, as **they** struggle day by day,
> If flowers be sweet or skies be blue or gray:
> **For me**, the lone, cool way by purling brooks,
> The solemn quiet of the woodland nooks,
> A song-bird somewhere trilling sadly gay,
> A pause to pick a flower beside the way.

Which choice best describes the overall structure of the text?

A) The speaker illustrates the heedlessness of others, then reflects on his own mistakes.

B) The speaker expresses sorrow over the misfortune of others, then admits his own loneliness.

C) The speaker acknowledges the value of a goal-oriented life, then considers how he might make a change in his priorities.

D) The speaker indicates how some choose to live, then details a different lifestyle that he has chosen.

✗ **Choice A:** The first part of the poem does describe how people are heedless of the natural world around them, but the second part doesn't discuss the speaker's mistakes.

✗ **Choice B:** The text focuses on the others' choosing a certain life: they "prick themselves" with "self-made goads." There is no indication they suffered any misfortune, nor does the speaker express any sorrow. Although the speaker mentions choosing "the lone" way himself, this means he is going a way that few choose, not that he is lonely.

✗ **Choice C:** The speaker describes the goal-oriented life of others but doesn't mention whether it has value. He then illustrates his own, different priorities but does not suggest he intends to change them.

✓ **Choice D:** The first part of the text discusses how others hurry and struggle through life without paying attention to nature, and the second part describes how the speaker chooses to engage with the natural world in a calmer, quieter life.

Practice

1. The following text is from Sarojini Naidu's 1905 poem "Alabaster." Alabaster is a stone similar to marble often used in ancient societies to create storage containers for oils or perfumes.

   Like this alabaster box whose art
   Is frail as a cassia-flower, is my heart,
   Carven with delicate dreams and wrought
   With many a subtle and exquisite thought.

   Therein I treasure the spice and scent
   Of rich and passionate memories blent
   Like odours of cinnamon, sandal and clove,
   Of song and sorrow and life and love.

Which choice best describes the overall structure of the text?

A) It contrasts the appearance of the alabaster box with the turmoil of the speaker's heart.

B) It describes the speaker's heart using the image of an alabaster box.

C) It illustrates how the vulnerability of the speaker's heart is the result of past sorrows.

D) It depicts the present state of the speaker's heart, then the speaker's dreams for the future.

See Appendix for answer

2. Two early twentieth-century writers, Ellen N. La Motte and Ernest Hemingway, were prompted by their experiences in World War I to write about the horrors of war. They both used a plain style of short, factual sentences to depict war's destruction and ugliness. La Motte's work *The Backwash of War* was published in 1916, while the conflict was ongoing, but it was quickly censored due to its criticism of the war. Hemingway's novel *A Farewell to Arms*, however, was published in 1929, more than ten years after the war ended. It became a bestseller and established him among America's great writers.

Which choice best describes the overall structure of the text?

A) It discusses the ways in which war influenced two writers, then explains how their styles changed over time.

B) It describes the style of two wartime writers, then shows similarities between their works.

C) It makes several assertions about two writers, then elaborates on one of those assertions with an example.

D) It describes similarities between two writers, then indicates a difference in how their works were received.

See Appendix for answer

Things to Remember

- Paraphrase the text to make it easier to understand.
- Find shifts in the text to identify its different parts.
- State the function of each separate piece of the text.
- Eliminate an answer if any part of it is incorrect.

Purpose: Structure
Check for Understanding

1. The following text is from the 1906 poem "Bird Nesting" by Ellis Parker Butler.

   O wonderful! In sport we climbed the tree,
   Eager and laughing, as in all our play,
   To see the eggs where, in the nest, they lay,
   But silent fell before the mystery.

   For, one brief moment there, we understood
   By sudden sympathy too fine for words
   That we were sisters to the brooding birds
   And part, with them, in God's great motherhood.

   Which choice best describes the overall structure of the text?

   A) The speaker details an animated effort, then questions the motivation behind that effort.

   B) The speaker introduces a childhood discovery, then calls attention to a misunderstanding about that discovery.

   C) The speaker describes a lighthearted scene, then reveals a profound insight following that scene.

   D) The speaker evaluates an experience in nature, then describes a conflicting experience.

2. One of the biggest unknowns for scientists studying climate change is what effect clouds will have on future temperatures. To investigate this, Brett McKim and his team created simple equations to build a model that predicts how the changes in the surface area of tropical storm clouds will affect future global warming. After confirming the model's reliability by testing it on observed clouds, they determined that changes in the clouds' surface area will have a smaller impact on future temperatures than anticipated. The study did not consider the brightness of the clouds though, which remains a topic for future research.

   Which choice best describes the overall structure of the text?

   A) It introduces a question that scientists have yet to answer, presents the methodology and results of a study exploring that question, and then indicates another aspect of the question that still needs to be investigated.

   B) It states a problem that scientists have been unable to solve, explains the results of a study that attempted to solve the problem, and then describes the reason the study was unsuccessful.

   C) It explains a hypothesis that has intrigued climate scientists, discusses the methods used to investigate the hypothesis, and then offers an alternative method that researchers might use in the future.

   D) It identifies a topic that needs further research, summarizes researchers' attempts to explore aspects of that topic, and then indicates a challenge researchers faced in their work.

Connections

Between Texts

Some SAT questions ask you to make connections between two texts that express different ideas about the same topic. The question will ask you to infer how the author of one text, or someone discussed by the author, would respond to information in the other text. The question might focus on the main idea, the conclusion, or a specific detail found in the text.

To identify how someone mentioned in one text might respond to ideas in another text, you must compare the passages and look for similarities and differences in what they express about the topic. This section will explain how to approach questions about connections between texts.

Strategies

- Identify what the question asks.
- Summarize each text.
- Compare the details to identify similar or contrasting ideas.
- Use the process of elimination.

Identify What the Question Asks

Identifying what the question focuses on before you read the texts will help you look for the relevant information. For example, if the question asks about the conclusion presented in Text 1, then you should identify that conclusion as you read. If the question refers to a specific detail or claim, then you should focus on understanding that detail in the context of the whole text.

After considering the relevant ideas in Text 1, look for information in Text 2 that agrees with or disagrees with those ideas.

Examine the question below and note its requirement to focus on the likely response of one text's author to the "overall argument" of another text.

Example

Based on the texts, how would the author of Text 2 most likely respond to the overall argument presented in Text 1?

A text's *overall argument is its main idea*, so the question requires you to understand Text 1's **main idea**.

Here are some other phrases that might appear in the question:

Language in the Question	Reading Focus
"overall argument"	main idea
"main idea"	main idea
"conclusion presented"	detail
"characterization of"	detail
"underlined claim"	detail

Summarize Each Text

Briefly summarizing a text provides clarity about its main idea. Awareness of what each text states about the topic helps you compare how they are similar or different. Read Text 1 and state its main idea in your own words. Then go on to Text 2 and do the same.

Example

Text 1

Audiobooks are the fastest growing book format in the world, but they shouldn't be relied on to help children learn to read. Reading is a multifaceted process of recognizing words and using letter sounds to decode language; audiobooks do not allow hearers the opportunity to make sense of the symbols on the page. Audiobooks are experienced as sounds and not as written language, making them unsuitable as a means for developing the ability to read.

Summary: Listening to audiobooks doesn't help children learn to read because it doesn't involve decoding symbols on the page.

Text 2

Audiobooks allow the sense of hearing to be used to recognize words. When students feel uncomfortable reading out loud, audiobooks can help them become better readers as they follow along on the page while the words are being spoken. In fact, some teachers are adding audiobook stations to their classrooms to encourage struggling readers who need an additional support system.

Summary: Listening to audiobooks helps children become better readers by engaging their sense of hearing to recognize words that they see on a page.

Summarizing the ideas of each text reveals their authors' contrasting claims about audiobooks. Thus, you can infer that the author of Text 2 would be likely to **disagree** with the argument of Text 1.

Compare the Details to Identify Similar or Contrasting Ideas

If the question asks about a specific detail, locate the relevant information in the first text and explain it in your own words. Then, look for a reference to the same detail in the second text and explain how it agrees or disagrees with the first.

Consider the example question below. The question texts will be presented later.

Example

Based on the texts, how would the curators (Text 2) most likely respond to the general belief presented in Text 1?

Given this question, look for a reference to a "general belief" in Text 1. After stating that belief in your own words, read Text 2 and look for information either agreeing or disagreeing with the idea from Text 1. Once you have that information, state in your own words how the "curators" in Text 2 would respond to the idea from Text 1.

Example

Text 1

Traditional drawings of the Continental Army during the American Revolutionary War highlight the lives of male soldiers, but few sketches exist showing the lives of women and children at that time. It is generally believed that women stayed at home because it was safer, performing tasks such as organizing fundraising drives, providing the troops with supplies, and nursing wounded soldiers.

Text 2

Curators at the Museum of the American Revolution assert that during the war, in defiance of regulations, women followed the men in wagons. In a recently discovered sketch, two female camp followers are shown—one holding an infant—in a wagon alongside the North Carolina Brigade's equipment. The sketch corroborates the statement of General George Washington, who complained that women and children slowed down his troops, calling them "a clog upon every movement."

Based on the texts, how would the curators (Text 2) most likely respond to the general belief presented in Text 1?

The "general belief" explained in Text 1 is that women remained at home during the Revolutionary War. Text 2 directly contradicts this idea by saying that the curators assert that women "followed the men in wagons." Since the information in Text 2 disagrees with Text 1, you might expect that the "curators" would respond to the belief presented in Text 1 **by arguing against the idea that women stayed at home during the war.**

Use the Process of Elimination

Read all the answer choices and look for anything that is inaccurate or not mentioned in the texts. Answers expressing ideas that conflict with the points of view stated in either text are incorrect because a correct answer will accurately reflect what is stated *in both texts*.

When any part of an answer is wrong, the entire answer is incorrect; eliminating wrong answers increases your odds of selecting the correct answer.

Example

Text 1

Audiobooks are the fastest growing book format in the world, but they shouldn't be relied on to help children learn to read. Reading is a multifaceted process of recognizing words and using letter sounds to decode language; audiobooks do not allow hearers the opportunity to make sense of the symbols on the page. Audiobooks are experienced as sounds and not as written language, making them unsuitable as a means for developing the ability to read.

Text 2

Audiobooks allow the sense of hearing to be used to recognize words. When students feel uncomfortable reading out loud, audiobooks can help them become better readers as they follow along on the page while the words are being spoken. In fact, some teachers are adding audiobook stations to their classrooms to encourage struggling readers who need an additional support system.

Based on the texts, how would the author of Text 2 most likely respond to the overall argument presented in Text 1?

A) By stating that hearing spoken words plays a more significant role in learning to read than the author of Text 1 acknowledges

B) By admitting that the author of Text 1 has identified a drawback that prevents audiobooks from being useful to children learning to read

C) By proposing that audiobooks get students excited about reading, a point that the author of Text 1 has failed to acknowledge

D) By concurring with the author of Text 1 that audiobooks don't allow students to see the spelling of unfamiliar words they might want to look up

Process of Elimination:

✓ **Choice A:** Text 2 mentions the benefits of both seeing and hearing as important in helping children learn to read, but the author of Text 1 dismisses the importance of hearing. Therefore, this answer accurately reflects the arguments of both authors.

✗ **Choice B:** This answer is inaccurate. Text 2 claims that audiobooks *do* help children learn to read, so its author wouldn't admit the opposite idea, that audiobooks don't help.

✗ **Choice C:** Text 2 doesn't mention whether audiobooks help get students excited about reading, so this answer is not supported by the text.

✗ **Choice D:** The texts don't discuss looking up words as a way for students to better understand what they are reading.

Practice

1. **Text 1**

The set of books that is commonly taught in classes across the country is referred to by literature scholars and English teachers as "the canon." Shakespeare's plays and classics such as *Of Mice and Men* figure prominently in the curriculum of most high schools nationwide. <u>But no new reading selections have been introduced, by and large, since the 1980s, so it is time to add more literature written in the last 50 years to the curriculum.</u> Literature study needs to include more diverse works to remain relevant to modern students.

Text 2

The "canon" of works studied in high school may not represent every student demographic, but it should be maintained because it instills a common culture by creating a national literary tradition. Despite the predominance of literature written before 1960 in school curricula, these classic literary works still capture the imagination of today's students. For instance, *To Kill a Mockingbird* and *The Great Gatsby* continue to be cited in online discussion forums as two of the best books read in high school.

Based on the texts, how would the author of Text 2 most likely respond to the underlined claim in Text 1?

A) By insisting that the "canon" is no longer relevant and by denying the suggestion that today's students enjoy reading traditional literary works

B) By admitting that contemporary students only read literature from the "canon" because it is required in their English classes

C) By stating that most English teachers could improve class engagement by offering more diverse literature selections instead of those found in the "canon"

D) By proposing that English teachers should continue to assign popular works from the "canon" rather than replacing traditional works entirely

See Appendix for answer

Things to Remember

- Identify what the question asks.
- Summarize each text.
- Compare the details to identify similar or contrasting ideas.
- Use the process of elimination.

Connections: Between Texts
Check for Understanding

1. **Text 1**

"Plasticity" refers to the human brain's ability to adapt to new experiences, like learning how to draw. But plasticity generally varies based on age, with the young usually having a greater ability than the elderly. Researchers are studying the connection between this mental adaptability and playing video games to better understand ways to enhance perception, memory, judgment, and reasoning. They are optimistic that this research will help the elderly and others who have weaknesses in these areas.

Text 2

Walter Boot and his team studied whether playing video games could help elderly adults combat cognitive declines associated with advancing age. They concluded that mental processing in elderly participants did not significantly improve, possibly because of a mismatch between the games that older adults enjoy playing and the types of games that result in the largest perceptual and cognitive gains. Additionally, Boot questions the extent to which a video game's platform affects mental improvement.

Based on the texts, how would the author of Text 2 most likely describe the view of the researchers presented in Text 1?

A) It is understandable given what Boot and his team discovered about the games played by different age groups.

B) It is overly enthusiastic given the additional research completed by Boot and his team.

C) It is predictable given that Boot and his team found decreases in cognitive decline for game players.

D) It is relatively discouraging given the findings that Boot and his team have reported.

2. **Text 1**

Evolutionary biologist David Jacobs conducted a study of rangeomorphs—prehistoric ocean-dwelling organisms that were among the earliest large organisms on Earth—to determine what competitive advantage they may have gained by growing up off the sea floor. Using simulations to model the flow of water through rangeomorph communities, he concluded that their size gave them a larger surface area to generate much greater "nutrient uptake."

Text 2

Earlier research concluded that increased size among rangeomorphs was driven by competition for nutrients. Researcher Emily Mitchell suggests that this conclusion fails to recognize that there were few competitors for resources in the nutrient-rich oceans. According to Mitchell, previous studies overlook the physical structure present in fossilized rangeomorphs that proves the organisms were not competing for food.

Based on the texts, how would Mitchell (Text 2) most likely characterize the conclusion presented in Text 1?

A) As surprising, because it is universally accepted that the size of rangeomorphs was directly related to their ability to obtain food

B) As incomplete, because researchers have only limited information to understand how the size of rangeomorphs influenced their chances of survival

C) As unfounded, because it fails to consider fossilized evidence and the unlikelihood of environmental competition

D) As confusing, because rangeomorph growth is difficult to simulate without accounting for ocean depth

Appendix

Practice and Check for Understanding Answers and Explanations

Standard English Conventions
Agreement: Pronouns

Practice

1.

> Plural subject
> Scientists use data visualizations to emphasize the significant results of
> Plural pronoun
> their studies....

Choice C is correct. To determine the right pronoun, ask who or what is emphasizing the results of the studies. The answer is "Scientists." Because "Scientists" is the plural noun being referred to by the pronoun, the answer should be the plural "their."

2.

> Plural noun phrase
> Masting...has been historically important for both animals and humans, who
> Verb / Infinitive / Plural reflexive pronoun
> depend on these sources to feed themselves.

Choice B is correct. The needed pronoun must function as an object of "to feed." The animals and humans are the ones being fed, so they are the object of "to feed." Because the subject and object of the infinitive "to feed" are the same plural noun, the correct answer must be the reflexive "themselves."

3.

> Singular antecedent / Singular pronoun
> ...forests can remove carbon from the air and store it in the trees....

Choice B is correct. To determine the correct pronoun, ask what is being stored by the trees. The answer is "carbon." Therefore, the correct object pronoun is the singular "it."

Check for Understanding

1. **Choice A** is correct. The plural "these animals" are the ones who may change where they go for food if wind turbines are installed, so the correct pronoun to refer to this plural noun phrase is "they."

2. **Choice D** is correct. The missing pronoun refers to who or what the food is hidden for, which is the subject of the sentence, "The chickadee." That subject is linked by "is" to "a bird," which is doing the hiding. Because "chickadee" and "bird" refer to the same thing and are both singular, the answer is the singular reflexive pronoun "itself."

3. **Choice A** is correct. Ask who is potentially going to experience a sugar crash: the answer is the participants who consume the drink. Because "participants" is a plural noun, the correct answer is the plural object pronoun "them."

Standard English Conventions
Agreement: Subject-Verb

Practice

1.

Singular subject — Interrupting participle phrase — Singular verb

The 1987 comedy film *Planes, Trains, & Automobiles* starring Steve Martin and John Candy tells the story of a businessman experiencing a variety of obstacles on his quest to get home so that he can spend Thanksgiving with his family.

Choice A is correct. The film's title is the subject, and its verb is the answer choice that correctly describes what the film does. The subject is separated from the blank by a participle phrase, which can be ignored when determining subject-verb agreement. Because *Trains, Planes, & Automobiles*, like all titles, is singular, the correct answer is the singular verb "tells."

2.

Singular subject — Prepositional phrase — Independent clause — Singular verb

...his limited use of equipment meant that an expensive investment in tools was not required.

Choice C is correct. Even though "tools" is a plural noun closest to the missing verb, it is part of a prepositional phrase beginning with "in." Instead, the subject of the "that" clause is the singular "investment." Therefore, the correct verb needs to be the singular "was."

3.

Plural noun — Plural verb

Water striders—tiny insects that walk on water and can go their entire lives without touching land—primarily inhabit humid, rainy regions.

Choice B is correct. "That," which begins the adjective clause, refers to the plural noun "insects." The plural verb that matches the plural noun is "walk."

4.

Singular subject — Singular verb

A research team who studied infants has found that an interest in socializing begins even before these babies develop language skills....

Choice D is correct. The dependent clause begins with "who" and refers to the singular "a research team." The only answer choice with a singular verb is "has found."

5.

Subject gerund		Singular verb	
...enjoying	mellow, sophisticated music	indicates	people....

Independent clause

Choice A is correct. The subject of the independent clause after the semicolon is the gerund "enjoying," so the verb that agrees with this subject must be the singular "indicates."

6.

Subject gerund — Singular verb

... viewing each person as someone with inherent worth is fundamental to numerous faith-based approaches concerning medical ethics.

Choice B is correct. The independent clause after the semicolon starts with "viewing," a gerund subject described as fundamental to numerous approaches. Because gerunds are always singular, the correct answer must be the singular "is" so that the subject and verb agree.

7.

Singular verb — Singular antecedent

...there is evidence showing that this type of aural therapy can decrease tension and fatigue....

Choice D is correct. The second independent clause that follows "and" begins with the pronoun "there" followed by the inverted antecedent "evidence," which is singular. Therefore, the correct verb is the singular "is."

8.

Prepositional phrase — Plural "be" verb — Plural subject

...among those who attend such assemblies are humanists who want to cultivate a sense of belonging and purpose.

Independent clause

Choice A is correct. After the semicolon is an independent clause that begins with a prepositional phrase. The clause's subject is the plural noun "humanists," referring to people who are among the ones who attend such gatherings. The only answer that offers a plural verb that would agree with this subject is "are."

Check for Understanding

1. **Choice D** is correct. Turgenev's novel is the subject exploring the tension, and book titles are always singular. The only third-person singular verb among the answer choices is "explore."

2. **Choice A** is correct. The inverted subject for the prepositional phrase "among those deemed somewhat successful" is the singular noun "construction." The only third-person singular answer choice is "was." For proof, note that if you reverse the order of subject and verb in the sentence, it would read, "The construction...*was* among those deemed somewhat successful."

3. **Choice C** is correct. The "that" clause describes the noun phrase "depressive symptoms," which is plural. The only plural verb offered as an answer choice is "are," making it correct.

4. **Choice C** is correct. Although the noun closest to the blank is the plural "theologians," it is the last of a list of four objects of the preposition "of." The subject of the missing verb is the singular "a group." The only third-person singular verb in the answer choices is "has taken," so it is the correct answer.

5. **Choice B** is correct. Because "eating " is the singular gerund subject of the sentence with the blank, the correct verb must be the only third-person singular one provided in the answer choices: "seems."

Standard English Conventions
Frequently Confused Words: Pronouns

Practice

1.

Singular noun Singular possessive pronoun

...as a patient's tumor and its position change.

Choice C is correct. The blank comes before the noun "position," so the missing word is likely a possessive pronoun. Ask who or what changes position. The answer is "the tumor." Therefore, the missing pronoun refers to the singular, nonhuman noun "tumor," and must be the singular "its."

2.

Plural noun

Research has found that individuals who focus on the immediate benefits

Plural possessive pronoun

rather than the delayed benefits of healthy habits increase their motivation.

Choice A is correct. The blank is followed by the noun "motivation," which is a clue that the blank requires the possessive form of the word. Because the blank refers to the plural "individuals" discussed earlier in the sentence, the plural possessive "their" is correct.

Check for Understanding

1. **Choice D** is correct. The blank precedes the noun phrase "varying colors," meaning that the desired word is probably possessive. In addition, the colors being referred to are the ones from the plural "bar codes" mentioned at the end of the previous sentence, so the correct pronoun is the plural possessive "Their."

2. **Choice B** is correct. The word in the blank comes before the noun "parts," so the correct word is likely possessive. The noun being referred to is the singular "ecosystem." Because "ecosystem" isn't a person, the singular "its" is the right answer.

Standard English Conventions
Parts of Speech: Verb Forms

Practice

1.

Subject Verb Infinitive = Adverb

Their observations led the two to discover that the sensation of taste helps pace the speed of eating.

Choice A is correct. The underlined verb form functions as an adverb that describes how or where the observations led the two scientists. Since an infinitive can function as an adverb, the correct answer is "to discover."

2.

Media scholars who research the online environment assert

Subject Main verb Indirect object Infinitive = Direct object

that various dangers require computer users to respond

Dependent clause

differently depending on the situation.

Choice D is correct. The needed verb form describes what is required. Because a direct object is needed to complete the sentence and because an infinitive can function in this way, "to respond" is correct.

3.

Subject Past participle

This settling, combined with a predicted sea level rise of between 20 and

Main verb

75 centimeters by 2025, further increases the city's vulnerability to flooding

Participle phrase

during coastal storms.

Choice C is correct. What follows "settling" must be something other than a main verb given that the sentence's main verb is "increases." Therefore, the first and last choices can be eliminated. Because "settling" can't have the intent to combine anything, the infinitive "to combine" is incorrect. That just leaves the past participle "combined," which is the correct answer.

4.

Main verb Noun Prepositional phase

"...it is rooted in a 2,500-year-old practice in which Athenian government

Present tense participle

officials were chosen from a pool of everyday citizens using a lottery system.

Choice B is correct. The needed word for the blank describes what the "practice" uses, so an adjective form is needed. Therefore, you can eliminate the verbs "used" in Choice A and "use" in Choice D. The practice can't have intent to use the lottery system, so the infinitive "to use" can be eliminated Instead, a present tense participle is needed to match "is," the sentence's present tense main verb.

Check for Understanding

1. **Choice B** is correct. Because the underlined segment functions as an adjective describing the noun "ability," the best choice is the infinitive "to provide."

2. **Choice D** is correct. The correct answer will be the object of the preposition "by." The only answer that can function this way is the gerund "positioning."

Standard English Conventions
Parts of Speech: Verbs

Practice

1.

Subject — Main verb

... the first known alphabet ever to exist was invented in ancient Egypt....

Independent clause

Choice B is correct. It is the only choice providing a main verb. The blank has to be filled with a main verb since it is preceded by a subject and no helping verb is provided. The other answers are either infinitives or participles, which can't be main verbs.

2.

Subject — Main verb

American pikas...gather bunches of wildflowers....

Choice A is correct. The subject is the plural "American pikas," and the only verb offered that would make the sentence complete is "gather." The others are either infinitives or participles, which can't be used as main verbs.

3.

...Gordon Parks is known for his photo essays highlighting social justice issues, which made an indelible impression on mid-20th century readers.

Main verb — Dependent clause

Choice D is correct. "Made" is the only answer choice that can be a main verb to complete the dependent clause. "Making" and "having made" both function as participles, and "to make" is an infinitive.

4.

Main verb

Recently, scientists discovered abundant fungi...that could hold the key for the development of new medicines.

Dependent clause

Choice C is correct. "Could hold" can function as a main verb in the dependent clause. "Having held" and "holding" are participles, and "to hold" is an infinitive, none of which can function as a main verb.

5. Past year / Past tense

> In 1832, Mexican army officers took all the pastries....

Choice C is correct. The year 1832 indicates the event being discussed occurred in the past. Because "took" is the only past tense verb, it is correct. "Have taken" is a present tense verb that indicates a completed action.

6. Past tense / Past tense

> Soubeyrand said she was unable to master the skill until she practiced for countless hours over the course of months to master this skill.

Choice D is correct. The past tense verb "was" indicates that what is being discussed happened in the past, making "practiced" the correct verb tense.

7. Past / Indicates a contrast / Present tense

> Previously the ink on these charred scrolls could not be read, but CT images and AI algorithms have allowed papyrologists to decode the text and gain a better understanding of these ancient documents.

Choice A is correct. The sentence begins by indicating that in the past the ink on the scrolls couldn't be read. The word "but" indicates a contrasting idea follows, which is that today's technology allows papyrologists to understand the text. Therefore, the present tense verb "have allowed" is needed.

Check for Understanding

1. **Choice D** is correct. Because the text discusses what "glycan structures" do in general, the correct answer is the present tense verb "store." The appositive phrase "networks...bonded together" is set off by commas, so although "bonded" seems to be in past tense, this participle does not determine the main verb of the subject.

2. **Choice B** is correct. The other answers are either participles or infinitives, which can't be main verbs. Because a main verb is needed to complete the independent clause that has "Environmentalists" as its subject, "want" is correct.

3. **Choice C** is correct. The year "1945" indicates that what is being described happened in the past, and "were working" is the only past tense verb offered as a choice.

4. **Choice A** is correct. The clause beginning with "that" requires a main verb. Because the other answers are either infinitives or present tense participles, the only verb that can complete the dependent clause is "reduced."

5. **Choice D** is correct. The first sentence's main verb is the present tense "has." Notice the first independent clause in the sentence with the blank has as its main verb the present tense "boasts." The second independent clause, with the subject "it," must be parallel to "boasts" because both clauses describe general situations that are always true. Therefore, the correct answer must be the present tense "lures."

Standard English Conventions
Punctuation: Apostrophes

Practice

1.

> Singular possessive
>
> The football coach for the University of Alabama encouraged the team's
>
> Plural noun
>
> veterans to lead by example.
>
> Apostrophe

Choice A is correct because it includes an apostrophe before the "s" for the singular possessive noun "team." A college team has more than one veteran player, so "veterans" is plural. Because there isn't a noun after "veterans" that can be possessed, "veterans" is possessive and shouldn't have an apostrophe added to it.

2.

> Plural possessive
>
> Possessed
>
> The technology expert scrutinized the salesmen's accounts
>
> and found no viruses.
>
> Apostrophe

Choice B is correct. An apostrophe is needed before the "s" because "salesmen" is a plural noun that doesn't end with an "s." The plural noun "accounts" doesn't have a noun after it that it possesses, so it should not have an apostrophe. This answer correctly includes an apostrophe before the "s" for the possessive noun (salesmen's) and doesn't add an apostrophe to "accounts," a plural noun that isn't possessive.

Check for Understanding

1. **Choice C** is correct. The phrase "several automobiles" indicates more than one car, so "cars" must be plural. Because cars have hoods, they would be considered the "hoods of the cars," revealing that "cars" is possessive. Because "a storm" indicates only one storm, this noun is singular. The "storm's fury" can be paraphrased as the "fury of the storm," so the noun "storm" is also possessive.

   Therefore, an apostrophe after the plural suffix "s" in "cars' hoods" correctly shows the noun "car" is plural possessive. An apostrophe plus "s" after "storm" correctly shows that this noun is singular possessive.

2. **Choice A** is correct. Because the first sentence refers to "a book," "book" is singular and should end with an apostrophe plus "s" because the book has many pages. The noun "pages" is followed by "are," but "pages" can't possess it because "are" is a verb, not a noun. Therefore, "pages" is not possessive, and no apostrophe should be added.

3. **Choice D** is correct. The sentence describes the eyes of the people, meaning the noun "people" is possessive. Because "people" is a plural noun that doesn't end in "s," an apostrophe plus "s" is needed. Eyes can't possess "widened" because "widened" isn't a noun and "widened of the eyes" doesn't make sense.

Standard English Conventions
Punctuation: Colons

Practice

1.

Independent clause 1

Savannah and Beau made a **big decision** when they were still in college: for

Explains

Independent clause 2

richer or poorer, they promised to love each other for life and **got married**

during their sophomore year.

Choice A is correct. Because the second independent clause explains what is stated in the first, a colon should go between them.

2.

Independent clause

During halftime, Coach Stevenson defined champions as those who played

Describes

Participle phrase

with "teamwork, tenacity, and total effort," claiming that these were the three

Comma

keys to victory.

Choice B is correct. A comma lets the participle phrase be joined to the independent clause while also setting it apart from the rest of the sentence for clarity about who is doing the "claiming." The other answers result in a fragment: "claiming…victory."

3.

Cause

Maya led the student council, participated in club soccer, and played for her

Cause and effect relationship

Result

Indicates effect

high school soccer team too. She didn't have much free time, as a result:

Explains

Comma

Colon

meetings, practices, games, and tournaments took up most of her evenings

and weekends.

Choice C is correct. Maya's lack of free time is a result of her participation in student council and soccer. Therefore, the conjunctive adverb "as a result" refers to the previous sentence (Maya…too) and indicates a cause-and-effect relationship. The activities described in the information after the conjunctive adverb explain the general idea of Maya not having much free time, so a colon is needed before the explanation that explains why. This means a colon is needed after "as a result" and before "meetings."

Check for Understanding

1. **Choice D** is correct. The sentence has two independent clauses: "At…disappointed" and ""in addition…unavailable." Because the second independent clause explains why people were disappointed, a colon should be placed after "disappointed" to show where the general statement ends and the additional information begins.

2. **Choice A** is correct. In Sentence 2, "He…diverse" is an independent clause stating the variety of pies. After the colon, the information explains how different they were by stating the wide range of pie types, from sweet to savory.

3. **Choice B** is correct. "Though" indicates a contrast and should be part of whichever sentence is in contrast to the one before it. The second sentence about job opportunities contrasts with the one before it about job losses. Therefore, "though" belongs at the end of Sentence 2. Sentences 2 and 3 do not contrast each other, so Choice C with "though" beginning the sentence cannot be correct.

Standard English Conventions
Punctuation: Commas

Practice

1.

Independent clause 1

Students in the theater program raised money to attend a competition in

Independent clause 2

Indianapolis, **and** they sold enough merchandise to cover all their expenses.

Choice A is correct. This answer has a comma between the independent clauses, "Students…Indianapolis" and "they…expenses." The comma is correctly placed before the FANBOYS "and," which precedes the second independent clause.

2.

Independent clause 1

The volleyball team promised to communicate better on the

Dependent clause

court, **but** when they played their next opponent, they didn't

Independent clause 2 — Dependent clause

talk to each other enough, which resulted in costly mistakes.

Choice C is correct. This answer properly includes a comma before the FANBOYS conjunction "but" that is needed to join independent clause 1 with the dependent clause following it.

3.

Independent clause 1

Some students enrolled in education courses, completed a semester of

Conjunctive adverb

student teaching, and became certified by the state to teach; consequently,

Semicolon Comma

Independent clause 2

most certified teachers were better prepared for the classroom than

uncertified educators.

Choice B is correct. The two independent clauses are joined by a semicolon, and a comma is correctly placed after the conjunctive adverb. "Consequently" belongs in the second independent clause because it refers to the outcome described in that clause—certified teachers are better prepared for success.

4.

Independent clause

Salvation Army workers decided to ring bells and collect charitable

Transition Participle phrase

donations, however, believing that funds for the poor were more important

Comma Comma

than their own discomfort.

Choice C is correct. The mid-sentence transition "however" has a comma before and after it. Choice D is incorrect because the information after the semicolon doesn't express a complete thought.

5.

Renames Nonessential appositive

John watched his boss, a micromanager, harshly

Comma Comma

criticize another worker in his department.

Choice A is correct because it includes commas before and after the mid-sentence nonessential appositive (a micromanager).

6.

When taking a walk, my neighbors used a leash to restrain their

Renames

Noun Noun

energetic dog, an Irish Wolfhound with fur the color of charcoal.

Nonessential appositive

Choice C is correct because it includes a comma before the appositive phrase "an Irish...charcoal" that comes at the end of the sentence and renames "dog."

7.

Describes
Noun — Participle phrase

The teacher split the students into several groups, assigning each a different part of the unit to present to the class.

Choice C is correct. The participle phrase "assigning…class" refers to the "teacher," but the phrase doesn't come immediately after the noun it describes. Therefore, a comma is needed before the participle phrase at the end of the sentence.

8.

Describes
Noun — Participle phrase

The competition required physics students to create a container protecting raw eggs from breaking after a 25-foot drop.

Choice B is correct. The participle phrase "protecting…drop" comes immediately after the noun it describes, so a comma is not included before the phrase.

9.

Introductory dependent clause

When Carlota and Juan compared their semester schedules,

Independent clause — Comma

they discovered that they had three classes together.

Choice D is correct. A comma is properly included after the introductory dependent clause (When…schedules).

10.

Describes
Introductory participle phrase — Noun

Escaping the violence in their home country, the refugees were relieved to be welcomed by the Red Cross team.

Independent clause

Choice D is correct. Because the participle phrase (Escaping… country) is introductory and comes before the independent clause, a comma should follow the dependent clause.

11.

Independent clause

…For example, the chocolates and soft candy were all displayed in a long

Subordinating conjunction — Dependent clause

glass case, while the hard candy was displayed in racks on another wall.

Comma

Choice A is correct. The subordinating conjunction "while" begins a concluding dependent clause, so a comma is needed before it.

Check for Understanding

1. **Choice B** is correct. The sentence has two independent clauses, ("The manufacturer's...expectations" and "the car's...declined") that are joined by a FANBOYS conjunction "but," so a comma is needed before the conjunction.

2. **Choice D** is correct. "The conjunctive adverb "though" is placed mid-sentence as an interruption that explains how Joel stayed was able to remain happy. Because "though" is placed in the middle of the independent clause "He...goals," it should be set apart with commas.

3. **Choice A** is correct. The nonessential appositive phrase (a singular...university) describes the noun "passion," so a comma should come before the appositive phrase to set it apart from the previous information.

4. **Choice B** is correct. The participle phrase "arguing...understood" doesn't come immediately after the noun it describes ("man"), so a comma should come before it.

5. **Choice B** is correct. "A poetic... Elizabethan age " is an appositive phrase renaming the noun "*Macbeth*." A comma is needed after this introductory information to set it apart from the independent clause.

6. **Choice D** is correct. The sentence concludes with an appositive ("the slapdash...sell") that describes the noun "paintings." Placed after the independent clause, a comma separates the concluding information from the previous clause.

Standard English Conventions
Punctuation: Commas + Semicolons

Practice

1.

Idea 1 · Points back · Conjunctive adverb · Idea 2

The band teacher enjoyed jazz the most; as a result, he had a large record collection that included his favorites—recordings by Jelly Roll Morton, Ella Fitzgerald, Duke Ellington, and Louis Armstrong.

Choice C is correct. The phrase "as a result" refers to the first idea, so the conjunctive adverb should follow the semicolon and precede the comma.

2.

Idea 1 · Idea 2 · Refers to · Conjunctive adverb · Idea 3

Lei Lei **smiled** and **laughed** during the party yesterday, **happy** to socialize with everyone. Her **pleasure** didn't last long, though; Corey, the boy she was attracted to, arrived late and ignored her throughout the evening.

Choice D is correct. "Her pleasure...long" points back to the first sentence because there is a contrast between Lei Lei's experience before and after Corey's arrival. Therefore, "though" must appear in the first clause in its sentence so that it can refer to the previous sentence, which means it must go before the semicolon but after a comma.

Check for Understanding

1. **Choice A** is correct. The second sentence ("Its jurisdiction…city") has two independent clauses that must have a semicolon to join them because the answers don't include any FANBOYS conjunctions. A semicolon should be placed before the phrase "for example" to include this conjunctive adverb with the second idea ("the BLC…city") that points back to a preceding idea ("Its jurisdiction…functions"). A comma is also needed after "for example."

2. **Choice D** is correct. The first sentence explains Regan's responsibilities, while the second sentence presents a contrast, telling what Regan isn't responsible for. "However" indicates a contrast to previous information; therefore, a semicolon after "however" correctly places the conjunctive adverb in the clause that refers to previous information. In addition, a comma correctly precedes the conjunctive adverb.

Standard English Conventions
Punctuation: End Marks

Practice

1.

Dependent clause — Direct question

When you sleep, do you snore? We want to know if earplugs will be needed.

Question mark

Choice A is correct because it ends a direct question with a question mark. Notice that the verb "do" is before the subject "you" and that the idea of wanting "to know" in Sentence 2 suggests that Sentence 1 includes a direct question.

2.

Direct question

If we have the cash to fund it, will this proposal solve the problem? The CEO wants to know if we have an effective plan.

Correct

Choice B is correct because it ends with a question mark and the verb "will" is before the subject "proposal." Stating that the CEO "wants to know" if the plan" would be effective in Sentence 2 indicates that Sentence 1 raised a question that hasn't been answered yet.

3.

Helping verb — Subject — Main verb — Independent clause

Would the topic meet the professor's criteria? The students needed to find out.

Direct question — Question mark

Choice C is correct because it places a question mark at the end of a direct question. In questions, the helping verb is placed before the subject. The helping verb precedes the subject and "Would" is a question word beginning the sentence.

4.

Independent clause 1 — Participle phrase

Carmen drove up in her 2023 Chevy Corvette Z06. Equipped with a powerful

Independent clause 2 — Describes

engine, the car went from 0 to 60 mph in 2.6 seconds.

Choice D is correct. The first clause is about Carmen arriving in her car. The second clause provides detail about the car's speed. Because "equipped" begins the participle phrase that describes the "car," the phrase belongs the second independent clause. Choices A, B, and C all create run-on sentences.

5.

Independent clause 1 — Prepositional phrase

Dominka's interrogation was rude and intrusive. During the interview, Gregorij

Independent clause 2 — Describes

was surprised at her disrespect and refused to respond to any more questions.

Choice B is correct. The first clause is about Dominka's behavior. The second clause describes Gregorij's surprise. Each can stand alone as a sentence, so they are independent clauses that are separated by a period. Choices A and C create run-ons, and choice D lacks a comma needed before the FANBOYS conjunction "so."

Check for Understanding

1. **Choice D** is correct. This answer begins the direct question with "would" after the introductory dependent clause ("If…week) and ends with a question mark. Notice the reversed order with the helping verb "would" before the subject "the grass," which indicates a direct question. Choice B is wrong because the next sentence "We…out" provides a clue that a question is being asked.

2. **Choice A** is correct. An essential participle phrase "discovered…are" follows the independent clause "Scientists…tracks." The other choices can be eliminated because they are not grammatical. Choices B and C create a fragment after the semicolon, and Choice D lacks the comma needed before the FANBOYS conjunction "and."

3. **Choice D** is correct. A period is needed between the independent clauses "The suburban…congestion" and "In the…drivers." The prepositional phrase "In the downtown area" describes the where the construction work occurs, so the phrase belongs with the second independent clause. Choices A and B create run-ons, and Choice C incorrectly adds the FANBOYS "but" after the semicolon.

4. **Choice B** is correct. Only this answer avoids a run-on sentence by inserting a period between the two independent clauses. The comma after "construction" indicates the prepositional phrases "within…construction" refers to the collapsing balconies and belongs in the second sentence.

5. **Choice C** is correct. A period after "city" correctly separates the independent clauses and keeps the participle phrase "Having…walkways" with the independent clause containing "the dark streets" that it describes.

Standard English Conventions
Punctuation: Dashes

Practice

1.

Interruption

There were two wild animals, a coyote and a bobcat, that were often on our property.

Comma   Comma

Choice C is correct. Matching punctuation (two commas) separates the interruption from the rest of the sentence.

2.

Interruption

Winston loved his new car—a fully loaded Jaguar—and wouldn't allow any food or drink inside it.

Dash   Dash

Choice C is correct. Matching punctuation (two dashes) separates the interruption from the rest of the sentence.

Check for Understanding

1. **Choice B** is correct because the interrupting information concludes with a dash after "*storm*" to show where the interruption ends; therefore, it must also have a dash after "*Dark*" to show where the interruption begins.

2. **Choice D** is correct because a comma is included before the interrupting information that begins with "including," and the answer needs a matching comma after "vinegar" to set the interruption apart from the rest of the sentence.

Standard English Conventions
Punctuation: Semicolons

Practice

1.

Independent Clause   Infinitive phrase

Dagobert and Reginald walked through the forest to search for leprechauns, ogres, and trolls.

Choice D is correct. The sentence has only one independent clause, which concludes with an infinitive phrase. Whenever an independent cause concludes with an infinitive phrase, no punctuation is used to separate them.

2.

Independent clause 1   Independent clause 2

My twin brothers care for each other and seem inseparable; I wish I had a twin.

Choice A is correct. The two independent clauses require separation, which must be with a semicolon, not a comma. Choice C is incorrect because the FANBOYS conjunction "so" turns the second independent clause into a dependent clause.

3.

Independent clause 1

Jimmy said the movie had puzzling challenges and an intriguing plot; Jonathan

Independent clause 2

and Tim decided to watch something else.

Choice C is correct. The two independent clauses are joined by a semicolon. Choice A has a semicolon, but it adds a FANBOYS conjunction.

4.

Independent clause 1

In 2022, Graciela and Pedro were married in the city's cathedral; in 2023, they

Independent clause 2 — Semicolon

celebrated the birth of their first child, Horacio.

Choice C is correct. "Graciela and Pedro" is the subject and "were married" the main verb in the first clause. The subject of the second clause is "they" and the verb is "celebrated." A semicolon between the two independent clauses correctly joins them. Choice A is incorrect because it adds the FANBOYS "and" after the semicolon.

5.

Independent clause 1

Aaron and Sue reduced the number of organized activities chosen by their

Describes preceding idea — Conjunctive adverb — Independent clause 2

nine-year-old daughter; consequently, the whole family found the free time

Semicolon — Comma

added to their new schedule delightfully liberating.

Choice D is correct because it uses a semicolon between independent clauses, and because it places the adverb after the semicolon so that the adverb belongs to the second clause while pointing to the first clause.

6.

Previous sentence — Independent clause 1

The restaurant's food was bland, and service wasn't the best. Xavier will eat

Conjunctive adverb — Refers to — Independent clause 2

there again, though; his parents own it, and he works with them as part of

the family business.

Choice C is correct. The conjunctive adverb "though" refers to the previous sentence, so it belongs in the clause "Xavier…again." The semicolon correctly separates the 2 independent clauses.

7.

Independent clause

The elderly military veteran respectfully placed his hand on his heart when the

Dependent clause — No punctuation

national anthem was sung.

Choice B is correct. The sentence begins with an independent clause, "The elderly… his heart," which could stand by itself as a grammatical sentence. It is followed by a dependent clause, "when…sung," which can't stand by itself as a grammatical sentence because of the conjunctive adverb "when."

8\.

Independent clause 1 | Conjunctive adverb | Introduces

Blanche seemed unable to control her buying impulses; for example, she went

Independent clause 2

to the store for a blouse but came home with 4 large bags of new clothes.

Choice A is correct. The two independent clauses are correctly separated by a semicolon. The conjunctive adverb "for example" belongs in the second independent clause because it builds on the idea in the first clause, indicating an example of that idea.

9\.

Item 1

Batman fought crimes perpetrated by the Riddler, who planned a bank heist;

Semicolon

Item 2 | Item 3

Poison Ivy, who was capable of mind control; and Scarecrow, who had

Semicolon

released fear toxin in Gotham.

Choice A is correct because it separates the list's first item from the second with a semicolon to avoid confusion with the commas within each item.

10\.

Ignacio decided on a road trip to visit several places on his bucket list,

Item 1 | Item 2

including Santa Fe, New Mexico, in 2020; Dallas, Texas, in 2021; and

Item 3 | Semicolon | Semicolon

Gulf Shores, Alabama, in 2023.

Choice B is correct. The complex list includes items containing commas, so semicolons provide clarity between each item. The first item ends with a semicolon after "2020," which is a clue that a semicolon should also be used after "2021."

Check for Understanding

1. **Choice C** is correct. A semicolon joins the independent clauses that describe the two sides of the coin. In the first, the subject is "One side" and the verb is "features." In the second, the subject is "the other side" and the verb is "shows." Choice B also includes a semicolon, so it shouldn't be followed by a FANBOYS conjunction such as "and."

2. **Choice B** is correct. The sentence lists three purposes of the named gardens. Because a semicolon separates the last two items listed after the blank ("plants; and"), a matching semicolon should be included in the blank after the first item. Choice C is incorrect because "both locally and worldwide" must describe "promoting," not "educating."

3. **Choice B** is correct. The sentence includes a list of games with descriptive information (such as "a digitized...habitats") about each game. Because the list items contain commas, semicolons should be used between the items to clarify which game belongs with which description.

4. **Choice D** is correct. The sentence has two independent clauses: "To her friends...herself" and "she...her boyfriend." They should be joined with a semicolon. The conjunctive adverb "however" describes the contrast between the preceding idea about how Yukina seemed ("cold and distant") and the idea of how she truly felt ("exhausted and...drained"). Therefore, "however" should be included in the second independent clause.

Standard English Conventions
Punctuation: Unnecessary

Practice

1. In her popular book *The House on Mango Street*, Sandra Cisneros includes a series of short, descriptive sketches of things taking place over the course

   Plural noun

   of a year that reveal the significant experiences of Esperanza Cordero, a 12-year-old Mexican American girl.

   Choice C is correct. Because "experiences" ends with an "s" and is followed by the preposition "of," it is plural but not possessive. Therefore, apostrophes should not be included either before or after the "s." An apostrophe should not be used with the singular noun "Cordero" because it doesn't have another noun after it to possess.

2. On Gordon Ramsay's television show *Hell's Kitchen*, when two or three

   Plural possessive Possessed

   contestants' mistakes are spotted, the famous chef often responds with explosive outbursts.

   Choice D is correct. The phrase "two or three" indicates more than one contestant is in Hell's Kitchen, so "contestants" and their "mistakes" are plural nouns. Because "contestants" ends with an "s," an apostrophe is needed after it to indicate that the mistakes belong to them.

3. Object 1 Object 2 Object 3

   On Wolfgang's final exams in English, Spanish, and Introduction to

   Prepositional phrase

   Philosophy, he performed better than others in class by focusing intently on taking good notes and reviewing them each day.

   Choice A is correct. The prepositional phrase "in…Philosophy" has a compound object ("English," "Spanish," and "Introduction to Philosophy"). Punctuation shouldn't come between a preposition and its objects.

4. After finishing dinner and washing the family's dishes, Cletis expressed his

   Prepositional phrase

   concern about "strolling to the cave," which is how he describes walking down

   No punctuation

   the rickety steps to his basement office.

   Choice C is correct because it doesn't add punctuation between the preposition (about) and its object ("strolling to the cave").

5.

Independent clause
As Eunice helped to organize the small home, she put things her mom used
Subordinating conjunction
Dependent clause
frequently in convenient places where they might be easily accessible, and
No punctuation
anything not used in the last year was donated or thrown out.

Choice B is correct. This answer doesn't add unnecessary punctuation before the dependent clause that follows an independent clause.

6.

Both Jack Brown, an attorney for the husband seeking divorce, and Gladys
Independent clause
Knight, an attorney for the wife, objected to the judge's decision. Together they
Dependent clause
filed a Motion for Reconsideration that encouraged the judge to take a second
look at the decision.
No punctuation

Choice B is correct. No punctuation should come between a dependent clause and the preceding independent clause. Choice D is incorrect because it lacks the subordinating conjunction "that," which begins the dependent clause describing the motion.

7.

Subject 1 Interrupting appositive Main verb 1
Craving the Cold, a psychological thriller, creates an intense, "edge of your
Correct Correct Subject 2 Main verb 2
seat" movie experience, whereas *Escaping the Heat* offers a slowly paced
No punctuation
drama about prison life.

Choice D is correct. The name of the first movie is a subject noun followed by a comma because it sets apart the appositive after it from the rest of the sentence. However, the second movie isn't followed by an appositive, so no punctuation should come between the noun "*Heat*" and the verb "offers."

8.

Last year, sophomore student Cameron Mackery, who had never performed
Noun
in a theater production before, earned a supporting role in the school play
Restrictive appositive Identifies
Our Town and received high praise for his acting, increasing his confidence
No comma No comma
that he might be given a starring role this year.

Choice D is correct. The name of the play identifies which play Cameron Mackery got a supporting role in, so "*Our Town*" is a restrictive appositive. Therefore, commas are not placed before or after the appositive.

9\. In 1971, Mexican American singer Selena Quintanilla was born in Texas, a state known for producing talented musicians, and was so successful that she was called the Queen of Tejana Music.

Noun

Nonrestrictive appositive

Describes

Choice A is correct. The appositive "a state...musicians" provides bonus information that isn't needed for the meaning of the sentence to be clear. This nonrestrictive appositive, therefore, should have commas before and after it.

Check for Understanding

1. **Choice C** is correct. The two nouns that begin and end the answer choices are not immediately followed by another noun that they can possess. The first noun, "accounts," is followed by the preposition "of," and "workers" is followed by a comma and the participle "explaining."

2. **Choice B** is correct. No punctuation should come between the preposition "with" and its object, which is the gerund "finding" that begins the quotation. Because a gerund functions as a noun, it can be an object of a preposition. The comma after "stressful" at the end of the quote follows the rule about adding a comma before or after forms of the word "say" when used in conjunction with a quotation, but this has no bearing on the preposition and its object.

3. **Choice C** is correct. "Carolyn Ruth Bertozzi" is an appositive that identifies the American chemist who won the Nobel Prize in chemistry in 2022. Because many people could be called "American chemist," Bertozzi's name is not offset by commas because "American chemist" must be restricted to her. Furthermore, "American chemist" is not itself an appositive that can be offset with commas, and it is incorrect to use exactly one comma between a subject and its verb.

4. **Choice A** is correct. No punctuation should come between the dependent clause "when...colonize" at the end of the text and the independent clause that precedes it.

5. **Choice A** is correct. In the second sentence, a comma is placed between the first subject *Eats, Shoots, and Leaves* and its verb ("is") because an interrupting transition ("for example") must be set apart by two commas. However, the next clause doesn't include an interrupting transition after the subject. Therefore, no punctuation should be placed between the subject *The Girl's Like Spaghetti* and its verb, "focuses."

Standard English Conventions
Sentence Structure: Modifiers

Practice

1.

> Performing before an audience caused many students to be nervous
> Descriptive phrase
> and concerned about mistakes. Despite the positive feedback from his
> Noun Describes
> parents, Stefon Washington claimed that more practice would be
> needed for his next concert.

Choice A is correct. The introductory descriptive phrase refers to a person with parents, so "Stefon Washington" is the noun that should immediately follow that phrase. Choices B, C, and D incorrectly make the descriptive phrase refer to "claim," "practice," and "statement," but none of these can perform.

2.

> Enemies for the last twenty years, the villagers and the elves continued
> fighting despite both sides losing many great warriors and suffering
> Descriptive phrase
> deprivation caused by the ongoing clashes. After defeating the ogres in
> Noun Describes
> the winter, Finnegan resumed his fight against the elves.

Choice D is correct. The one who defeated the ogres was Finnegan, so that noun is correctly placed immediately after the introductory description.

3.

> Mexican American Ignacio Rodriguez was a popular student at his high school
> Descriptive phrase
> in Corpus Christi, Texas. Voted as Most Likely to Succeed by his senior class,
> Noun Describes
> Ignacio willingly helped others with homework and difficult math concepts,
> which inspired his peers to like, respect, and admire him.

Choice C is correct. The descriptive phrase refers to Ignacio, so that noun must immediately follow that introductory phrase. Choice A is incorrect because "Ignacio's" is possessive and functions as an adjective, which would inaccurately state that his "willingness" was the thing that was considered likely to succeed.

4.

Hamilton is a highly acclaimed musical created by Lin-Manuel Miranda that premiered Off-Broadway in 2015. Based on the biography by Ron Chernow, *Hamilton* covers the life of Alexander Hamilton, a founding father of the United States who fought in the American Revolutionary War and died after being shot in a duel with Aaron Burr.

Descriptive phrase — Describes — Noun

Choice A is correct. Because what was based on Chernow's book is the musical, the noun Hamilton should immediately follow the descriptive phrase "Based on...Chernow."

Check for Understanding

1. **Choice C** is correct. The introductory phrase "Depicting...submersible" begins with the word "depicting," which means showing something with a picture, movie, or performance. Because it is the dance drama *10,909* that depicts what the Chinese researchers did, the first noun after the introductory phrase should be *10,909*.

2. **Choice B** is correct. The introductory phrase "Although...coach" describes someone who was put on the bench instead of being allowed to play. Therefore, the noun "Hurts" should be placed immediately after the introductory phrase that describes his benching. Choice C is incorrect because the possessive noun (Hurts') functions as an adjective, making "career" the first noun after the introductory phrase. However, it was Hurts, not his career, that was benched by the coach, so "career" shouldn't be the first noun to follow the introductory phrase describing what happened to Hurts.

3. **Choice D** is correct. The introductory phrase "In evaluating...2009" describes a person because "evaluating" is an action performed by people; "evaluating" cannot be performed by "Cameron's use," "there are," or "the focus." Therefore, the first noun after the introductory phrase should be "viewers," who are the ones who can evaluate films.

4. **Choice C** is correct. The introductory participle phrase "Distinguished...Surgery" describes Alexa Canady, so the noun "Canady" should be placed immediately after the phrase modifying it. Choices A, B, and D are incorrect because they don't place "Canady" immediately after the introductory phrase.

Standard English Conventions
Sentence Structure: Parallel

Practice

1.

In addition to teaching history at Central High School during the academic year, Anne would also volunteer at a soup kitchen **and** (would) attempt to learn Spanish.

Verb — Understood — Verb

Choice B is correct. Two actions are joined by the conjunction "and." Because "volunteer" follows the helping verb "would," the verb "attempt" must work the same. The helping verb "would" before "attempt" is understood.

2.

Verb 1

When I travel to England, I plan on attending a professional soccer

Verb 2

match at the stadium **or** viewing a soccer game on television with the local people because I don't want to spend the entire time visiting museums and monuments.

Choice A is correct. The conjunction "or" joins two verbs. Because the first verb "attending" is an -ing verb, the second verb should also be an -ing verb.

Check for Understanding

1. **Choice D** is correct. To create parallel structure, the two actions that resulted from Moore's promotion of community engagement should be expressed with the same verb form. Therefore, the verbs "assist" and "give," which are joined by the FANBOYS conjunction "and," should match in tense. The helping verb "would" before "give" is understood and matches the parallel verb phrase, "would assist."

2. **Choice B** is correct. The FANBOYS conjunction "or" connects two things that Coeli became interested in. Because the first idea that follows the preposition "in" is the –ing verb "working," the –ing verb "providing" should be placed after "by" to create parallel structure. The correct verb forms are similarly structured: "in working" and "by providing."

Expression of Ideas
Synthesis: Notes

Practice

1. **Choice C** is correct. The goal is to describe the artwork *Autumn Surf* to an audience **unfamiliar** with Sam Gilliam. Thus, the answer must give information about the artwork as well as background information about the artist. Choice A does not give any information about the artist, Choice B focuses on the artist but doesn't describe the artwork, and Choice D focuses on Gilliam's *Drape* paintings in general, instead of *Autumn Surf* specifically. Choice C describes relevant details about the artwork and introduces Gilliam as an "American abstract artist," so this choice fulfills the goal.

Check for Understanding

1. **Choice D** is correct. The goal is to emphasize the aim of the research study, so the answer must focus on what the researchers were trying to learn. The phrase "because they wanted to know" in Choice D introduces the researchers' aim of understanding how the expansion of West Nile virus relates to climate change, so this is the correct answer.

2. **Choice C** is correct. The goal is to explain an advantage of induction stoves. Choice C fulfills this goal by indicating that induction stoves have a smaller risk of burns than traditional electric stoves do. Although Choice B indicates that induction stoves avoid a problem of electric stoves, it does not specify what that problem is or how induction avoids it, so it does not adequately explain an advantage.

3. **Choice A** is correct. The goal is to introduce 1001 Pages to an audience unfamiliar with the artwork and its artist. Therefore, the answer must provide information about the artwork and also give background information about the artist. Choice A satisfies those requirements by introducing Amighi as an "Iranian-born American artist" and the "award-winning" artwork as featuring "intricate, hand-cut designs inspired by Iran's Islamic past and present."

Expression of Ideas
Transitions: Conjunctive Adverbs

Practice

1.

Indicates contrast

...while students have traditionally taken AP courses in high school to

Idea 1 Increase

gain college credit, evidence indicates that more students are choosing a

Indicates contrast

different option. Increasingly, students are enrolling in dual credit courses

Idea 2

to gain both high school and college credit—a trend shown by a significant

Increase

rise in dual credit...

Choice B is correct. The sentences before and after the blank discuss how "more students" are choosing dual credit courses with a "significant rise" in that enrollment. The words "rise" and "more" indicate an increase, a clue that the correct transition is "increasingly."

2.

Most insect species in the Arthropoda phylum of animals are oviparous.

Contrast

That is, they lay eggs that hatch outside of their bodies. However, not all

Idea 1 Example

species of Arthropoda are oviparous. Scorpions, for example, produce

Idea 2

eggs that hatch within the mother's body.

Choice A is correct. Sentence 3 introduces an idea that some insects don't hatch eggs outside of their bodies, which contrasts with the previous information. The final sentence supports the contrasting idea with an example of scorpions that hatch eggs inside their bodies.

3.

Claim

...Robert Frost creates meditative poems inspired by a person, object, or

Example 1

event. His poem "The Road Not Taken" centers on a fork in a woodland

Example 2

path that sparks reflection about life's journey. Similarly, Frost's poem "Birches" describes trees bent over by ice that leads to contemplation...

Choice C is correct. Two examples support the claim by describing experiences with nature that are similar. A woodland path and birch trees both inspire the speaker to think deeply in a meditation on how those experiences connect to life.

Check for Understanding

1. **Choice A** is correct. Using the past tense verb "uncovered," sentence 2 explains how researchers searched for kivas in "years past." With the verbs "are helped" and "detect," Sentence 3 describes new technology currently used by researchers. The logical transition connecting a present action to past methods is "Currently."

2. **Choice D** is correct. Sentences 1 and 2 explain geckos' setae, a feature that gives them the ability to adhere to a surface. Sentence 3 states that because of their setae, geckos can climb most surfaces. Because the final sentence explains the effect caused by the idea expressed in the previous sentences, the answer "Consequently," logically connects the two ideas.

3. **Choice D** is correct. Sentence 1 makes two claims about the Blemmyes people: they worshipped Egyptian gods, and they also practiced a unique ritual. Sentence 2 begins with "First" and provides one piece of evidence about their worship of Egyptian gods. Because Sentence 3 provides another piece of evidence, "Second" is the most logical transition between the sentences.

4. **Choice C** is correct. The sentence before the blank states that a septic tank can be installed when a sewer system isn't available. The sentence after the blank describes a different way that waste can be disposed of—placing it in a compost pit. The sentences discuss different alternatives, making "Alternatively" The best transition.

5. **Choice B** is correct. Sentence 1 is a general statement about how some writers have combined poetry and plays. The next sentence discusses Shakespeare's Hamlet as a specific work that includes poetry in a play. Because Sentence 2 provides an example of what is described in Sentence 1, "for instance," is the best transition to connect those ideas.

Information and Ideas
Evidence: Nonfiction

Practice

1. **Question:** Asks about weakening a claim

   Located claim: Found in first sentence of the text: "political candidates...claim that these civil servants contribute to the inefficiencies of [government]."

   Answer Summaries and Process of Elimination:
   Choice A: Government employees confessed that their position's benefits and job security were important factors for why they chose their jobs. This information doesn't show that they are effective in those careers.
   Choice B: Government workers have time off to reduce their stress when Congress shuts down their jobs due to a lack of money. This answer doesn't say whether these workers are productive.
   Choice D: Government workers didn't follow presidential orders if they were part of a different political party. This answer would support, instead of weaken, the claim about civil servants not being efficient.

   Choice C: Leaders of some government organizations carried out plans to make work performance more efficient so that they could be better at serving people. Because this is the opposite idea of civil servants being inefficient, this answer is the only one that would weaken the claim.

2.

Question: Asks for a response to support the researchers' explanation

Located claim: Found in last sentence of the text stating that researchers believed that more people living in cities requires greater cooperation because it helps everyone.

Answer Summaries and Process of Elimination:
Choice B: Using public transportation to explore new places isn't related to cooperating with strangers.
Choice C: Being someone who supports the subway system and uses it regularly is unrelated to the idea of social cooperation.
Choice D: Saving money and being healthier are individual benefits, not the benefits of collaboration.

Choice A: Because this response indicates that both the person riding the bus and the driver of the bus benefited from their interaction, this quotation would support the researchers' explanation that when strangers cooperate, everyone is better off.

Check for Understanding

1. **Choice D** is correct. The last sentence of the text states that the researchers hypothesized that combining h-BN with c-BN would result in a material that could withstand heat. Because this answer indicates that the combination of the two compounds was used to manage overheating, it supports the researchers' hypothesis.

2. **Choice B** is correct. Atkins-Weltman and Snively asserted that more dinosaur species could be discovered by looking closely at fossils in museums and changing the classification if they are incorrect. One way to weaken this assertion would be to analyze the categorized fossils, only to discover that they have been classified correctly.

Information and Ideas
Evidence: Novel and Short Story

Practice

1.

Claim Paraphrase: Alice has lost a part of herself that she previously had before her marriages.

Answer Choice Summary:

Choice A: Waythorn realizes that women have more difficulty than men in letting go of their pasts.

Choice C: Waythorn imagines how Alice looked and acted in a past life.

Choice D: Waythorn notices that even though Alice looks pretty, she isn't smiling and looks more worried than he has ever seen her be before.

Choice B is correct. The claim asks for lines that show Alice has given up something during each of her marriages. This answer lists all of her married names and indicates that she has given up her privacy, personality, and inner self as a result of each of her marriages.

2. **Claim's Paraphrase:** Alymer says or does something to show that he doesn't like how Georgiana looks.

Process of Elimination:

Choice A: This quotation discusses Aylmer's realization that he is troubled and will do anything to find peace, but it doesn't say that the reason he is upset is because of Georgiana's appearance.

Choice B: This quotation describes how he watches his wife and believes he can protect her from harm; it doesn't mention how he feels about his wife's looks.

Choice C: This quotation says that Aylmer is using his science knowledge to calm down Georgiana, but it doesn't mention that he is upset with how she looks.

Choice D is correct. The claim asks for lines that show that there is something about Georgiana's looks that Aylmer doesn't like. This answer mentions a "frightful" birthmark that causes Aylmer "horror." Therefore, this quotation illustrates the claim that Aylmer has a negative view of his wife's appearance.

Check for Understanding

1. **Choice B** is correct. This quotation mentions Winterbourne not having associated with women who are flirts, which he believes Daisy to be. Because it fulfills the criteria about Winterbourne being "unaccustomed to women like Daisy" asked for in the claim, this quotation is the correct answer.

2. **Choice A** is correct. In this quotation, the narrator states that another character is being disrespectful by making negative comments about Harvey Merrick, a person who couldn't be corrupted or limited by others. Because this quotation expresses the narrator's disapproval, it meets the claim's criteria and is the correct answer.

Information and Ideas
Evidence: Play

Practice

1.

Claim: Higgins is confident he can change Eliza from a working-class girl to an upper-class lady.

Formulated Answer: Higgins speaks confidently about how he will change Eliza.

Summary and Process of Elimination:

Choice B: Higgins admits that as a teacher, he will be hard on Eliza, which is information unrelated to the claim.

Choice C: Higgins explains to his friend how men and women bring each other down, but this answer doesn't address how confident Higgins is.

Choice D: Higgins tells Eliza's father that it was her idea to learn to speak better, an assertion unrelated to Higgins' abilities.

Choice A is correct. The claim is about Henry's confidence that he can transform Eliza. This answer reveals his belief that within three to six months he can "pass her off as anything he wants." In other words, he can make other people believe that she is anything he wants her to be, and this includes an upper-class lady. Therefore, this answer meets the claim's criteria.

2.

Claim: Gwendolen and Cecily are confused about their engagements.

Formulated Answer: They think they are engaged to the same person.

Summary and Process of Elimination:

Choice A: Gwendolen says that she doesn't know how anybody important can live in the country. This idea doesn't mention any confusion about their engagements.

Choice B: Cecily says she will fight to save her man from the schemes of another woman. This statement doesn't indicate any kind of confusion about their fiancés.

Choice C: Gwendolen says she was worried and that she wouldn't want anything bad to happen to prevent them from being friends. Her statement shows no confusion about her engagement to Earnest.

Choice D is correct. The key to the claim is that "confusion arises." Because a "misconception" is a wrong or inaccurate idea, this answer shows that Cecily believes Gwendolen is confused about being engaged to Earnest, which does illustrate the claim.

Check for Understanding

1. **Choice C** is correct. The claim asks which set of lines shows how Othello is upset about his wife cheating on him. The only lines that do so indicate that he is saying goodbye to a peaceful mind and contentment.

2. **Choice B** is correct. All the answers mention a god—either Jove or Mars—but only one of them discusses Tamburlaine's belief that he is protected by the gods. In this quotation, Tamburlaine claims that if anyone tries to hurt him, Jove will reach down from heaven to protect him.

Information and Ideas
Evidence: Poem

Practice

1.

Claim Summary: The poem describes being sensitive to other people's feelings and experiences.

Predicted answer: The lines will describe sympathy or understanding for another person.

Process of Elimination:
None of these answers indicate empathy:
Choice A describes feeling grateful to be alive.
Choice C describes viewing the sky.
Choice D describes smelling something that makes the speaker happy.

Choice B is correct. The claim asks for lines that show empathy, which is the ability to understand and feel what others experience. The lines in this answer describe a situation in which the speaker sees a man who is hungry and understands that painful feeling.

2.

Claim Summary: A difference of opinion regarding how important his mother's affection was to the speaker.

Paraphrase of Quotations:
None of these answers indicate two different opinions:
Choice A: The speaker describes feeling his mother's kiss on his forehead.
Choice B The speaker acknowledges his worldly success but treasures the thoughts of his mother.
Choice D The speaker is old and ready to be with his mother again just as he was as a child.

Choice C is correct. This answer addresses what "you" say, which indicates someone other than the speaker believes his memory of his mother's kiss is "a fancied thing," or something imaginary. Conversely, in these lines, the speaker indicates that he views this same affection as deserving to be respected and kept as a cherished prize, so this quotation shows contrasting views.

Check for Understanding

1. **Choice A** is correct. The claim asks for lines that show that the speaker doesn't understand how her neighbor can have negative life conditions and a positive outlook. These lines state that the speaker is puzzled by how the woman across the street can be so cheerful given how few good things she has in her life. Because this quotation addresses ALL the parts of the claim, it is the right answer.

2. **Choice D** is correct. The claim asks for a quotation that shows a restlessness due to looking forward to something. These lines indicate that it feels like their progress through the woods is slow because "It is so hard to wait!" Thus, the speaker anticipates arriving and feels impatient, making this answer the one that best fulfills the claim.

Information and Ideas
Explicit Meaning: Novel and Short Story

Practice

1.

Text Paraphrase: After Kirsanov's wife died, he was upset, and it aged him. To distract himself, he thought about going overseas but instead took some time off, then improved his property. A few years later, he took his son to college where Kirsanov isolated himself from everyone except Arkady and his friends.

Process of Elimination:
Eliminate **Choice A** because even though the text mentions Kirsanov's hair turning gray, it says he wants to distract himself from his wife's death, not from getting older. Although the text does say that Kirsanov works on his property, it doesn't say the reason is so that it will be more valuable for his son, making **Choice C** incorrect. **Choice D** is wrong because Kirsanov's priorities are not mentioned in the text.

Choice B is correct. The first sentence mentions the death of Kirsanov's wife, which was devastating for him. The next sentence states that Kirsanov considers going out of town to divert his attention from her death.

2.

Text Paraphrase: The cowboy was someone who hit the card table. Whenever he had the best cards, he forcefully slammed them on the table and won the rounds with such pride that those playing against him felt upset. Playing with someone who hits the table gets "intense." His opponents looked unhappy when the cowboy slammed down his good cards, but his partner was happy.

Process of Elimination:
Although the text mentions "tricks," it is a reference to winning rounds of cards, not to practices meant to deceive others. Therefore, **Choice A** isn't supported by the text. The cowboy seems to enjoy playing cards when he is winning, but there is no information in the text that indicates that he prefers playing cards to other methods of entertainment, making **Choice B** wrong. The cowboy clearly likes to win, but the text doesn't discuss his priorities, so **Choice C** lacks text support.

Choice D is correct. Slamming down his aces and kings and being proud when he has the best cards are examples of how the cowboy displays his winning cards, so this answer IS supported by the text.

3. **Text Paraphrase:** Mr. Gradgrind asks Sissy what she used to read to her father. She says she read about several mythical characters. He tells her not to ever reveal this again and tells Bounderby that she must be strictly trained and that he will be interested to see how she does.

Predicted answer: He does not approve of reading about things that aren't real.

Process of Elimination:
Eliminate **Choice B** because even though Sissy remembers happy times with her father, it isn't because Mr. Gradgrind asks her to do so. **Choice C** is incorrect because there is no indication in the text that Mr. Gradgrind disapproves of her upbringing or Sissy's lack of education. **Choice D** is wrong because the text doesn't contain information about Mr. Gradgrind questioning Sissy's skill in subjects other than reading.

Choice A is correct. When Sissy tells Mr. Gradgrind that she read stories to her father about imaginary characters like fairies and genies, he stops her in midsentence (as indicated by the dash at the end of the fourth paragraph) and tells her to never again talk about such nonsense. Therefore, this answer is supported by the information in the text.

Check for Understanding

1. **Choice D** is correct. The first sentence gives Fanny's opinion about her brother. The second sentence indicates that she might think differently about him if she had seen him once he was out of her sight because then he changes his appearance and actions. Therefore, Fanny's brother acts differently around her than when he is out of her sight.

2. **Choice A** is correct. According to the text, Mrs. Pontellier has a "natural aptitude" with how she handles her brushes, meaning that she has some talent. She also is "unprofessional," meaning that she is an amateur. Therefore, unlike the other answers, this one is supported by the text.

3. **Choice C** is correct. The text talks about Gabriel Oak looking at the sky and appreciating how beautiful it is, like a "work of art." The other answers aren't supported by the text.

Information and Ideas
Explicit Meaning: Poem

Practice

1.

Question: Asks about narrator's isolation.

Text Paraphrase: Ever since I was young, I haven't been like other people. I see things differently, and my interests are different. Both my sadness and happiness come from different sources than others', so I have loved all by myself.

Predicted answer: Narrator is different from others.

Process of Elimination:
Eliminate **Choice A** because the text doesn't discuss a physical disability. **Choice B** is incorrect because the text doesn't mention the narrator feeling ashamed. **Choice D** is wrong because no loss is mentioned in the text.

Choice C is correct. The poem discusses how the narrator is different from others because he sees things in a unique way. The text indicates that both the narrator's sorrow and love come from a different place than these emotions in others, which makes him feel alone. Because the entire excerpt describes the narrator as not viewing things in the same way as others, the answer that expresses this idea is correct.

2.

Question: Asks how the sunset and saying goodbye are similar.

Relevant Text Paraphrase: The sunset is like two friends saying goodbye: they bow and shake hands just as the sun departs at a distance.

Possible answer: Both use accepted ways of parting.

Process of Elimination: Get rid of **Choice B** because the text doesn't discuss consistency. **Choice C** is incorrect because the text doesn't mention anything about connection. **Choice D** is wrong because even though both are natural and inevitable, neither of these ideas has text support.

Choice A is correct. The second line of the second stanza makes the comparison: "sunset like the parting of old acquaintances." The next line mentions bowing and shaking hands as the two individuals part, which is how many people say goodbye to each other. So, just as a sunset signals the end of a day, a bow and handshake signal two people who are going separate ways. Because it is supported by the poem's details, this answer is the right one.

Check for Understanding

1. **Choice D** is correct. The first four lines present the speaker's suggestion that the children pick flowers in meadows. The rest of the poem gives the children's answer: they would rather be left alone than spend the energy to leave the city, because they are too "weary" (tired) to enjoy playing. The answer that states something similar is the one indicating the children are tired and want to rest.

2. **Choice B** is correct. The poem indicates that there are showers blowing newspapers around and beating down on things like "broken blinds and chimney-pots." The speaker also mentions only one horse and cab that can be seen before the streetlights come on. Because no other people are mentioned as being out in the rain, the best answer indicates that "the streets are mostly deserted due to the inclement weather."

Information and Ideas
Explicit Meaning: Nonfiction

Practice

1.

Question's Criteria: *What* researchers learned about how baleen whales create sound

Possible Answer: Baleen whales push air past a cushion in the larynx, which results in sound.

Text Paraphrase:
S1: Baleen whales can vocalize due to a special voice box.
S2: Researchers looked at three baleen whales and found U-shaped structures that push against a cushion in the larynx.
S3: Researchers determined that air moving past the cushion caused the vibrations that resulted in sound.

Process of Elimination:
Although the text states that baleen whales create low frequency vibrations, it doesn't say that these are different based on the species. **Choice A** also doesn't explain how whales create sounds.

The question asks about how, not why, whales make sounds, so **Choice B** is incorrect.

Although **Choice D** mentions how whales create sounds, the answer is incorrect because the text doesn't say anything about whales reversing air flow to make sound.

Choice C is correct. The last two sentences in the text discuss how a special apparatus—"a large U-shaped structure that pushes against a fatty cushion inside the larynx"—causes a vibration when air from the lungs moves past it, resulting in "very low frequency sounds underwater."

2.

Question's Criteria: *Why* water specialists worry about groundwater levels.

Possible Answer: Once groundwater has been used up, it takes hundreds of years to renew itself.

Text Paraphrase:
S1 states that groundwater provides drinking water and water to grow food.
S2 indicates what water specialists say: once ground water is gone, it takes a long time to renew itself.
S3 explains that even though groundwater levels are decreasing in many places in the world, certain societies have taken actions to stop its loss.

Process of Elimination:
Choice A is wrong because the text says groundwater can be restored even though it takes a long time.

Choice C is incorrect because even though the text states that it takes groundwater a long time to renew itself, there is no discussion of a mass extinction occurring.

Choice D isn't right because the text doesn't say people won't be able to use groundwater anymore.

Choice B is correct. The text says that once people have used all the groundwater, it will not be available for hundreds of years, which could cause a shortage.

Check for Understanding

1. **Choice D** is correct. The question asks why finding Er is important. The answer can be found in the last sentence: the discovery of Er would benefit doctors treating problems that occur when the blood used in a transfusion is not compatible with the blood of the patient receiving that blood. Because this answer basically states the same idea, it is the correct choice.

2. **Choice A** is correct. The question asks what prevents people with an amputated limb from feeling hot or cold temperatures in their prosthetic. The answer can be found in the second sentence of the text: a prosthetic does not have nerves that would allow it to detect sensory information. This answer contains similar information, making it the correct choice.

Information and Ideas
Graphic Displays: Bar Graph

Practice

1. **Choice C** is correct. The question calls for graph information that supports the growing popularity of EVs, which is measured by how many are purchased. In addition to China's 8 million in EV sales, the US had between 1 and 2 million in sales. This information completes the text with accurate graph data that shows the popularity of EVs.

2. **Choice A** is correct. The correct answer must weaken the conclusion that women prefer other activities over watching television. This answer provides graph information that women spent more time watching television than participating in other activities, which counters the conclusion that women prefer other activities rather than watching television.

Check for Understanding

1. **Choice D** is correct. The graph's bars for women are each lower than any of the bars for men, indicating that women's average salary was lower than men's for all three years in the graph.

2. **Choice B** is correct. The graph's bars representing women are higher than all the bars for men, indicating that more women work part time than men do. Therefore, the difference in percentage rates was greater based on gender than on differences in race or marital status of part-time workers.

Information and Ideas
Graphic Displays: Table

Practice

1. **Choice D** is correct. Victims aged 60 and older had over 101,068 complaints and $3.4 billion in losses. Given that data, higher rates of complaints and losses were experienced by those aged 60 and older. The other age groups each had fewer complaints and lower financial losses than people aged 60 and older.

Check for Understanding

1. **Choice C** is correct. The researchers' conclusion is that the methods for measuring bite force influence the estimate of that force. Thomason and Kiltie both used an equation to measure bite force and reached similar measurements of 300–600 newtons while Lindner's method determined bite force to be 13–1,394 and Ellis's method 147–926, estimates with much broader ranges of bite force.

Information and Ideas
Graphic Displays: Line Graph

Practice

1. **Choice A** is correct. The student concluded that one region had the lowest number of new homes built during the years examined. The *lowest* line represents the Northeast, so it had the least number of homes built during 2021 to 2023.

2. **Choice B** is correct. The question requires support for the claim about Samsung selling more smartphones than Apple. The line representing Samsung's market share of sales was the highest, reaching just over 20%.

Check for Understanding

1. **Choice D** is correct. In all four academic years, the line representing certified social studies teachers is higher than the lines representing certified teachers of the other subjects.

2. **Choice B** is correct. The student's claim deals with the number of AP tests taken in US History in 2023. Looking at the Y-axis confirms that there were between 200 and 250 students who took the test in 2023, whereas in previous years the totals were between 150 and 200.

Information and Ideas
Inference: Completes Text

Practice

1. **Choice C** is correct. Because the same genetic factor enabled three bird species to change their color, it is logical to conclude that other bird species that are red possess this same gene.

2. **Choice B** Is correct. The text states that wind, humans, and flotation couldn't carry Koa seeds to Réunion, which means they must have been carried by an animal. Fish can't transfer seeds to land like a bird could, so a sea bird most likely carried the seed because birds often transfer seeds in this way.

Check for Understanding

1. **Choice A** is correct. According to the text, the *Harry Potter* series appeals to younger audiences because its "fast-paced plot" involves "familiar, universal themes." The *Cormoran Strike* series includes greater book length, less familiar themes, and a slower pace than the *Harry Potter* books, which likely makes the adult *Cormoran Strike* series less interesting to younger readers than the *Harry Potter* books. Therefore, it is logical to conclude that young readers will find the *Cormoran Strike* series less appealing than the *Harry Potter* books. Notice the contrast indicated by the word "but" that begins the sentence about *Cormoran Strike*.

2. **Choice D** is correct. The cave-dwelling tetra responded to a food source when surface-dwelling tetras did not. If cave-dwelling tetras evolved larger nose tissues that gave them a superior sense of smell, that ability enabled them to detect unseen food and survive in a dark habitat. The text's opening word "Between" may suggest that a comparison or contrast likely follows, in this case about food detection in blind and sighted tetras.

3. **Choice C** is correct. Archeologists state that there isn't sufficient evidence to support researchers' claims about *H. naledi*. Therefore, archaeologists doubt the researchers' conclusions about the cave evidence. This means that the ability of *H. naledi* isn't demonstrated conclusively (without a doubt). Notice the word "However" at the beginning of the second sentence, which indicates the two views about the cave evidence differ from each other.

Information and Ideas
Main Idea: Novel and Short Story

Practice

1. **Choice A** is correct. Mrs. Garstin isn't generous as a host because of her "parsimony" (stinginess). Her *actions* as a host of "thrifty" dinners with cheap wine that guests believe is champagne show her hateful *feelings* about spending money.

2. **Choice C** is correct. The girl *feels* the "pain of parting" and is "tormented" by their separation. These details show how much she cares for Edmund. Giving him her locket—her "most precious earthly possession"—is an *action* that indicates how much she loves him.

3. **Choice B** is correct. Mathilde has "suffered" and is "distressed," "tortured," and "angry" about not having "all delicacies and all luxuries." Her *feelings* indicate her unhappiness with lacking what she *thinks* she was "born to" and should have.

Check for Understanding

1. **Choice D** is correct. Mr. Clacton is described as feeling love for the response of "obedience" to his written call for a meeting. He also "loved" his sense of feeling "visibly important" when he exited the "inner chamber" that is his office. Like a powerful "Prime Minister" enjoying command of a country, Mr. Clacton loves his ability to command a committee meeting.

2. **Choice C** is correct. The text describes Nathalie's thoughts by revealing that she "meant to accept" Brantain's marriage proposal when he declares his love for her, even though she thinks he is "insignificant and unattractive." There is no mention of Nathalie feeling love for Brantain, but she thinks about becoming "enormously rich." Nathalie feels confident that Brantain loves her and will provide a lifestyle that she feels is desirable, including an entourage she "liked and required."

3. **Choice A** is correct. Baba feels a loss, missing the sugarcane fields, gardens, visitors, bazaar, and knowing people who share a common past. The comparison of Baba to a widower expresses his feeling of sorrow. Mourning the loss of those past experiences shows that he previously enjoyed them.

4. **Choice D** is correct. The text describes Mrs. Sommers feeling of joy and sorrow as she "laughed" and "wept" during the play. The fact that Mrs. Sommers is "absorbed" by the play and "gathered in the" the stage, actors, and audience demonstrates her attentiveness to the performance. Her unique "attitude" allows her to think of a broad "impression" created by the different theatrical elements.

Information and Ideas
Main Idea: Nonfiction

Practice

1.

> Scientists have suggested that humans originally hunted horses as prey and later began to protect and breed horses to ensure a steady supply of meat. [Initial use] The domestication of horses seems to have occurred independently in different areas of the world over the centuries. New uses of horses developed over time as humans used them for milk, hides, and transportation, [New, varied uses] but these animals may also have been domesticated to help with the hunting of wild horse herds. [Additional use]

Choice A is correct. Sentence 1 mentions how horses were initially hunted for food and then were captured to maintain that food supply. Sentences 2 and 3 discuss how horses were domesticated around the world for various uses.

2. **Choice D** is correct. Sentence 1 describes Standley's belief that technology connects artists and art successfully. Sentence 2 explains a process used by Standley to make art, and Sentence 3 discusses "universal" elements of his work that create a "unifying effect" on viewers, the artist, and the work. This answer expresses these ideas about the complexity of Standley's art and its unifying effect.

Check for Understanding

1. **Choice A** is correct. The text describes Historical Criticism and Ransom's argument against it. Sentence 3 discusses Ransom's belief that Historical Criticism "distracted" the reader from a literary work's "meaning" and argued for a New Criticism that more clearly reveals a work's meaning.

2. **Choice B** is correct. The text explains how Milk's art installation engages visitors because it "immerses the viewer" in three stages of creativity. Sentences 2–4 provide details about how the viewer interacts with the screen, casting a shadow that transforms into birds and moving arms to flap the wings. This "engages" viewers in an "interactive art experience."

3. **Choice C** is correct. The text describes how a "positive relation" between extroverts and intelligence "may seem surprising," but extroverts' activities involve advanced cognitive abilities, which means that they have more intelligence than might be expected.

Information and Ideas
Main Idea: Poem

Practice

1.

Idea 1
I travelled among unknown men,

In lands beyond the sea;

Idea 2
Nor, England! did I know till then

What love I bore to thee.

Idea 3
'Tis past, that melancholy dream!

Idea 4
Nor will I quit thy shore

Idea 5
A second time; for still I seem

To love thee more and more.

Choice C is correct. In lines 1–4, the speaker realizes his "love" for England when he travelled to "lands beyond the sea" and lived "among unknown men" in what he calls a "melancholy" (sad) time. In lines 5–8, he claims he won't "quit" (leave) the shores of England again because he loves his country "more and more." These details show that the speaker's love for England increased when he was away.

Check for Understanding

1. **Choice D** is correct. The speaker imagines that in the future "when I am dead," the friend will suffer great sorrow. Not wanting the friend to "mourn" or feel "woe," the speaker prefers that after his death the friend will forget their relationship if that prevents painful sorrow.

2. **Choice A** is correct. Although the night seems to be a time to "sleep," the speaker claims instead that people who love each other should be kept together. The night was designed to keep friends together, and the evening "together brings" each person to "his love at night." This idea of night bringing closeness is emphasized by the repetition in lines 4 and 7 of the word "together."

Craft and Structure
Connections: Between Texts

Practice

1. **Choice D** is correct. Text 2 claims the canon contains works that still "capture the imagination." The author would most likely suggest that teachers continue to assign traditional books that are "popular" with students.

Check for Understanding

1. **Choice B** is correct. The researchers in Text 1 were hopeful that having older people play video games would improve their brain plasticity. The author of Text 2 presents details about a study conducted by Boot and his team that showed that the mental processes of elderly participants did not significantly improve after playing video games. Therefore, the enthusiasm expressed by the researchers in Text 1 proved to be overly optimistic.

2. **Choice C** is correct. In Text 1, Jacobs used simulations to support his theory about the size of rangeomorphs being related to how much food they could obtain. Mitchell debates this idea based on the historical lack of competition for food at this time and her observations of fossilized rangeomorphs, asserting that the physical structure of rangeomorphs shows that these creatures weren't competing for food.

Craft and Structure
Purpose: Main

Practice

1. **It was in those two summers that we came to know Babanchik best and to adore him accordingly.** It was he who led our marvelous expeditions to the neighboring peaks, his clothes steaming with the effort of that leadership—he who showed us where to look for mushrooms, and later fried those mushrooms for us. His mind settled, wisely and fairly, all our momentous quarrels, and invented countless new and fascinating games when we had tired of the everlasting croquet.

   Choice A is correct. The first sentence serves as a topic sentence and indicates that the narrator and the others came to "adore" Babanchik. The repeated "he" or "his" as the subject of each following sentence suggests that this is a result of Babanchik's actions. Thus, the purpose is to show what Babanchik did that led the others to admire him.

Check for Understanding

1. **Choice A** is correct. The speaker starts by mentioning a "debt" that must be paid for "one riotous day," and goes on to say he must pay it "to the end." This implies he made some mistake one day that will affect him for the rest of his life, bringing "regret and grief, / Sorrow without relief." Although he thought the debt was "small," it has led to great anguish.

2. **Choice B** is correct. The text begins by identifying a belief that many scientists hold about the development of handedness. This is followed by the contrast word "However," indicating a shift in ideas. The rest of the text discusses William Hopkins's research and explains that it led to a

conclusion different from what was previously mentioned, thus conflicting with commonly held ideas. The text does not suggest that this research "resolved" an issue (Choice D), but just that it supported a different point of view.

3. **Choice B** is correct. The first sentence states that Carrie had time to "study the flat." The following paragraph describes the poor conditions she notices throughout the apartment, leading to her impression of financial struggles, or a "lean and narrow life."

Craft and Structure
Purpose: Portion

Practice

1. **Choice D** is correct. The text discusses Jenks's unpleasant attitude and rudeness to everyone around him. By emphasizing that Bill Jackson is the "one friend" who "continued to brave" Jenks's "vile" words, the text implies that Jenks had other visitors before, but they stopped coming due to Jenks's behavior. This suggests that if Jenks had not been so rude, he would have still had other friends who visited him.

2. **Choice C** is correct. The text discusses how the people of North Platte contributed to the morale of the American troops traveling through their town. By giving details of what the residents provided for the soldiers, the underlined portion illustrates the claim that they made the soldiers "feel welcome."

Check for Understanding

1. **Choice B** is correct. The first sentence claims that groundwater levels can be restored if "appropriate measures" are taken. The underlined portion emphasizes that these measures are necessary because "without efforts" like those in Tucson, Arizona, groundwater levels will "continue to decline" more and more quickly. Thus, the underlined portion draws attention to the claim that intentional measures are necessary to stop groundwater levels from decreasing.

2. **Choice A** is correct. The underlined portion explains that many people think that GDP represents a nation's progress; this perspective leads to policies that "prioritize economic growth." The text goes on to discuss the alternative view of two specific economists who believe that focusing on "other indicators of well-being" would lead to better policies. Thus, they believe that the common perspective on GDP ignores many important factors that contribute to a society's well-being.

Craft and Structure
Purpose: Sentence

Practice

1.

> Plants rely on their root systems and on photosynthesis for nutrients, but some plants acquire additional nutrients by catching and eating insects or even small reptiles or mammals. The round-leaved sundew attracts and captures its prey with sugary droplets on its leaves that appear to be nectar or dew. Insects trying to feed on these droplets become trapped in the sticky substance. The sundew plant then uses enzymes to digest the insects and obtain the nutrients it needs.

Choice B is correct. The first sentence states that some plants get nutrients by "catching and eating insects." The underlined sentence talks about how a specific plant, the "round-leaved sundew," "attracts and captures" insects with "sugary droplets." Thus, the underlined sentence indicates how the plant performs the action of catching insects.

2.

> Those well-remembered opening chords, they were by this time not merely musical sounds. They had become something within [Marise], of her own being, rich with a thousand clustered nameless associations, something that thrilled and sang and lived a full harmonious life of its own.

Choice C is correct. The text says that the "well-remembered" chords Marise plays "had become something within Marise," suggesting the musical piece has some deep significance to her. The underlined sentence elaborates on that significance, showing that Marise felt a connection with the music.

Check for Understanding

1. **Choice C** is correct. "His thoughts ran back" indicates the character is remembering something. This sets up the description in the following sentences of the memories he recalls from his morning at home with his family.

2. **Choice A** is correct. The first sentence introduces a study about air pollution and teamwork. The underlined sentence explains what data the researchers used for that study and what they did with the data, thus presenting a method they used in their investigation.

Craft and Structure
Purpose: Structure

Practice

1.

Like this alabaster box whose art
Is frail as a cassia-flower, is my heart,
Carven with delicate dreams and wrought
With many a subtle and exquisite thought.

Therein I treasure the spice and scent
Of rich and passionate memories blent
Like odours of cinnamon, sandal and clove,
Of song and sorrow and life and love.

Choice B is correct. The beginning of the poem indicates "my heart" is "like this alabaster box." The following lines continue to offer descriptions of the speaker's heart using images of the alabaster box. For example, the "spice and scent," which might be stored in an alabaster box, represent the "rich and passionate memories" stored in the heart.

2.

Two early twentieth-century writers, Ellen N. La Motte and Ernest Hemingway, were prompted by their experiences in World War I to write about the horrors of war. They **both** used a plain style of short, factual sentences to depict war's destruction and ugliness. La Motte's work *The Backwash of War* was published in 1916, while the conflict was ongoing, but **it was quickly censored** due to its criticism of the war. Hemingway's novel *A Farewell to Arms*, however, was published in 1929, more than ten years after the war ended. **It became a bestseller** and established him among America's great writers.

Choice D is correct. The first two sentences discuss how La Motte and Hemingway both wrote about the same topic, the "horrors of war," and used a similar "plain" style. Sentence 3 discusses the publication and reception of La Motte's work *The Backwash of War*, while Sentences 4 and 5 show that Hemingway's work *A Farewell to Arms* was published at a different time and received a much different response than La Motte's writing.

Check for Understanding

1. **Choice C** is correct. The first three lines of the text show the speaker and others "eager and laughing" as they climb a tree to see a nest with eggs. This lighthearted scene is followed by a shift with the phrase "But silent fell." The rest of the poem describes the speaker and others in awe as they encounter the nest and have a momentary understanding of how all creatures are connected.

2. **Choice A** is correct. The text begins by introducing the question of "what effect" clouds will have on climate change. Sentence 2 introduces the methodology of a study that investigated that question, and Sentence 3 continues giving information about the researchers' methods and the study's results. The last sentence introduces an aspect of clouds that the study did NOT address, which "remains a topic for future research."

Practice

1.

In a project known as ScanPyramids, which began in 2015, Cairo University and the French HIP Institute (Heritage Innovation Preservation) are using muon tomography, among other technologies, to **uncover previously hidden** spaces inside the Great Pyramids.

Choice D is correct. The strongest clue is "previously hidden." If something was previously hidden, then it is not hidden anymore. This fits with "uncover," which means "to reveal" or "discover."

2.

In 2023, the US Census Bureau **predicted** that, although the rate of growth is decreasing, the global population will reach 10.2 billion by the year 2060. **This projection** is slightly higher than the 10.1 billion **estimate** made by the United Nations Population Division.

Choice C is correct. The word "This" at the beginning of the second sentence indicates the following word, "projection," is an idea that was mentioned previously. A projection is a prediction, so "predicted" makes sense to fill in the blank. Also, the word "estimate" later in the sentence is another clue that fits with "predicted."

3.

Contrast word

Many people **enjoy** the flavor of the herb cilantro, **but** others find it

1st clause

unappealing due to a genetic variation that makes them sensitive

2nd clause

to a soapy-flavored chemical compound in the herb.

Choice B is correct. "But" is a contrast word indicating that the two clauses should have opposing ideas. The first clause says people "enjoy" the flavor. "Unappealing" means "not pleasing," which is opposed to enjoying, so this word fits in the second clause.

4.

Leon Botstein, president of Bard College, believes that by treating adolescents as children, the typical American high school provides an **unhealthy** environment for teens: he argues that keeping teens separate from the adult world has **damaging** effects on students and on society.

Choice B is correct. The colon indicates a context clue following it that should be similar to the missing word: "damaging effects" suggests the environment is "unhealthy."

Check For Understanding

1. **Choice B** is correct. The word "this" before the blank points back to the "obstacle" mentioned in Sentence 1. In this context, the "obstacle" is a problem the researchers are trying to solve, so "problem" is the best choice.

2. **Choice D** is correct. The best context clue in the sentence is the word "showing." "Reveal" means to "make known or show to others," so this goes with "showing."

3. **Choice A** is correct. The colon indicates that the following clause should have an idea similar to the missing word. Since the "technique" is described as "creative," the "treatment" should be described similarly. "Innovative" means "new and original," which matches the idea of "creative."

4. **Choice C** is correct. The word "but" in the second sentence implies a contrast with the first sentence. Since the following clause says that modern economists DO NOT rely on land value taxation "alone," that suggests that the person in the previous sentence DOES rely on it alone. Thus, the answer should be similar to "alone." "Sole" means "the only one," so this is the best choice.

Craft and Structure
Vocabulary: Most Nearly Means

Practice

1. **Choice C** is correct. The text implies that the "drowsy spell" of the scene affected the character so that he lost track of the "passing time." "Becoming influenced by" is the best choice to show that he was affected by the quiet scene.

2. **Choice B** is correct. The text indicates that Amory was "rattling off" lists of book titles like a "Brentano's" bookstore clerk. The phrase "rattling off" suggests he was able to name them with little effort, or with "ease."

Check for Understanding

1. **Choice C** is correct. "Attracting to" means "causing to come to a place." The text says the room has been "taking on character" over time, suggesting it has been gaining characteristics that create a sense of "fineness and greatness," or causing these characteristics to come to itself.

2. **Choice A** is correct. "Behavior" means "the way someone acts." The text describes how Bartleby acted "calm" and at ease, and how his acting in this way influenced the narrator's response to the situation.